IN SEARCH OF THE

Ninja

In Search of the

Ninja

The Historical Truth of Ninjutsu

Antony Cummins

The History Press

This book is dedicated to my Mother
Judith Wilkinson.

First published 2012

The History Press
The Mill, Brimscombe Port
Stroud, Gloucestershire, GL5 2QG
www.thehistorypress.co.uk

British Library Cataloguing in Publication Data.
A catalogue record for this book is available from the British Library.

ISBN 978 0 7524 8093 0

Typesetting and origination by The History Press
Printed in Great Britain

Contents

Acknowledgements

The following people have given their time and help and I would like to thank them all for their hard work.

All Japanese translation by Yoshie Minami and the Historical Ninjutsu Research Team. Her translations of ninjutsu documents provide the backbone to this work and the entire foundation of my research is based on her kindness. Research into ninjutsu's connection to Kusunoki Masashige was aided by Steven Nojiri, who was a huge help in all aspects of Japanese history and Buddhism. I thank Jayson Kane for his wizardry in the area of graphic design and endless help with covers and jacket designs. All chemical analysis was undertaken by Alex Allera of the Chemistry Department of Turin University, whose help has brought clarification to the provenance of some of the art. Also, a thank you to Christa Jacobson, for her help in relation to the *Koka Shinobi no Den Miraikai* and the *Koka Ryu Ninjutsu Densho* scrolls. Thanks to Peter Brown of Brighton, England, for allowing the use of his copies of the *Rodanshu* transcription.

Thank you to Mieko Koizumi for her hard work transcribing documents from very difficult 'Grass-style' into something readable. Also, to Masako (Natori) Asakawa and Yasuko (Natori) Hine, who are the last of the Natori line and to monk Juho Yamamoto for his continuing care of the Natori clan graves. I am grateful to Mr Yoshida Shigeo for his help in authenticating scrolls.

All Chinese translations are quoted from the work of Ralph D. Sawyer unless otherwise stated. His work has been chosen for its academic excellence and to give a uniform translation of the Chinese Classics.

This scroll should be passed down to one person. That person should train as a Musha-warrior and be familiar with the mountains and fields, the forests and the oceans and he should understand the tactics of war, how to form military camps, understand castle planning, topography and travel around the provinces. Master Matsumoto [Jirozaemon] did this for a long time without stopping and he trained for years on end. These are the secrets of Koka.

Iga-ryu Koka-ryu Shinobi Hiden

Introduction

You should build watch fires in front of your position, close all the gates and allow no one to come or go without questioning, this is done to block the enemy's shinobi.

Heiho Nukigaki Hippu No Sho Gunshi No Maki, 1689

Finding the Ninja is a task that is harder today than it ever has been in history. Whilst the contemporaries of the ninja had to search moonlit thickets and windy bamboo forests with only the shadows of the night to contend with, a modern searcher for the illusive shinobi has to hunt through dusty libraries and negotiate with collectors who guard their treasures with ferocity.

The first step in this quest is to emphasise that there has never been any authoritative form of academic research conducted into these Japanese figures, even though they are one of the most popular Japanese exports; no one has ever really explored the question, who are the ninja? Many think that they know the answer and that the ninja figure is well defined, however, most of their information comes from films, comics, hearsay and a splash of fantasy, mixed with a little faith. In truth, the medieval documents that describe the actions of the ninja – sometimes written by the actual agents themselves or by those around them, or by those defending against them – have never actually been seen in full in the west and are rarely seen outside of certain circles in Japan.

You are about to venture deep into the history of the ninja, hopefully your preconceptions will be torn away as we unmask the shinobi and break him down into his component parts, stripping away the fantasy and arriving at the truth.

To begin with, this will be done by exposing what is believed to be the origin of the ninja and then replacing it with the facts. Like Hansel and Gretel we will then trace the breadcrumbs into the darkness, through the grammatical gore and the slippery surface of syntax. We will fully investigate the issues, trying to identify if an ideogram in the historical record means 'ninja' or 'in secret' or even 'to persevere', as a slight change in grammatical form can radically alter a document's meaning.

We shall cut through the ninja versus samurai mythology and find the stark reality that there never was a struggle between the samurai and the shinobi. The myth of the ninja underdog fades to reveal the reality of the highly trained samurai-spy, who is well known and utilised by the Japanese generals of old. From this point, we will survey the evolution of the Japanese scout and his deep connection with the ninja and the subtle differences between the two.

Having found who the ninja are, the quest will turn to where they came from, a query that ends in the Japanese 'Dark Ages', where literature for the ninja is non-existent and all trails fade away. But the shape of the ninja footprint can be discerned hundreds of years earlier in China, where we find a series of highly interesting connections to the shinobi and a collection of undeniable ninja skills being used on mainland Asia, centuries before the ninja.

These Chinese elements of *ninjutsu* are rarely touched upon, but all are fascinating – and all are screened here by academic investigation and even chemical analysis. These skills are then cross-referenced to many original Japanese manuals to find that the ninja did have common themes and skills, similar enough to show a central curriculum shared by all the old ninja of Japan, but different enough to show that evolution had occurred within the clans. The text will then analyse the secret oral traditions and concentrate on two of the most famous ninja families, the Hattori and the Natori clans, who have left us documents to follow. This will explain why the people from the provinces of Iga and Koka became legendary in their own time, being hired out and recognised as the premier ninja of the day and retaining that pre-eminence for generation after generation. The myth of the female ninja is then explored.

At this point, we consider 1603 as the date of the sowing of the seed of destruction for the ninja and one which means over 200 years of decay; gradually the core of the ninja arts weakens and eventually dies – the headstone reads 'Killed by the abolition of the samurai class and the Meiji Restoration in 1868'. In this ninja graveyard we can view the ghost of ninjutsu as it briefly reappears in the Second World War. The investigation will touch upon what is best described as 'ninja tomb robbery', as pretenders and frauds feed off the modern ninja boom and change the once devastatingly effective, practical arts of the ninja into a global brand, manipulating the ninja into a dark hero figure for profit.

With the revelation that the ninja have long been dead and their arts only to be found on library shelves, the manuals and documents pertaining to the ninja as translated by the Historical Ninjutsu Research Team finally give an all-round understanding of the path of the ninja. The evidence of the true skills and the manuals that record the decline of the ninja during a shift towards the mythical are examined for the first time in the English language.

For some this book will shake their long-held beliefs about ninjutsu, for those who are new to the ninja, it will be as a scribe inking on fresh paper. It may even offend some. For all, it should lay the foundation for future ninja research, destroying the false and promoting the real.

Notes on the Text

Any ideas or statements that do not appear in the original text but are assumed from the context are in square brackets. All measurements are given in their Japanese form, such as *Bu, Momme, Sun,* etc and their equivalent can easily be obtained from various sources; however, a select table of measurements is supplied on page 195.

The small selection of notes that follows has been written for those readers who are new to the world of the ninja. I will describe certain points that need to be understood to avoid confusion when reading the Japanese terms.

A ninja or shinobi is a mixture of spy, guerrilla tactician, night time infiltration agent, explosives expert, thief and arsonist. The ninja have been named in various ways in many parts of Japan, however, historically they were known as 'shinobi' before they became ninja. Both of the names 'shinobi' (also *shinobi no mono*) and ninja come, in the main, from the same combination of Chinese ideograms 忍者, which can be read in the two ways described above.

It is a misconception that the ninja are a separate force outside of the samurai, as they are in fact a subgroup of the samurai with some members being from the foot soldier or *Ashigaru* class; this will be discussed in depth later in this volume. A ninja could come from any class in Japan but many were low level samurai retainers.

We are concerned with two main time periods. The Sengoku period – translated as the 'period of the Warring States' – which began in the mid-fifteenth century, followed by the Edo or 'peace period', which began in 1603 and ended in 1868. In short and unsurprisingly, the Warring States period was an age of bloodshed, where ninjutsu (also *shinobi no jutsu*) was at its height, whilst the Edo saw the steady decline of the ninja skills but at the same time an increase in the recording of ninjutsu.

In the mid-twentieth century a Japanese enthusiast (and mayor of Iga) named Okuse described a ninja hierarchy, which in his work consisted of three levels: *Jo-nin, Chu-nin* and *Ge-nin,* or high, middle and low level ninja; this is incorrect. In truth, a person's social class was dictated by many factors but skill in the arts of the ninja had no bearing on social or political standing. *Jo, Chu* and *Ge* describe a ninja's level of skill, high, middle and low, but historically they never referred to his social position. Examples include: *Jozu no* ninja (good ninja); *Joko no* ninja (skilful ninja); *Chukichi no* ninja (ninja of middle level skills); *Yo-nin* (ordinary ninja); and *In-nin no jozu* (a skilful performer of night-time infiltration skills). This mistranslation by the enthusiast Okuse has affected academic work, such as that of Professor S. Turnbull and the popular author Steven K. Hayes, which has led to a widespread misunderstanding. The misprision is seen in immensely popular television shows such as the Japanese anime *Naruto* and the cult Japanese film *Shinobi no mono*.

The explosion of the 'ninja martial art' phenomenon has muddied the historical waters more than anything else. From around the mid-twentieth century a small selection of individuals arrived on the ninja scene, claiming to be heirs to full ninja lineages and shinobi schools. A few of these individuals have gone further and promoted the idea that ninjutsu contains a specialised form of hand-to-hand combat skills that were used solely by the ninja and were kept secret for hundreds of years, including from their samurai 'opponents'. This 'specialised combat system' is not only without basis but also goes against the grain of Japanese history and how ninjutsu was used in war. No ninja lineage claimant has ever supplied any form of historical record or documentation that predates the 1950s to help solidify the claim and in Japan, no one is considered a true heir of ninjutsu with certainty. The popularity of this new martial art took the world by storm in the mid 1980s and has gained a considerable following since. No form of ninja martial art exists that has come down through any recognised school of Japanese warfare and it must be considered purely as a modern invention.

The modern idea of a suit worn by the ninja is historically incorrect, though it does have some details right. Modern ninja suits are based on traditional Japanese clothing. A ninja would, of course wear contemporary garb, cut in the same way as the 'ninja suits' that are on the market. Also, the ninja would have had access to masks, which were were worn (especially by husbands visiting brothels!) and there are even historical records of the ninja dressing in black, mainly on a night without moonlight. So the image of a ninja all in black and masked is one that was historically recorded. However, it appears to be more correctly identified as the image of *Nusubito,* or thieves, who were active in the period of peace and who wished to hide their identity. This concept of the 'Nusubito thief' is intermingled with the history of the ninja and the two have become one in modern understanding. During the Sengoku period of Japan, when ninja*s* were truly active, this image of the black masked ninja is without foundation, there is no record from this time of any such garb. Why bother to wear a mask when anyone sneaking around at night in time of war was automatically considered to be the enemy? Ninja manuals seldom talk of covering the face and in fact describe groups of ninja wearing white head bands during night raids, so that they could identify each other in the dark.

Lastly, ninja manuals; during the Sengoku period, few ninja manuals were written and fewer survived and it is only with the adoption of peace that the recording of ninjutsu begins to take place. Throughout this book you will find references to a selection of shinobi scrolls and other literature. The four major sources for ninjutsu at present and their authors – in date order – are these:[1]

- The *Shinobi Hiden* (commonly known as the *Ninpiden*) by Hattori (Yasunaga) Hanzo and various authors. Dated 1560 with only a few transcripts surviving and the original lost.

- The *Gunpo Jiyoshu* by Ogasawara Saku'un Katsuzo, *c.*1612, of which three inner scrolls are dedicated to the arts of the ninja.
- The *Bansenshukai* by Fujibayashi Yasutake, dated 1676, of which various transcriptions exist; considered by most to be the premier ninja manual in existence.
- The *Shoninki* by Natori Masazumi (sometimes Masatake), dated 1681, of which various transcripts exist.

It is advisable to familiarise yourself with this list, as many references within this book are to these four manuals or name their authors as a source. All quotations are attributed to the relevant scroll.

1

What Is a Ninja?

Shinobi are also called Suppa or Rappa. These are people who hide themselves and infiltrate an enemy position and observe and listen to the status of the enemy and then bring this information back to their allies. For these shinobi, there are various teachings and they are called; the 'tradition for a moonlit night', the 'tradition for a night with a hazy moon' and the 'tradition for a moonless night'. In the area of Koshu they were called Suppa and in Bando (Kanto) they were known as Rappa. These days they are known as *Iga no mono* or *Koka no mono* and they are well trained in the arts of the shinobi.

The writings of Arisawa Nagasada, 1689

To discover the historical truth behind the ninja, one must negotiate a network of dead ends, fabrications (both historical and modern), geographical differences, varying terminology and an evolution of skills which change with the political climate.

Often the word ninja comes with two main suffixes, 'ninja assassins' and 'ninja spies' both of which have a claim to correctness, yet fall short of the reality. Ninja were used as assassins, but evidence for this is scant and represents a minor part of their role. Ninja were spies; secret agents have existed throughout history and yet ninja remain the most enigmatic and most complex. In truth, the terms 'assassin' and 'spy' do not do the ninja justice, nor do they describe fully the arts of *shinobi no jutsu,* the way of the ninja.

A ninja or *shinobi no mono* is a person with a specific set of skills and the term has no connection to their level of ability. Also, the term *shinobi* can be used for a person who is undertaking any form of stealthy mission, even if they have not been trained in any arts. However, it is considered that most shinobi no mono were at least trained to some level in the ways of the ninja. These skills include the arts of spying and working as an undercover agent, the ability to scout in extreme proximity to the enemy – scouting inside enemy castles and defensive positions or even temporarily acting as a member of an enemy force to gain information before returning to one's own side. A ninja was also a person involved in the making and the use of explosives in a clandestine military capacity, including arson, and who could use the skills of breaking and entering to gain entrance to a fortified household in order to steal. He would gather information through eavesdropping, would take documentation and valuables and on occasion would murder the residents and set fire to the buildings. A shinobi was a person who acted as a guide in no-man's-land for attacking units, normally under the cover of darkness. Alongside this, they acted as messengers and utilised secret codes via horns, drums, symbols and the written word to transfer information. In short, the ninja was a spy-scout-arsonist-thief-killer.[2]

The following is from the 1656 *Bukyo Zensho* military manual and outlines the requirements and uses of the ninja.

Those who should be chosen as Ninja[3]

1   Those who look stupid but are resourceful and talented in speech or are witty.
2   Those who are capable and act quickly and who are stout [and can endure]. Also those who do not succumb to illness.
3   Those who are brave and open-minded and those who know much about certain districts and people all over the country, with the addition of being eloquent.

Items you should be aware of in order not to allow a spy or Shinobi to infiltrate your position

1   Strictly guard the gates and checkpoints and arrange for signal fires and signal flags and also 'dual section' tallies,[4] identifying marks and passwords.
2   Examine merchant travellers or travelling monks who are training or collecting for their home temple.
3   If any of your allies have relatives within the enemy, they should declare this immediately.
4   If you receive an offer [from one of the enemy] to spy for you, then you should report this immediately.
5   Understand the difference between truth and untruth.[5]
6   If the enemy offer reconciliation and they say they are sincere, then be careful not to be deceived by them.
7   Do your best to defend against double agents.

Of Shinobi Scouts

Shinobi[6] – Scouts have people called shinobi who go to and come from the enemy provinces and they acquire information. There are traditions and skills exclusive to them and they spy on and ascertain the status of the enemy.

Tasks Assigned to the Shinobi

1   To take advantage of enemy gaps, in reference to both information and [the enemy] position.
2   Getting through doors.
3   Body warming device (Donohi) and ignition tools.
4   Signal fires and passwords.

5   The art of quickly changing appearance.

6   Tools used to climb fences, stone walls, earth walls or to cross over rivers.

7   The carrying of various tools.

8   To hide that which is hidden and to display that which should be shown.[7]

9   Attaining [a certain] mindset.

Two major categories of ninja begin to emerge through historical analysis. The categories are not distinguished grammatically.

Firstly, a ninja can be a man or woman with no training whatsoever, who is simply exploited for their innate abilities, even if only minor. For example, a man with a good memory may be used as a shinobi to go forward into an area and gather a mental record, simply because he has the ability to recall information. Or a man who has knowledge of a local area (*Kyodo*) may be called on to act as a ninja and go into that area and gain information. This untrained individual is considered a shinobi by the tacticians of medieval Japan and is not what we would consider a ninja from our modern prospective.

The second category is the archetypal ninja figure, that is a man trained in the arts first outlined above (to any skill level) and who is used as required by a general. Documentation is often vague in distinguishing between these two. The only way to identify each is to understand the context of each historical reference.

Therefore, remember that at times we may be considering a relatively incompetent person, sent out at the whim of the lord, but at other times, the ninja are a group of individuals who were highly trained specialists, who took part in actions that have made them the legends they are today; creeping into castles, passing armed guards as they slip through the shadows, leaving a trail of destruction or silence behind them. Before we can investigate their skills, we have to understand where they came from.

2

the Origin of the Ninja

The people of the Qi dynasty trained themselves with these skills [of ninjutsu], and Xu Fu[8] inherited the traditions and brought them to Japan.[9] He went to the Kumano Mountains and tried to find [the elixir of life,] however, he could not find what he was looking for in the land of Japan but he did not return to China. From here, he then went into the mountains in Iga province and passed down these subtle secrets of military skills to two of the children he brought with him.

The 'lost' chapter of the Nagata version of the *Shinobi Hiden*, 1646

While the true origin of the ninja has been lost, this chapter will record for the first time in English their appearance in accordance with the actual historical record.

No reference to date of the word ninja or *shinobi no mono*, in any of its forms, has been discovered earlier than the end of the fourteenth century. As research stands, nothing is written describing the act of espionage or infiltration using the ideogram 忍 as a name for the agent before this date. This sets the base point for the entry of ninja into written history.

The Chinese Idea

Separating the ninja from a Chinese[10] ancestry is almost impossible, as much of what the ninja stands for has some connection to Chinese skills in one way or another and as will be shown in a later chapter, the ninja or their skills most likely did originate from the Asian mainland. The evidence for this Chinese connection is immense, yet still myths and misnomers proliferate within the ninja enthusiast communities around the world. One such unfounded (yet maybe not wholly incorrect) story is that, under oppression from the harsh Chinese totalitarian system, Chinese refugees fled to Japan and found their way to the soon-to-be ninja homeland provinces of Iga and Koka, where in the mountains they taught the locals the way of the ninja. This is a modern construct and has no historical record, and whilst it is undeniable that Chinese immigrants came to Japan in many waves and at various points – including the Chinese origins of the famous 'ninja family' Hattori – there is only one piece of 'evidence' to connect Chinese migration with *ninjutsu,* which comes from the Nagata version of the *Shinobi Hiden* manual (quoted above) but any attempt at constructing theories based on this is impossible as the document was written over 1000 years after the event and is only a family tradition based on a famous ancestor – a common thing in the manuals – and results in pure speculation.

What we do know is that in Japan around the end of the fourteenth century the word *shinobi* appears, and then begins to appear more frequently until it becomes known all over the world today. When written evidence cannot be found, speculation is our only recourse.

The Mythological Origin

The *Igamondo Ninjutsu Kazamurai no Makoto* scroll of the Edo period states that ninjutsu originated at the time of the Emperor Jimmu and was transmitted by a man named Doushin No Mikoto, who was a descendant of the god Amatsu-shinobi, who achieved a great success in a place called Shinobi-kaza.

This myth is not shared by the three major works of ninjutsu and is probably an Edo period historical fantasy. The use of the ideogram for ninja appears in the name of the god and in the place name. These place names or names of gods were inscribed well after any period of importance for the ninja and must be ignored in any attempt to find the origin of the ninja, as they seem more wishful than historically verified.

The Ninjas' Origin Beliefs

The shinobi themselves did possess origin myths or origin theories. Whilst these stories can be found in credible manuals, it does not mean they are correct. Just as the Spartans claimed to be 'descended from Hercules' and the Nazis from pure white Aryan ancestors, the ninja did not necessarily descend from the 'historical' persons they mention. The *Shoninki* manual states: 'Shinobi have existed in Japan since ancient times'; the *Shinobi Hiden* states: 'In our country these skills [of ninjutsu] are found as late as in the era of the Emperor who was called Tenchi 天智天皇 (626-672).' The *Bansenshukai* explains:

Question: When did this way [of ninjutsu] come into use in our country [of Japan]?

Answer: A brother of the 38th Emperor Tenchi was Emperor Temmu. In this period when Prince Seiko plotted treason against him and holed up in a castle that he had constructed in Atago of Yamashiro Province, the Emperor Temmu had a shinobi named Takoya 多胡弥 and he infiltrated the fortress. Takoya got into the castle and set fire to it, as a result the emperor penetrated its defences and the castle fell without difficulty. This is the first time that ninjutsu was used in our country. This is written in the Chronicles of Japan. Since then no general has not used this skill. It is also said that those generals who fully exploited ninjutsu were Ise no Saburo Yoshimori, Kusunoki Masashige and his son, Takeda Shingen, Mori Motonari, Echigo Kenshin, and Lord Oda Nobunaga. Of them, Yoshimori produced 100 poems about the shinobi and they have been passed down to this day.

As can be seen, the ninja themselves believed in a history which stretched back well before the actual period that ninjutsu appears in the historical record, predating that appearance by hundreds of years. It can be argued that the *Bansenshukai's* origin story was based on Fujibayashi consulting the *Shinobi Hiden*[11] manual, as he may have had access to it. If that is the case it helps to support the idea of a unified and well connected ninja community, which possibly shared a common origin story. However, the problems are compounded by the fact that after the *Bansenshukai*, many documents simply copy the latter manual's information and origin story.

It can be stated that the ninja believed that their skills had an origin in China and that at some point, by an unknown medium, the arts of the ninja were brought to the shores of Japan, where they were then perfected, altered or honed by the warriors of Japan and that the people in the regions of Iga and Koka were the exemplars of the skills of the ninja. With the Chinese immigrant origin not based on historical records, we need to look at the documents we have.

The Seventh-Century Myth

One recurring myth is that of a seventh-century use of the word shinobi. This myth has its foundation in the scroll the *Ninjutsu Ogiden* (1840) where it says that the origin of the name shinobi was established in the seventh century; Otomo no Sahito, who was a retainer of Prince Shotoku, worked as his agent and was called a 'shinobi' 志能便.

The *Ninjutsu Ogiden*, 1840.

The *Ninjutsu Ogiden* is the second scroll of that name, the first being from the Sengoku period, however the one used here is from 1840, near the end of the Edo period. The word shinobi was not only well established by this point but also at the end of its military significance. Therefore, this information appears to be highly dubious as there is no historical documentation to support this statement in any way, and it should be considered to be a fabrication of the author, which means that the actual first mention of shinobi is in the *Taiheki* war chronicle.

The *Taiheiki* War Chronicle

The first historically identifiable use of the ideogram for ninja 忍 as a definite name for a military role, dates to the late fourteenth century, where two descriptive segments discuss the shinobi and show their first confirmed usage, the document is the famous *Taiheiki* war chronicle. Volume 20 states:

> One night, as it was windy and raining, Moronao took advantage of the weather and sent out an *Itsu mono no shinobi* 逸物ノ忍 [excellent ninja] to infiltrate Hatchiman Yama and to set fire to the buildings.

Volume 24 continues with the second use of shinobi:

> The Shogunate's military governor, Tsuzuki-nyudo, led 200 armed people on a night raid, and approached Shijomibu, from the direction where *Kukkyo no shinobi* 究竟ノ忍 (robust ninja) were hiding. Those soldiers [ninja] in the complex did not care for life or death and went to the top of a building and after spending all their arrows committed suicide[11] (*hara kaki yaburu*).

This document of the late fourteenth century deals primarily with the Nanboku-cho, the period of war between the Northern Court of Ashikaga Takauji in Kyoto and the Southern Court of Emperor Go-Daigo in Yoshino. It features the tactics of the famous general, Kusunoki Masashige; only a few early copies survive. The manual viewed by the Research Team was the *Seigenin Bon* version at Tokyo University and dates to between 1520 and 1550. The *Kanda Bon* manual is the oldest but only a single chapter remains and unfortunately it contains neither of the above references.

This finding initiates some debate. Firstly, most 'anti-ninja' historians argue that the term shinobi was an invention of the Edo period, which is without doubt incorrect, as through this find (and others) we know the term shinobi predates the Edo period. The *Seigenin* version –viewed by the team – has the correct ideogram and as this was written in the early 1500s it shows that the ideogram shinobi is clearly recognised in the Sengoku period, putting the ninja in Japan well before the time of peace. Secondly, the fact that it comes with no explanation as to what a 'shinobi' is, proves that the word was in common usage and was accepted as a fact, implying that the shinobi as an entity was present in the early 1300s and possibly before.

Further shinobi-like skills are clearly displayed in other sections of the *Taiheiki*,[12] such as the following episode concerning Kasagi Castle:

> Under the cover of this night's rain and wind, let us secretly enter the castle precincts to amaze the men of the realm with a night attack!
>
> Thereupon all drew holy pictures to wear in preparation for death, since they were resolved not to return alive. They took two lead ropes for horses, 100 feet long, knotted them at intervals of a foot, and tied a grapnel at the end, that by hanging ropes from branches and boulders they might climb over the rocks.
>
> On that night one could see nothing, however much one looked, for it was the last night of the lunar month. Moreover it was a night of furious rain and wind, when opposing armies would not go forth to clash in battle. With swords and daggers on their backs, the 50 men began to climb the northern rampart of the castle, a rock wall 1500 feet high, where even a bird could not fly so easily. In diverse ways they went up for 750 feet, until with perplexed hearts they beheld rocks like folding screens, rising up in layers above them in a place of smooth green moss and ancient pines with dropping limbs.
>
> Thereupon Suyama Tozo ran up lightly over the rocks, hung the lead ropes [with grapnels] onto a branch of the tree, and lowered them from above the rocks, so that the warriors passed over the difficult place easily by laying hold of them. And there was no other great precipice above. Toiling sorely, they grasped Kuzu roots in their hands and walked over the moss with

their toes, until with the passing of four hours they came to the edge of the [castle] wall. And when they had rested their bodies awhile, every man of them climbed over.

Then in stealth they spied upon the castle interior by following a sentry making his rounds. They saw that 1000 warriors of Iga[13] and Ise guarded the front gate on the west side of the mountain…

…Could it be that the defenders trusted the steepness of the cliffs of the north side? No warriors watched there, but only two or three soldiers of low degree, who had lit a campfire and gone to sleep on straw matting spread below the tower.

When Suyama and Komiyama had gone around the castle to see the enemy positions on four sides, they turned their footsteps toward the main hall, thinking to search out the abode of the emperor. Hearing them, a man of the Battle Office asked a question saying:

'It is strange indeed that many men pass thus stealthily in the night, who are you?'

Quickly Suyama Yoshitsugu answered him saying:

'We are warriors of Yamato, guarding against attackers slipping in by night, for the wind and rain are very violent and there is much noise.'

'To be sure' said the voice and there was no other question [from him].

Thereafter they ascended calmly to the main hall without seeking concealment, shouting aloud 'All positions be on the alert!' When they beheld the hall, they saw that it was indeed the imperial abode, where candles burned in many places and a bell rang faintly. There were three or four men in high crowned caps and robes serving in an anteroom.

'Which warrior-guards are you?' they asked.

And the warriors [who had just crept into the castle] lined up close together in the winding corridor, giving the names of such and such a person and from this and that province.

When Suyama and his men beheld everything, even to the imperial abode, they made their hearts strong, bowed down in front of the god of the mountain, climbed the peak above the main hall, lighted a fire in a deserted compound, and raised a battle cry together.

This fourteenth-century episode rings out with skills that can be seen in the major ninja manuals of the seventeenth century, such as the *Bansenshukai, Shinobi Hiden* and *Shoninki*. Using two apparently 'specialised' men to lead them on their night raid, they climb impossible cliffs or 'difficult areas' as ninja manuals state, then scale the castle wall and get into the main compound. Here they turn stealthy infiltration (*In-nin*) to open disguise (*Yo-nin*), using classic tricks such as claiming to be searching for enemies and giving false background stories, leaving them to wander freely around the castle, until they reach the required area, set it ablaze and attack. Of course, this is a classic stealthy night raid and should not be confused with a 'pure' shinobi infiltration. In the night raid, it is often the case that a shinobi will lead the warriors, as did the two figures in the story. A shinobi raid is by a group of trained infiltrators who creep in in a similar fashion and set fires, but remain hidden. Either way, the above extract shows classic ninja skills that are indisputably in the 1300s.

Two further points can be taken. Firstly, the men of Iga (a place famous for ninja) who were guarding the gate showed no signs of understanding these tactics and in fact were guarding the one place that a shinobi would not come from. This, combined with other references to the men of Iga in the *Taiheiki*, shows that the warriors of Iga province are not trained in shinobi ways at this point and it is not until the late 1400s, about 150 years after this attack, that the men of Iga and Koka are famed for their skills in such attacks. This shows that stealth and infiltration techniques were not born in Iga but were perfected there. Secondly, the translation claims that the warriors had 'swords and daggers on their backs', one of the earliest references of a 'ninja' style use of the samurai sword on an infiltrator's back whilst climbing.

This period, between the time before the *Taiheiki* and the solid incarnation of the ninja in the Sengoku period, could be what most shinobi in their writings consider 'Ancient Times' one that the ninja authors of the early Edo period were reflecting back on. However, in this blind period before the Sengoku period, and before the example given above, there is one reference that that will spark the imagination of all ninja researchers.

The Strange Case of the Stealer-Samurai

In 1232 the *Goseibai Shikimoku Shokai* document or the 'Formulary of Adjudications' was written by the Kamakura Shogunate to help provide a fair basis of law and a regulated judicial system. It was aimed primarily at the samurai class and outlined the punishments for selected crimes. One of the 51 articles, Article 33, has a fascinating section which allows us to delve into the possible early years of the ninja in Japan:

Article 33 of the *Goseibai Shikimoku Shokai* document from the 1300s.

> The punishments administered to those who steal by force and by infiltration, including arsonists are well established [in our country]. Therefore, those thieves (Tozuku) should be decapitated and arsonists should be treated in the same way, this is done to exterminate this type of crime.

The most vital point is that the word for shinobi does not appear in this text and the ideograms used are descriptions of crimes and are not used as titles to describe a task or a function. However, that being said, when put into context it gives an insight into shinobi-like activity in the early thirteenth century. Article 33, as translated above, mentions two forms of theft: 'forced' theft, such as street robbery and banditry and theft by 'infiltration' or 'sneaking in'. The two forms are expressed in a complex way and need to be teased out of the text, but to a Japanese reader they are clear. The full term is 強竊二盗 and can be broken down as follows:

1 強   by force
2 竊   by creeping
3 二   two of
4 盗   thievery

The four ideograms.

As you can see, a literal translation would 'by force, by creeping, two [ways] of stealing'. For a native Japanese speaker of the thirteenth century this would reference two methods of theft, terms still used in the Japanese language today. The first two single ideograms can be added to the last ideogram in the example. Here is how it would look:

- 強 force and 盗 stealing   強盗
- 竊 creeping and 盗 stealing   竊盗

It is the second example of 竊盗 (*Setto* or shinobi) that is of interest to us and whilst on its own the find is not significant, when it is combined with other elements it becomes hugely important.

The term 竊盗, as explained above, has multiple interpretations in Japan, one of which is *Setto* and the other of course is shinobi.[14] Remember that in this thirteenth-century case, it is not the name of a position or title, because the syntax demands 'the art of stealing into a house by using creeping methods'. The amazing fact here is that it is samurai who were using the art of infiltration to break into domestic buildings and steal for profit. It refers to early shinobi-like activity by the military class in a time of relative peace. It shows that the samurai were 'restless' and using their skills for personal gain. We also see that 150 years later, the *Taheiki* war chronicle mentions samurai who have special infiltration skills and talks about them as 'shinobi' whose skills are identical, that is they 'creep in' and infiltrate, but this time it is for the purpose of destruction. So these 'ninja' skills are considered of military value in wartime but when in times of peace, such skills could be and were used for personal gain and were therefore classed as a crime.[15] We see the ideograms 竊盗 being used to mean samurai who steal by stealth and later used to represent the military figure, the shinobi.

The relationship between military infiltration (shinobi) and theft (*Nusubito/Tozoku*) becomes more complicated as time progresses. By the mid 1500s the ideograms of 竊盗 explained above and the classic example of 忍 both have identical readings and both are recorded with the phonetics 'shinobi'.

What does this mean? It means that by the end of the 1300s, people understood that a shinobi was a person who infiltrated camps or houses and that the word shinobi could be written in the two ways, that is 竊盗 and 忍. It is only by considering the individual context of each example that a reader can determine if it is the name of a specialised person (a shinobi) or if it is the action of creeping in.

To compound the problem, ninjutsu manuals use both of the above versions (and more) in the same section of text and there appears to be no reason why they switch between the two. The *Shinobi Hiden* uses both versions, as does the *Bansenshukai*, whereas the *Taiheiki* war chronicle and the *Gunpo Jiyoshu* military arts manual only use one version each. The *Gokuhi* manual uses only phonetic markers 忍び or 志のび. However, the *Koka Shinobi Den Mirakai* manual dictated by the samurai-ninja named Kimura Onosuke states that the tacticians of his time do not understand the difference between these two forms of ninja, so he differentiates between the two types of ninja agent. Cross-referencing with other documentation, it can be concluded that in the minds of some chroniclers the ninja can be separated into those who spy in a classic sense, that is, those included in Sun Tsu's five spies, and those ninja who steal in by stealth alone.

In summary, the term shinobi was well established from the time of the *Taiheiki* in the late fourteenth century. It continued to be used through to the Sengoku period. The word shinobi as a title is by no means a modern invention, making the ninja at least 700 years old, if not older.

Ninja or Thief?

To understand the difference between the term *Nusubito* (thief) and shinobi we need to know what kind of stealing they were doing. First it must be understood that the term *Nusubito* is a generic word for thief. Which means that simply finding the word *Nusubito* in a document does not confirm a shinobi reference, however, further markers in the text will help prove if the form of stealing was similar to that of a ninja or not. The following two examples are taken from the military writings of Todo Takatora, a distinguished Sengoku period general who was active at the height of the Japanese civil wars.

> If you have been robbed by a Nusubito, do not investigate the issue, it may turn out that you will be ridiculed in the end for your carelessness [for allowing the theft to take place]. Furthermore, even if you identify who the thief is, do not pursue the acquisition because it may turn out that he is a part of a retainer's group, therefore you should reduce any form of punishment [if the case arises]. Otherwise you will have to submit notice that these hired retainers are of the same ilk [as the associated thief]; and further, you should consider the stolen object to be lost and not pursue the criminal and also, you should restrain your greed.

The words are for the samurai class and imply that the thief in question is either of lower samurai status or an aide connected to a samurai retainer. By the context of this description we know that Todo is talking here of infiltration into a house. The idea that the victim does not know who the culprit is and the fact that he did not simply cut him down in the street implies this was not face-to-face banditry or street robbery. Also, the loss of an object precious to you would suggest it was contained in your living area. So the *Nusubito* here was using the arts of infiltration to gain entrance into a house or restricted area with the intent of stealing for profit.

Todo continues his message about the art of the Nusubito: 'Whilst you are young, learn all kinds of arts, as it is easy to throw them away at a later point. You should even learn the art of the Nusubito thief, as it will teach you the ways of defence against thievery itself.'

So the samurai class is exhorted to learn the art of thievery, something that seems to have been more common than we thought. This perfectly matches the teachings of the *Tenshin Katori Shinto Ryu* sword school of Japan, a 600-year-old sword school that teach the arts of the ninja to their students to help them defend against ninja theft.

The following two quotations from the *Jinkaishu* statute imposed by the Date clan, probably around the year 1536, speak about the concept of *Nusubito* and indirectly the issue of arson, and show the way in which people thought about *Nusubito* thieves:

Setting ablaze to a person's property is a serious crime which is equivalent to that of Nusubito thievery.

Those peasants who do not pay tax or the required dues to a Jito estate steward and who flee to another province should be charged with a seriousness equivalent to that of a *Nusubito* thief. Therefore, those who give them quarter should give notice and hand them over. If they do not and continue to give them shelter, then they too will be as guilty as the fugitives themselves.

Remembering that the skill of the shinobi is akin to that of the *Nusubito* and in truth are only separated by motive, then we can see where a negative opinion of shinobi may have come from.

Lord Kujo Masatomo (1445–1516) was a court noble who left behind the document *Masatomo Ko Tabi Hikitsuke* or *Record of Masamoto's Travels*, in which we see more laws and punishments concerning the *Nusubito* thief.

The sixteenth day of the second month of 1504

It was raining when the headmen of Oki and Funabuchi Village reported to the Lord and they said:

'Because of the drought of last year, a lot of peasants have died. So we have gathered bracken and barely managed to survive. However, someone is stealing our food from us and as we would die if our stocks run out, we decided to keep guard over it. Recently, some came to steal from the storehouse and we gave chase and found them running into the house of a woman fortune teller of Takimiya shrine. When we entered we found they were her two sons and because they were the *Nusubito*, we killed all three of them, the mother and her two sons. We have come to report this with respect.'

Lord Masatomo's wrote about this case:

It is quite harsh that they killed them all, even their mother and that there are no witnesses left. However, accounts of *Nusubito* activity have been frequently rumoured of late and the punishment for lower village people should be decided among themselves, so this cannot be helped as they [the thieves] must take the consequences of their own deeds as *Nusubito*. *Namuamidabutsu* [a Buddhist prayer].

So as early as the 1200s, samurai and military personnel were already proficient in clandestine operations and they used their knowledge of the art of creeping in to profit by theft. In times of war, these skills were being used by generals for clandestine infiltration into enemy positions. Also, at some point, the shinobi become a specialisation within the military class. Two versions of the word 'shinobi' are used to describe a person with a selection of specialised skills later known as *shinobi no jutsu*. In addition, theft was common and considered a skill among all classes including the samurai, who were active thieves throughout much of samurai history.

The Shinobi in the Fifteenth Century

In 1487, the ninth *Ashikaga* Shogun, Yoshihisa, took up position in a temple in Magari, where he was in conflict with Rokkaku Takayori, who was the governor of Omi province. One night during the long encampment, 1600 from the Rokkaku camp including men of Koka and Iga conducted a surprise night raid on the Shogun's quarters. It is said they succeeded in getting in the Shogun's bedroom and injuring the Shogun himself, an injury which caused his death the following year. For their abilities and conduct, 21 families of Koka were given a letter of appreciation for their achievements and the *Omi Onkoroku* document (1684–1687)[17] states the following:

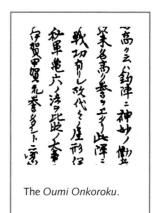

The *Oumi Onkoroku*.

> The *shinobi-shu* of Iga and Koka are renowned because they accomplished an amazing feat at the battle of Magari-no-jin, earning the respect of the massive army gathered there. Since then they have achieved great fame.

The document then continues to describe the tactics of the warriors as *Kiroku no Ho* or the 'six way method of the turtle', which is a reference to how a turtle retreats into its shell.

> Like a turtle, which pulls in its four legs, head and tail, the people from Iga and koka conducted surprise attacks on the Shogunate's massive army and quickly retreated into the mountains. The army was lured in after them, where [the Iga and Koka people] were waiting for them and thus they attacked by dropping logs or stones from above, trapping them in pits, etc.

How Records Differ in the Sengoku and Edo Period

During the Sengoku period, records of the ninja, such as the *Gunpo Jiyoshu*[18] and others[19] make their mark, however, as the Sengoku period was a time of war, records are not easy to obtain. Accounts of the Tokugawa family hiring shinobi for campaigns exist, the term *Iga* and *Koka no mono* or 'Men of Iga and Koka' become bywords for the ninja and talk of *Iga-shu* and *Koka shu* becomes more common, possibly more so than the word 'shinobi.'

Ninja manuals from the Sengoku period are rare. The *Ogiden* document claims and is believed to be from the late 1500s and the *Shinobi Hiden* manual by Hattori Hanzo I claims to be from 1560. Both use the word shinobi as we know it. One possible reason for the lack of manuals is the destruction of Iga in 1581, as the warlord Nobunaga burnt his way through the land and brought the independent states of Iga under control, leaving nothing but ashes behind. Secondly, the need for manuals in the Sengoku period was significantly less then in the period of peace, as skills were used in everyday life and a level of practical ninjutsu was needed to be effective in war.

The Sengoku period military manual, the *Gokuhi Gunpo Hidensho*[20] uses the word *shinobi*:

> Understanding if the Enemy are Experiencing Famine:
> To identify the status of the enemy, you should send a shinobi しのび to pretend to be a woodcutter or mower in the enemy's territory. He should have the lower ranking people of that area drink[21] [alcohol] and then he should listen to their conversation for clues.

It continues with:

> How to Know if there is an Ambush Ahead:
> To Know if there is an ambush in a forest, send a shinobi しのび from the leeward side so that they can smell Hinawa [musket] fuses and so that they can listen for sounds on the wind.

This manual also discusses the shinobi しのび adopting the painted lantern crests of the enemy, so that the ninja can infiltrate the enemy ranks at night, a skill which is known in the *Bansenshukai* as *Bakemonojutsu* or the skill of transmutation (literally 'Ghost Skill').

The *Edo* or Peace period – the manuals and records from which will be explored in depth as this volume progresses – is the period of the ninja manual 'boom'. Basically, the Edo period starts with accurate accounts of the ninja, but then they start to deteriorate in quality and in some cases build the foundations for future ninja misinformation.

Understanding the Unrecorded History of the Ninja

Whilst Shinobi as a word can be taken back to the *Taiheiki* war chronicle, what is *not* recorded that can also help to find the ninja. When diving deeper into the tomes of ninjutsu, certain figures crop up time and time again: Yoshitune, Masashige, Shingen and others are names that ring out in ninja and samurai history. However, the tactics of all of these famous warriors were written down after their time, including references to their ninja and shinobi usage. Therefore, whilst these works were not recorded by their own hand or by their contemporaries, we know the ninja existed and we know that they conducted asymmetrical warfare. We can consider the tactics of these famous samurai and investigate what the ninja themselves thought of these patriarchs of ninjutsu.

The Ninjutsu of Minamoto no Yoshitsune

Yoshitsune was a twelfth-century figure who fought in the wars of the early Kamakura period. He is a well known figure in Japanese history and also a character in the Japanese epic poem *The Tale of the Heiki*. Fighting alongside him was Ise no Saburo Yoshimori, who was the supposed author of the *100 Ninja Poems*.[22] These two figures, closely acoiated with the origins of ninjutsu, are shadowy figures, as no contemporary literature exists to confirm or deny their involvement in the development of the shinobi ways. However,

500 years after they were active, both the *Shoninki* and the *Bansenshukai* ninja manuals class them as the forerunners of the ninja, and in fact go so far as to imply that ninjutsu was already developed and that they utilised its strategies.

The *Shoninki* states: '[The shinobi's] existence was highlighted at … the Genpei War, when Minamoto no Kuro Yoshitsune picked up and utilised brave men like Ise no Saburo Yoshimori.'

The *Bansenshukai* goes on to state that both of these characters indeed used ninjutsu, and further, the *Bansenshukai* lists the forms of fire tools and torches attributed to *Yoshitsune* and quotes from the *100 Ninja Poems* of Yoshimori.

It will never be known just how much these two figures contributed to the origins of *shinobi no jutsu*, but what is certain is that the ninja themselves considered both figures to be active commanders of shinobi.

The Ninjutsu of Kusunoki Masashige

Masashige is a figure whose deeds are recorded, but whose tactical abilities are mythical. He is described as a general who utilised ninjutsu extensively, however, sorting fact from fiction is very difficult. Contemporary records are scarce and the annals are filled with manuals and lineages of the *Kusunoki-ryu* school that arrive well after his time, showing his continuing popularity. One thing is sure, he is considered as a major figure in the world of the ninja, and by the ninja themselves. The *Shoninki* states: 'In the Kemmu period [of 1334–1336], Kusunoki Masashige used shinobi several times.' The *Bansenshukai* states:

> It is also said that those generals who fully exploited ninjutsu were Ise no Saburo Yoshimori, Kusunoki Masashige and his son,[23] Takeda Shingen, Mori Motonari, Echigo Kenshin, and Lord Oda Nobunaga. Of them Yoshimori made 100 poems about the shinobi and they have been passed down to this day.

Before Kusunoki Masashige was turned into a hero of the post-Meiji Restoration and for the purpose of the Second World War a propaganda tool, he was a much beloved and respected hero of the shinobi and is recorded in various manuals as one of the greatest utilisers of ninjutsu. Shinobi traditions (including the *Bansenshukai*) have considered Kusunoki Masashige and the Kusunoki family to be some of the most important figures in the development of ninjutsu. Masashige is thought to have engaged in both conventional and unconventional warfare, including the use of shinobi.

According to the *Bansenshukai*, Kusunoki Masashige called his shinobi 'Yutei' and 'Yushi', terms that originated in China, as will be discussed later. The *Bansenshukai* clearly sees him in a positive light and explains the methodology of his ninjutsu:

> In Kusunoki Masashige's ninjutsu, there was a skill where he divided 48 ninja into three and always had one of the groups of sixteen people staying in Kyoto. They observed the situation by utilising various plots and kept Kusunoki informed. This is exactly what the word *Yutei* means.

Contrary to popular belief, Kusunoki Masashige did not live during the Nanbokucho period, as he died in 1336, just as the Nanbokucho wars were beginning. Therefore, the ninjutsu he employed was utilised in the Kemmu Restoration of 1333 to 1336, when the Imperial Court defeated the Hojo Clan. The Kusunoki family member who used ninjutsu during the Nanbokucho period was Masashige's son, Masanori (who presumably gained his knowledge of the use of shinobi from his father). It would be the ninjutsu of Kusunoki Masanori that would spread from Kawachi to the rest of Japan, being known loosely as '*Kusunoki-ryu*' or systems based on Kusunoki family techniques.[24] This *Kusunoki-ryu* is referred to in numerous ninjutsu manuals and scrolls.

In short, the ninjutsu of Kusunoki Masashige is a specific form of scouting and spying. As previously stated and according to the *Bansenshukai*, he used the word '*Yushi*' for his shinobi, a Chinese-derived word which translates as 'playing warriors',[25] revealing that he conceived of them as scouts who interfered in other's plans. However, rather than the generic 'Monomi scout', who ventured to the edge of the enemy position to gain information, Kusunoki's *Yushi* were deployed into the territory of the enemy to gather information by blending with the population (the ninja skill of *Yo-nin*) and also, to creep around undetected[26] (the ninja skill of *In-nin*). The Kusunoki Clan serves as an excellent historical focus for understanding the inseparability of ninjutsu and politics and the transmission of Chinese *Yushi* skills to Japan and their evolution into Japanese shinobi. Regardless of political position, clan loyalty and even origin, all shinobi seem to conceive of Kusunoki Masashige as one of the developers of ninjutsu.

The Ninjutsu of Takeda Shingen

Takeda Shingen, the highly respected adversary of Uesugi Kenshin and Togugawa Iyeasu, would probably have become military ruler of Japan, had not his death through illness[27] taken him from the field of battle. Again, literature from his hand or about him by contemporaries has not been dicovered. His connection to ninjutsu is strong and it is thought that he used ninjutsu to a high level. The *Shoninki* states: 'Shingen of Koshu employed those called *Suppa*, who were also thieves of Kai province.'

This statement is perplexing when we consider the Natori family. Here the author of the *Shoninki*, Natori Masatake, calls them 'thieves' and does not form any connection with them. This is strange as the official records of the Kishu-Tokugawa clan record the originator of *Natori-ryu* ninjutsu as Natori's own grandfather, who was a samurai under the Takeda clan. Natori omits this fact, and it is well established that the Natori clan did serve the Takeda family and that they originated *Natori-ryu*. It is strange that Natori in his own ninja manual states that they are 'thieves of Kai', considering the connection to his own family. Sadly, we will never know why Natori chooses to ignore his own ancestry.

The ninjutsu of the Takeda was not recorded at the time that it was utilised, that is during the Sengoku period. However, afterwards it was said to have branched off into many variations, including the *Koshu-ryu, Takeda-ryu, Koyo-ryu,* etc and the tactics are recorded in the *Koyo-gunkan* military war manual. It is unknown how close these schools actually are to the original Takeda system that was used in war.

The *Iga-ryu Koka-ryu Shinobi Hiden* scroll talks of Shingen's connection to the ninja and establishes how he used them. It is said that Takeda Shingen instructed his three retainers, Babamino no Kami, Yamagata Saburobei and Yamamoto Kansuke, to hire four men to command his *Denuki* or *Suppa*, both considered to be shinobi in some form. Shingen then ordered two of the three, Babamino no Kami and Yamagata Saburobei, and a third man, Mutokihei Yoshibei, to have a further and secret meeting with Yamamoto Kansuke, who was told to pass the skills of this type of warfare on to a select number of people. It must be noted here that the *Gunpo Jiyoshu* manual of *c*.1612 does in fact name Yamamoto Kansuke in its shinobi scrolls as a person with this kind of knowledge. It is not known how many people he passed the arts on to, but the following names are recorded within the Matsushiro domain.

Kosaka Danjo
Oi Zuioken
Osawa Dojusai
Obata Kanbei
Hara Hayato
Tomagawa Daini
Hasegawa Zenbei

Interestingly, the scroll also claims to have a connection to two Iga and Koka ninja, who were named Tada Jibuemon and Takada Gozaemon and that the teachings of the scroll itself are based on the oral teachings of these two men. The scroll lists 72 skills of the ninja.

Takeda Shingen is considered to be a general who used ninjutsu, and after his death numerous schools used his name to form their own military strategies. It is certain that Shingen used the ninja and that he was an adept at their deployment. An independent study of the individual Takeda-based systems would display commonalities that would identify his tactics.

The Rise of Iga and Koka

Often, the words 'Iga' and 'Koka' are found next to 'ninja homeland', which often incorrectly changes to 'ninja birthplace'. The name '*Koga*' is a modern representation of the word 'Koka'. The older version is still used in the region to this day, as can be seen by the train station sign opposite.

The next step in understanding the ninja and its connection to the regions of Iga (Modern day Mie Prefecture) and Koka (modern day Shiga Prefecture), is to know that zero documentation exists tying the birth of the ninja to the regions and that ninja documentation itself does not state that these regions gave birth to ninjutsu. As described above, historical figures who do not originate from either Iga or Koka have better claims to be involved with the origin of ninjutsu and predate the mythical 'Iga and koka ninja birth story'. The *Shoninki* states that Yoshitsune and Yoshimori practised ninjutsu and that

The train station in Koka, showing the correct spelling and pronunciation.

from there, ninjutsu also moved to the areas of Iga and Koka, where it was developed into a highly sought-after skill set.

The *Shoninki* states:

> Later, the people from Koka, next to[28] Iga, followed this path of ninjutsu having made the oath of *Ichigun Ichimi*, the friendship oath of 'one district and one band', joining the people together. They went out far and wide to various provinces to utilise their skills. Thus, being universally recognised as the premier shinobi, they exchanged a firm written form of oath, which says 'If I come to where you are, you should show me everything of your province, and if you come to where I am, I will show you everything about my province.'

Yoshie Minami, the Historical Ninjutsu Research Team's translator, feels that there is a subtle hint of disapproval buried in the text focussing on Iga and Koka's mercenary behaviour as opposed to loyal service; however, it is considered that the author Natori acknowledges that these men were at the 'top of their game'. Confirming this, the *Gunpo Jiyoshu* manual clearly identifies the position of the men of Iga and Koka:

> It is common knowledge that there used to be people who were good at this path [of ninjutsu] in Iga and Koka in ancient times. Their skills have been handed to their descendants and that means they still exist. Thus, the people in charge of this job are called *Iga* or *Koka shu* [people of Iga or Koka] and are hired in every clan across Japan.

The *Omiyochishiryaku* (1734) document written by Samukawa Tatsukiyo, a retainer of Zeze domain in Omi, states the following about the men of Iga and Koka.

> *Shinobi no mono* ... are named using the words Iga or Koka and are those people who infiltrate the enemy castle freely and obtain enemy secrets by listening or watching, and then bring this information back to their allies. In China they are called *Saisaku* and among military tacticians they are also called *Kagi* or *Monogiki*. During the Eiroku period (1558-70) there was a great and peerless performer [of ninjutsu] whose name was Tobi Kato (Flying Kato).

The document refers to the famous event when the Iga and Koka retainers found their way through a battle camp into the heart of the enemy Shogun's quarters (as previously described).

> The reason why the ninja from Iga and Koka are spread all over the country is their outstanding achievement when the Ashikaga Shogun [Yoshihisa] was positioned at Magari [in 1487]. All of the armies of Japan immediately got to know of this deed and their fame flourished. At the above event of Magari no Jin [the warrior] Kawai Aki-no-kami and his retainers who were from Iga achieved this outstanding performance of the shinobi [arts], and they were called as *Iga-no-mono* from generation to generation after that. This is the origin of the name of *Iga-no-mono*.

The term *Iga no mono* has become more popular in recent years than *Koka no mono*. However, from a researcher's perspective, the study of the distribution of *Iga no mono* across Japan is difficult to track. According to the research of Associate Professor Isoda, the Sokoushi record states that in the summer of 1615, at the famous siege of Osaka Castle, the province of Iga[29] employed ninja, hiring a total of 50 shinobi. The following year they only retained 40 men.

A further record of the warriors of Iga being used as ninja comes from the *Igaji no Shirube*, which is a record of the Iga ninja who served the Shogun, Tokugawa Ieyasu. It states that in 1584 when the Shogun attacked and besieged a castle, too many '*Iga no mono*' were shot whilst scaling the castle walls and that in total 75 were killed. As a result of this loss of ninja, Lord Ieyasu gave the order to have them equipped with 'iron shields', supposedly to cover them as they scaled the battlements.

So the basic components used by the ninja were most likely a Chinese[30] import that influenced Japanese military skills, producing what is considered the art of ninjutsu. This was then perfected to a high level in the regions of Koka and Iga, where the independent samurai clans would hire out their retainers (with the skills of ninjutsu) to all the provinces of Japan. The method of transaction or means of contract is unknown. However, it is likely that most *Iga no mono* or ninja were hired for around 25[31] Koku,[32] which would place them at the lower end of the samurai class.

How did these men become the elite of the professional commandos of the medieval Japanese world, second to none across the entire nation? The answer can only be theoretical as documentation is lacking. Geographically, the areas are isolated within mountain rings,

The *Iga-ji no Shirube* document.

partly divided from external powers (but not from cultural influence). This semi-secluded area held a collection of samurai families who were at war with each other and as ninjutsu researcher Steven Nojiri points out, the area of Iga and Koka was a 'hell-hole of violence'. This judgement is supported by the historical pacts of both Iga and Koka,[33] which declare a peace in these regions to unify against external aggressors. The *Bansenshukai* is loaded with historical descriptions of where the ninja practitioners of Iga fight with other warriors of Iga by using the arts of ninjutsu. Even in the *Tensho Iga no Ran* war, which saw the crushing of Iga by the Oda family, the Iga samurai (*jizamurai*) clans divided and argued in the end, despite the threat of annihilation. Therefore, on the whole, the image of the freedom-loving and equality-driven 'ninja families' of Iga and Koka is a modern myth. This independent state was a microcosm of Japanese feudal life, with its own wars, dictators and 'rivers of blood', and out of this were born the best ninja in all the land.

Ninja – a Job or a Name?

Is the word 'ninja' a name for a warrior or is it the title of a profession? Terms like 'he is a ninja' or 'he is a samurai' proliferate in the martial arts and history communities. As it will be explained in greater detail later on, a 'samurai' is a social status whilst 'ninja' should be considered as a profession. This conclusion is arrived at owing to the fact that anyone from any social class can be a ninja, yet not everyone can be a samurai. So a shinobi is a man (rarely a woman) who is employed to engage in espionage, guerrilla tactics or arson and can be from any social class but predominantly from the military class at varying levels.

The following quote is from the *Onmitsuhiji Shinobi-daii* ninja manual. It clearly displays the shinobi working above rank and file samurai and taking the position of leaders, as their skill dictates in this situation: 'The shinobi from Sotogane have a method of firing arrows at battle-camp huts to establish the situation [inside of the hut] and thus take the lead over fighting samurai 働士.'

It can be said that ninja was the title of a profession and skill set, as a lawyer is a lawyer and a butcher a butcher. Some ninja were from the lower levels of the samurai elite and some were from the *Ashigaru*, or foot soldier divisions. When the word ninja arises, we must see it as a job title and less as a name for a class of people.

3

Naming the Ninja

Concerning Kagi and Monogiki – Guards [against the ninja] are called Kagi or Monogiki, they are called this because [Kagu] is to 'feel' or 'smell' the presence and Chi of people, whilst Monogiki is to listen to the sounds around. These people circulate around your position as a precaution against the enemy's shinobi no mono.

Heiho Nukigaki Hippu No Sho Gunshi No Maki, 1689

What makes the word 'ninja' so popular today? It is without doubt that the word 'ninja' 忍者 is a relatively modern interpretation, instead of the historically correct and original version of '*shinobi no mono*' or 'shinobi'. However, this was not the only name for this division of warrior-spy. It is unclear when the term 'ninja' was first used, however early twentieth-century books tend to display phonetic markers which spell out '*nin-ja*' next to the ideograms 忍者 which displays a level of uncertainty. In contrast, the phonetic sound of 'shinobi' is dominant throughout history and can be found in many examples, with pronunciation normally aided with 'no' between the two, making the reading '*shinobi (no) mono*' 忍之(ノ)者. Where the ideogram is not accompanied by phonetic markers, then its pronunciation is uncertain but most likely a variant on the term 'shinobi'.

The word 'shinobi' appears in the fourteenth century and then disappears for around 200 years, until it starts to re-emerge at the end of the Sengoku period and the start of the Edo period. Which begs the question, where did it go? As the Sengoku period was filled with warfare and fire, it is possible that documentation regarding the arts of the ninja or even references to them have been destroyed or were simply never made. It is also possible that there are still references to the shinobi to be found in letters and documents as yet unread. Alternative ideograms or the use of phonetics and the use of alternative names is also a possible explanation for the silence; a silence that may be broken by further research.

The final and possibly most significant problem with the term 'shinobi' is the minefield of alternatives. There is a list of names that are considered to be alternatives for the word ninja, words like *Kanja, Suppa, Rappa, Kamari, Onmitsu, Oniwaban, Iga no mono, Koka no mono, Monogiki, Kagi, Yutei, Yushi* and many more.[34] There is no supporting evidence or any solid connection to show why each alternative word is considered to be equal to shinobi, they are just given. The identification of which alternative word actually means ninja is confused by a web of arguments and counter arguments. The level of research required to establish a correct and proven full list for the alternatives to ninja would be a thesis in its own right and has not been presented here. This book concentrates on the main groups and touches on the alternatives for the ninja but predominantly focuses its search on the term 'shinobi' and its specific historical 'footprint'.

The following quotes display the complexities of establishing a correct list of alternative names for the ninja, but will show that the ninja themselves considered the fact that there were many alternatives or titles for their art. The *Bansenshukai* gives a few options:

> Question: Is this art called ninjutsu in China as well?
> Answer: Shinobi is a name that was invented in our country. In the state of Wu[35] it was called Kan 間, and in the Spring and Autumn period, Cho 諜, and in and after the Warring States period [in China], Saisaku 細作, Yutei 遊偵, and so on. All these names refer to ninjutsu. Alongside this, in the Six Secret Teachings[36] it is referred to as Yushi 遊士 'playing warrior' and in the Yin Jing 陰経 manual written by Risen it is known as Koujin 行人. As seen in these, it has been called many different names according to the period, or the lord's intention. It is quite similar in our country, as we call it *shinobi Yato, Suppa, Nokizaaru, Mitsumono, Kyoudan*, etc.

The *Kusunoki-ryu Ninpo Dakko Shinobi No Makimono* also states:

> *Tōryu*[37] means the *Kusunoki-Ryu* and the skill of *Dakko* – which means depriving the world by mouth – and these are considered the art of the shinobi. Each family has their own name for this art and that name changes. In the Takeda clan it is called *Suppa*[38] and in the Hojo clan it is called *Fuma* and that clan uses *Tozoku* (thieves). A common saying is '*Suppa no gotoku*' that is to 'be like *Suppa*'; this phrase comes from the shinobi of the Takeda clan. Another saying is: '*Ame furi Fuma ni shinobu*' that is, 'to steal in during the rainfall, just like *Fuma*'.

There exists a historical whirlpool, where true alternatives for the word or idea of the ninja clash and mix with the waters of false or misunderstood variations. The modern ninjutsu community swims in this mixture, sometimes stating the truth and sometimes accepting the incorrect as fact.

4

Putting the '忍' in Ninja

After the defeat of Moriya, we were named with the ideogram shinobi 忍

The Ogiden manual, 16th century

忍 '*nin*' is the infamous ideogram that sparks the imagination of a myriad martial artists and historians, even the sight of its black form on a page fascinates most ninja enthusiasts. However, this should not always be the case. Firstly, the shinobi come under many guises, as discussed above, and secondly, this Chinese ideogram is not always considered to mean ninja. The ideogram itself is thousands of years old, yet the shinobi can only be traced back to the fourteenth century, and without doubt this symbol is not solely linked to the ninja in

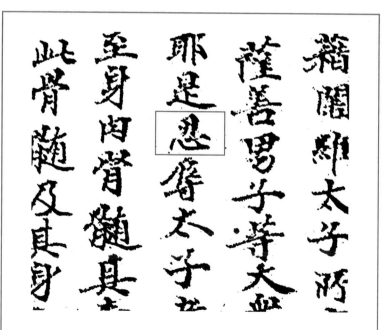

A ninth-century example of the ideogram '*nin*' can be seen in the centre, third ideogram down from the top.

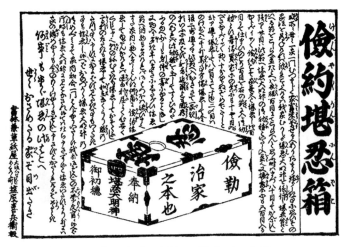

Nin can be seen on the right-hand side and is the fourth ideogram down.

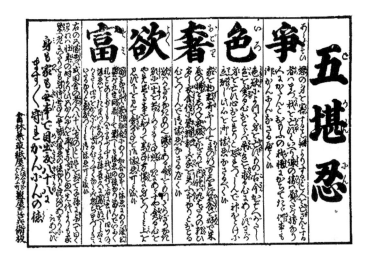

The ideogram *nin* can be seen on the right.

the Japanese mind or language. There are multiple meanings that can be extracted from this ideogram, such as stealth, perseverance, creeping, hidden, and others. It can hold a number of connotations depending on the syntax. For example, a *shinobi-amigasa* 忍び編み笠 (or *shinobi-gasa*) is often thought to be a 'ninja-hat'; however, this is not the case as its true translation is 'the hat that hides [the person's face]'. It was worn by those who wanted to hide their face when travelling to places they did not wish to be seen, such as brothels or gambling houses and had no connection to the ninja themselves. (It would be illogical for a ninja to have a specific hat, unles it served some specific military purpose.) Further examples of this can be seen in the two images above, where the ideogram '*nin*', not only has a different pronunciation to either '*nin*' or '*shinobu*' but in fact means to 'persevere', and not in the manner a ninja needs to.

There are three basic ways to investigate the ideogram, 忍, which help identify if it has anything to do with the ninja. The two phonetic ways to read Chinese ideograms in Japanese are known as *Onyomi* and *Kunyomi*, the mock-Chinese pronunciation and the Japanese respectively. It is not always known which way they are to be read.[39] For example, the famous manuscript in the Hattori family is commonly known as the *Ninpiden,* however the alternative (and most likely correct) reading is *Shinobi-hiden.* Also, *shinobi no mono* is the correct and older reading of *nin-ja.* It is not always so simple! The ninja manual the *Sho-nin-ki* can only be read as '*nin*' and not in an alternative way.

The following quotations highlight three main areas to consider when reading the ideogram 忍 and show how there are situations where this symbol represents a ninja, where it may do, and where it most definitely does not.

The following is an example of 忍 being used directly to mean ninja as a person and in the capacity we would understand.

忍びが敵陣に忍び入る
The shinobi crept into the castle undetected

The following is an example of 忍 where it is ambiguous and means 'stealthy' and could either relate to a ninja or have connections to infiltration. Remember here, it is unknown if this is a ninja, or someone acting in a stealthy manner.

忍び取の城は手づよく二番勢押し詰ぬれば乗とるとしれ
A castle taken by a stealthy action is captured only when strong secondary forces come to secure the occupation.

The following is an example of 忍 devoid of any connection to the ninja at all:

人目を忍んで会う
To go on a date in secret

One example of misunderstanding the ideogram for '*nin*' is in a martial arts scroll for a school called *Shinobi-ryu or Nin-ryu* 忍流 (1627), which led to the idea of a possible ninja style of fighting. The possibility soon fades as on closer inspection the ideogram means 'determination' or 'diligence' and uses the character for '*nin*' as 'perseverance' and describes no relation to the Shinobi.[40]

The following section will expand on the preceding examples and display the various instances when the word '*nin*' is in direct relation to the shinobi. Furthermore it will show the diverse ways in which the ninja were integrated into the military society of Japan, making them not an

This image leaps off the page for a shinobi researcher as it is the classic shinobi 忍び, however, in this case, it is a secret love or love affair.

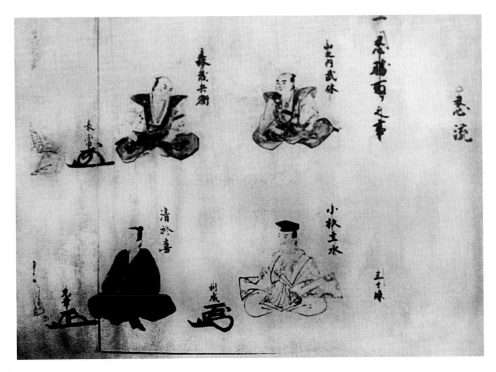

A section of the *Nin-ryu* manual.

alternative culture to the samurai, as somtimes thought, but an integral part of the samurai military machine.

The Ninja
Ideogram: 忍者
Onyomi reading: *Ninja*
Kunyomi reading: *Shinobi no mono*
A man whose profession is a ninja or is a person carrying out the arts of ninjutsu.

The Shinobi [no] Samurai
Ideogram: 忍士
Onyomi reading: *Ninshi*
Kunyomi reading: *Shinobi no samurai*

As an ideogram compound, this appears in various documents, attesting to the acceptance of the ninja at times as part of the samurai class. The word is made up of shinobi and samurai together, implying a samurai whose job is that of a ninja. A historical example of such a position would be Natori Masatake (though never used in connection to him directly) as he was a samurai of modest pay whose function was that of a ninja for the Kishu-Tokugawa and who headed the Natori secret military school. Therefore, we can infer that whenever this ideogram combination is used, the *shinobi* in question was of the samurai class, albeit probably of the lower grade. It is highly unlikely that any samurai of high status would be a ninja, as the ninja's function was direct and physically applicable, whereas the higher one is in the samurai class, the more the emphasis is on command and strategy.

The Shinobi-soldier
Ideogram: 忍兵
Onyomi reading: *Ninpei*
Kunyomi reading: *Shinobi no tsuwamono*

Literally, this is shinobi and soldier, a soldier who is also a ninja. However, unlike the previous example of shinobi-samurai, it is possible that this can refer to both foot soldiers and lower grade samurai. This is made possible by the fact that a higher scale warrior may use the term 'Hei' (soldier) to mean those lower than he is, including low-ranking samurai, which means it is not certain if this is a direct reference to the *Ashigaru* foot soldier class or not. Interestingly, the term soldier 兵 has even been used in relation to the high ranking samurai named Sanada Nobushige (also Yukimura).

The use of this compound sheds some light on the social hierarchy inside the shinobi ranks, as both Ninshi and Ninpei described above had 'ninja-captains' or *Shinobi-gashira* to lead them.

Ninja Captains
Ideogram: 忍頭
Onyomi reading: None
Kunyomi reading: *shinobi-gashira*

Here the phonetics *Shinobi no Tsuwamono* were next to the ideograms.

Having looked at the possible social aspects of the names *Ninshi* and *Ninpei* and the difficulties in aligning them with the correct social class, we come across the *shinobi-gashira*, a term that has definite social parallels. The suffix *kashira* (which becomes *gashira*) is a captain of a squad and this rank is found in several positions within the military framework. Examples such as *Yumi-gashira*, a captain of archers, establish that this military post was an authoritative one. What is not clear is if this position was given to samurai or high ranking *Ashigaru* foot soldiers. However, the main point to try to establish is the social position of a shinobi within an army and within the command structure of armed regimes. The following document is a record of the men left behind by the warlord Kato Kiyomasa to defend his castle of Kumamoto whilst he took part in the Keicho invasion of Korea (1597–98).

The list consists of names and positions, such as Mori Kanzaemon who took charge of 100 archers and Tadera Hisadayu who took command of eleven mounted warriors.

中川善林鉄拾三人

四宮藤五郎弓百人
毛利勃太夫預弓一百人
田寺久助預鉄十人
佐野弥三預頭十人
津田兵部三騎忍頭十人

The term 'shinobi-gashira [including] ten men' can be seen in the bottom left of this image.

Listed amongst them and equal at least in being mentioned is a man named Tusda Hyobu, a *shinobi-gashira* or ninja captain who has command of ten people, presumably ten ninjas. This example can be seen in the last four ideograms on the left hand side of the image; they read as '*Shinobi-gashira* [including] ten men'. In other records, the listing of three *shinobi-gashira* who commanded two or three shinobi each can be seen, showing that the shinobi groups were under the command of a ninja captain.

This truly scotches the myth of the samurai versus ninja and defines the ninja as actual samurai, who were well established within the ranks of standard armies.

Enemy Ninja
Ideogram: 敵忍
Onyomi reading: *Tekinin*
Kunyomi reading: *Teki no shinobi*
The simple concept of a ninja who serves a lord that is in opposition to 'your' lord and thus is considered the enemy.

Ninja Poems
Ideogram: 忍歌
Onyomi reading: *Ninka*
Kunyomi reading: *Shinobi uta*
These are in the form of Japanese *Tanka* poetry and are centred on themes that relate to ninja activity with the aim of disseminating knowledge to future generations.

Ninja Gunpowder
Ideogram: 忍焼薬
Onyomi reading: None
Kunyomi reading: *Shinobi yakigusuri*
A form of gunpowder used by the ninja in some of their tools.

Ninja Torch
Ideogram: 忍松明
Onyomi reading: None
Kunyomi reading: *Shinobi taimatsu*
A torch specifically used by the ninja or used for shinobi activity.

All of the above were found in relation to ninja activity within their grammatical placement and thus are known to refer to ninja. Having now established that more often than not the ideogram for '*nin*' is used without reference to ninja and that each example has to be checked for its own context, we will move on to show the various slight variations in the form of the ideogram itself.

Variations on the Ideogram 忍

The ideogram is of course of Chinese origin and means 'perseverance' or to 'steal in', and was established long before the shinobi of Japan came to be. Japanese text can be divided into *block* and *cursive* style, the former being a clear image and the latter being generally a form of connected or 'sloppy' writing. Examples found in Japanese literature:

The standard ideogram for 'nin'.

The ideogram 'nin' from the *Shinobi Hiden* (1560), transcribed in 1733.

The ideogram for 'nin' from the *Shoninki* of 1681, transcribed in the mid 1700s.

The ideogram for 'nin' from the *Otsubohon* school of horse riding, Edo Period.

The ideogram for 'nin' from the *Kusunoki Masashige Ikkan no Sho* manual of the Edo Period, accompanied by the phonetic spelling of 'shinobi'.

The following two examples come from the Edo period, however, both are in reference to the name of Oshi Castle and have no connection to the ninja, they simply spell out a name, which is a fine example of how the ideogram for shinobi is found with zero connection to the ninja and an example of how the pronunciation can be totally different. They are examples of *Sosho*, or cursive style writing and are difficult for most readers of Japanese.

A point of interest – the diagonal dash normally inserted through the upper left part of the 'blade' ideogram 刃 was originally extended and as can be seen in all of the historical examples, this dash cuts through both sides of the radical in early manuals but is drawn back and only dissects one side in later texts.

As we have seen, the use of the ideogram 忍 is a more complex subject than one might think, with variations in meaning and grammatical differences due to placement. The simple fact is that in most cases, it has nothing to do with the ninja of Japan. So when identifying if a document is in fact referring to the shinobi, the reader must establish if the ideogram is grammatically used in context with infiltration and whether it is referring to a person, a skill or activity, or even mindset. It is only after establishing these points that you can clearly state if a document is discussing the ninja or not.

5

The Samurai versus Ninja Myth

Next to the modern concept that ninjutsu is a specific form of martial art, the ninja versus samurai myth is the second most popular misconception. The idea that the ninja formed as a counter culture to the samurai has taken root, not only in Japan but also the rest of the world. This is not only a recent construction, it is also an outright mistake. The term ninja refers to a position and is not representative of social status. A ninja is a man undertaking a job who is trained in a particular set of skills, his social rank does not come into play. The majority of the population were not samurai and large sections of armies were in fact taken from the peasant class to form *Ashigaru*, or foot soldiers. This means that social status was not a factor in training the ninja and that any man could be taken from any social class and trained, depending on circumstance. Therefore, it is only logical that a high percentage of ninja were from the *Ashigaru* ranks and that an unknown percentage were from the samurai class. The only factors which militate against this logic are that it may have taken a fully retained person, i.e. a samurai, to have the time to concentrate on perfecting the skills of ninjutsu and that many of the listed retainers recorded as ninja were of the samurai class. Remembering that social movement was considerably easier in the Sengoku period, it was not too difficult for a peasant to achieve status as a mercenary and we must not become trapped in the modern connotations of the term 'peasant'. Vast armies were drawn from the peasant class; however, some of these men were promoted and did in fact help shape Japanese history.

Some ninjutsu lines were contained within families and passed down through the bloodline or to a relevant candidate in the family, but family connection was not a prerequisite as is commonly believed. Samurai martial arts and skills were passed down through the clan and to those attached to the family who would also be trained in these arts; ninjutsu is one of those samurai arts and thus was transmitted through a family but not always to those connected by blood. This is inevitable with ninjutsu as it requires a special type of person and therefore recruitment must have been mainly based on ability. It is not uncommon for manuals or documents to recount how certain shinobi would take people of worth in an army and proceed to train them in the arts of the ninja, sometimes with the help of *Iga no mono*. However, social positioning does play a part in the world of the ninja to a small extent and this will be discussed in the next chapter.

Ninja documentation and historical evidence for the fact that there was no divide between the ninja and the samurai comes in many forms and establishes without doubt that during the Sengoku and Edo periods, the ninja were considered as fundamental sections of an army and were indeed not only required elements of medieval defence but were also government employees. Samurai trained in the arts of the ninja or those who understand their use would command and govern their official but hidden ninja agents.

Ihara Yori Fumi was a samurai active in the early part of the 1700s and was retained by the Fukui domain to teach the *Gunpo* arts or the military arts to the clan. Further to this, he held the position of *shinobi no mono shihai* 忍之者支配 or 'ninja commander' and his job was to orchestrate the shinobi of that domain and ensure that their system of spies was working correctly. His position as a shinobi and ninja commander underlines the respect given to the ninja arts from a military perspective and the need for individual provinces to undertake espionage on a committed level. In his manual he states that raiding groups should consist of ten shinobi and 25 'fighting samurai' and that there are difficulties in leading and taking charge of 'fighting samurai' on night raids. These difficulties are highlighted in Yoshimori's ninja poems and show that shinobi are needed to lead squads of men at night, as they are trained in this matter. The *Shoninki* states that ninja used to be known as *Yato*, or leaders in the night, as they took command of samurai teams. So samurai bowed to the command of shinobi, men who were considered to be essential for the job. Ihara Yori Fumi has the shinobi as the leader in the following quotation from his manual:

> In peace times when you go to other provinces on missions you should take those of a lower [social] position[41] and carry alternative[42] rain coats, spare clothes and so on. You should reach for the appropriate contact and proper person. This is how you will be able to see and hear [what you need to]. Before you go to a place of importance you should leave your swords somewhere and you, as the master, should exchange places with those below you (*ge-nin*). Or you may take on the form of a merchant, pilgrim or yamabushi.

Alongside obvious references to social class, his writings also contain more subtle clues to the position of a ninja as here he advises changing places with servants to aid in disguise, showing that having servants was usual for a shinobi.

> When taking part in a mission within your own province, and as it is secret, you should frequent suspicious[43] places. Further to this do not carry luggage and do not hire labourers [to aid you] but stay stealthy and investigate. This way people will give you lodgings with ease.

Ihara Yori Fumi does not stop there as he instructs on measures to be taken by a shinobi commander to ensure the secrecy of his teachings: '[A shinobi commander] should have lower people sign a blood oath with their fingerprint before they teach them how to capture prisoners, of archery and of gunnery.'

The *Onmitsuhiji shinobi-dai* scroll gives an insight into rank within a ninja band:

When entering a battle, you should carry arrows, guns, an investigation or measuring rod, togikinawa,[44] tools to help cross moats and rivers, stone wall climbing tools, Donohi [body warmers and fire lighting equipment], torches and fire projectiles. The highest ranking person should plan the forthcoming infiltration. Remember not to throw away your tools as they may come into the possession of the enemy and your plan may be detected. Remove your armour when you steal in.

A later piece of evidence comes from the *Gohoko no Shina Kakiage* document, which is a record of the retainers who served in the Okayama domain. It has an interesting case that indicates the social level of the shinobi. In 1864 a ninja was punished for becoming involved in money lending with common people. The mention of 'ninja' in contrast to 'common people' in itself makes them of a higher social class. The restriction on money lending is a samurai prohibition, implying that the ninja in question was restricted from lending or borrowing due to his social position as a samurai. And finally, the document is a list of retainers, that is, samurai, or at the lowest, military staff above the peasantry.

Having established that ninja were taken from any class and that often shinobi were placed in charge of samurai, it is best to look at the more famous shinobi authors and ascertain their position. The three most prolific writers on the shinobi are Fujibayashi Yatsutake of the *Bansenshukai*, Natori Masatake of the *Shoninki* and Hattori Hanzo I of the *Shinobi Hiden*.

Fujibayashi lived on the borders of Iga and Koka 100 years after its decimation by Oda Nobunaga. At this point, the families of Iga had been displaced from their land as governors and were sometimes considered as *Koshi*, or displaced samurai. It is difficult to discern from which level Fujibayashi came but he writes that he is a 'retired warrior', which would make him of samurai status, or at least a displaced samurai. Natori is without doubt a samurai and comes from a relatively prestigious family (of around 250–300 Koku in income) and is in the personal employ of the Kishu-Tokugawa clan, one of the most prominent families in all Japan. He is also the head of the *Natori-ryu*,[45] which is considered one of the premier schools of war within that clan. Furthermore, Natori is a personal retainer of the family and his position will be discussed in depth in a later chapter. Continuing with the Kishu-Tokugawa clan retainer lists, in the Edo period they show payment in Koku for the *Iga* and *Koka no mono* (shinobi), a payment level which makes them lower grade samurai or even *Doushin*,[46] a reflection of their drop in status but still with one foot firmly on the samurai ladder.

The listings from 1638 state: '45 Koku is to be divided between three men of the Koka group [shinobi]' making it fifteen Koku each. The listings state that the Koka group was reduced to two people three years later but at 30 Koku between them. This arrangement later returned to the original three men. The listings from 1781 state:

- Ten Koku for the seven Iga Kumigashira or Iga group captains with the permission to hire two servants

- Nine Koku for each Iga mono – being 61 in total and each with permission to hire two servants
- Five Koku for each of the fourteen Iga kodomoyaku or trainee ninjas with permission to hire two servants

The *Iga mono* also are also listed with the extras that they were awarded or paid and consists of eleven items, including *Haori* jackets and uniforms needed, money for what appears to be lacquered raincoats, silk jackets, end-of-year bonuses and money to aid them in their service in Edo, the capital. Interestingly, the listings also state that in 1793, the original name of the men was *Okusurigome* or [those who handle] gunpowder but was changed to *Iga*. The listings describe the jackets as marked with a circle with a cross in the centre and state that these Men of Iga wore them at all times (presumably only in the castle grounds). These men were under a commander called the *Ohiroshiki Goyonin*. This Iga group, or at least a group which bears the name Iga, were said to have been founded from the remnants of the '*Koka shinobi no mono*', that is, ninja from Koka. Their job was similar to the '*Oniwaban*' or the Shogun's secret spy network when this listing was compiled at the time of the Meiji restoration in 1868. The document even goes as far as to list their duties, paraphrased as:

> The Iga group undertook *Onmitsu no Tantai* espionage and received *Gonaimei* or secret orders directly from the lord. To add to this, if needed, the lord would give them secret orders and they could be told to infiltrate a distant province at short notice.

Hattori Hanzo I was the father of the famous Devil-Hanzo and was a man of Iga retained by the future Tokugawa family of Mikawa prefecture, making him and his son samurai retainers. (His son was of a very high rank and personal friend to Tokugawa Ieyasu.)

From these examples, it is obvious that being a ninja did not mean being part of a counter-culture, in fact it was quite the reverse. A ninja was an integral part of medieval Japan and was a recognised part of samurai life. However, this being said, it must not be forgotten that historical documentation is most often created by the social elite and we must not fall into the trap of imagining that all shinobi were of samurai status. Whilst the shinobi from the foot soldier class did not leave manuals or documentation, we can infer that the position of ninja was one based on training and ability, not social standing. With this in mind, and with the understanding that the ninja were samurai and that they were an accepted part of Japanese life, we must ask the question, where did the negative image of the ninja come from?

Generally, ninja manuals based in the teachings of the Sengoku period or even military manuals which deal with battlefield conditions, speak of the ninja in two ways. Firstly, they either expand on the importance of the shinobi and their usage and the proper method of employment or, alternatively, they talk about defending against the shinobi and highlight how poor defences against the ninja can lead to disaster or at least the penetration of the camp. Remembering that the literature was brought to us by a select group, it can be understood that these elites had good reason for discussing the use of the ninja, however, they always use a syntax which talks of the ninja as 'lower', of a low status. This has been interpreted by most to mean the ninja were low in social position, which is an error. The authors of these prestigious battle manuals were the samurai elite, highly educated and usually employed as tacticians and generals or even clan warlords; therefore, by definition they are of higher status than any ninja and will naturally talk of them as lower class people – not people of the lower class. Records show that some ninja were a part of the lower samurai class, which puts them towards the top end of the social ladder when observing Japanese society as a whole, making even the lowest of the samurai an 'officer' in the army, distinguishable from the *Ashigaru* troops. Furthermore, we can assume that some of these *shinobi-samurai* 忍士 were in command of troops of lower level shinobi, who were *Ashigaru* foot soldiers, still considered men of war and not at the bottom of the social scale.

There is a blank in the recorded history of the ninja and that blank is what the average person thought of a shinobi. Doubtless the shinobi would have been hated by many and even feared. It was a ninja's job to lie, kill, deceive, cheat, steal and burn people's property and root out conspiracy. The basic nature of their job elicits hatred in others and it is no wonder that an undercurrent of fear and even contempt has followed the shinobi throughout history. The ninja themselves were aware of this, the *Bansenshukai* and the 100 ninja poems, amongst others, discuss this fact and reassure the ninja that lying and cheating are seen in a positive light by the gods when used in the service of a lord. However, when not in such service, then their actions are seen as base. This is the point at which the evolution of the 'heroic samurai' and the 'evil ninja' begins.

The modern myth of samurai versus ninja is a mixture of the echoes of Edo period literature and the (sometimes perhaps wilful) misunderstanding of those in the modern media. In the early 1940s – which was before the modern ninja craze hit the world – authors such as Tamabayashi stated that the ninja were of samurai stock and that a ninja could come from most levels of society:

> Ninja were common ranking samurai such as *Soshi*, or even *Ashigaru* (foot soldiers) or *Doshin* 'half-samurai', also they sometimes came from more humble backgrounds, and were part of the *Toppa*, *Suppa* and *Rappa* groups of bandits.

The class issue in relation to the people of Iga was a touchy subject. Up until 1582 Iga was an independent state of samurai families, who governed their own lands. But after Oda Nobunaga brought Iga to its knees, the samurai of the domain were replaced or displaced. When the wars ended, the people of Iga were placated with an 'in-between' status, not samurai and yet not peasant. They were known as *Musokunin* and were classed as village leaders under their new samurai lords, a situation that must have been painful to endure, yet a transition that some modern scholars have ignored, defining the once-proud samurai of Iga as merely lower class people.

We can safely say that the shinobi have been misrepresented to a modern audience and that they were a functional part of any army. It was only after the coming of peace that the ninja were 'blacklisted'.

6

Medieval Japanese Scouting

When you construct your camp and you have to raise the watch towers, lay Kusa ambush [scouts] to watch the opponent's camp

Medieval War Poem

Throughout all of my work concerning the shinobi I am always referring to ninja 'scouting skills'. Whilst a high proportion of a ninja's role was indeed scouting, there are some fundamental differences between the work of the ninja and the work of a 'conventional' war scout.

The term 'scout' in Japanese is translated as '*Monomi*' 物見 and has a different application to the word 'shinobi'. In short, the art of the *Monomi* is predominantly mounted scouting, taken up by groups or individual samurai, who are sometimes accompanied by foot soldiers or samurai on foot, who observe the enemy up close but at a 'safe' distance.

The *Monomi* rode into no-man's-land with the intention of getting within visual range of the enemy to record and bring back information about the enemy forces and their activities or to scout out an army route and acquire topographical information. These *Monomi* scouts are 'external scouts', who do not penetrate the enemy's position but observe from a distance.

On the other hand, shinobi, in general, gather information from either very close by an enemy position or from inside the opponent's camp or fortress. Whilst a *Monomi* may discover the general outlay, position, route and strength of an army, a shinobi will gather passwords, detailed positions, names of commanders and their command team, code words, secret signals and information in detail; information that normal scouting would never garner.

Whilst the above distinction is a simplified one, it shows how the two are distinct and provides an 'anchor' to hold on to, as often the two concepts of *Monomi* and shinobi merge.

There is no way to establish if the shinobi and the *Monomi* scouts were the same people performing two separate jobs, or if they were separate individuals, or if there was an overlap between the two, meaning that some people were specialists in either shinobi or *Monomi* and that some individuals were trained in both. Whilst there is evidence to show that shinobi used horses (which is discussed later on), the general lack of documentation about shinobi using mounted tactics leads to the conclusion that it was rare. In addition, a shinobi may not have been paid enough to support a horse and gear, keeping him on foot. Logically it seems that shinobi were a separate group to the *Monomi*, with a small margin of cross-over. Fujibayashi, author of the *Bansenshukai,* argues for the use of shinobi over *Monomi*, implying an actual distinction in qualified personnel as opposed to a distinction in employment of the same person. The *Rodanshu* military secrets scroll appears to provide some evidence for a mixture of *Monomi* and shinobi forms of scouting, but we cannot know how many people shared shinobi and *Monomi* skills.

There are four main types of scouting (with some minor variations), normally found in samurai armies, using the term '*Monomi*'.

大物見 Large Scouting Groups (*O-monomi*)

Up to 100 men (out of 1000) can make up an *O-monomi* group, if not more. The military tactics appendix found at the end of the *Bansenshukai* states that this form of scouting party can be made up of mounted samurai, each with up to five *Ashigaru* or foot soldiers accompanying them. On the whole, this group was sent out before the army moved out and would scout ahead, checking the route and lay of the land. This is a large armed group who are not trying to hide their activities. In some cases an *O-monomi* group was said to reach the level of 1000 mounted warriors.

To-monomi, To-miban and *To-me* all mean 'far reaching scouts'. It is unknown if this was a large band of mounted warriors or only a few in number.

中物見 Middle-sized Scouting Groups (*Chu-monomi*)

Chu-monomi or middle-sized scouting groups appear to be made up of around 40–50 people out of 1000. This group were also heavily armed and prepared for engagement with the enemy.

小物見 Small Scouting Groups (*Ko-monomi*)

Ko-monomi or smaller scouting groups are a small number of warriors, possibly mounted, of up to five people, most likely used to keep up to date on enemy movements from a distance. However, some scrolls which feature *Ko-monomi* skills are almost identical to shinobi activity.

忍物見 Secret or Stealthy Scouting (*Shinobi-monomi*)

Stealthy scouting is by far the most illusive kind to pin down. There are differences in title, differences in usage between clans and also grammatical issues. On a basic level, this is a form of scouting that is done in secret and away from the eyes of the enemy, be it mounted or on foot, the latter being far more popular. Examples of secret mounted scouting can be seen in a later chapter, with the study of the *Otsubo Hon* equestrian school and their use of their shinobi skills on horseback.

According to Edo period records, *Shinobi-monomi* is also known as: *Shibami, Kamari,*[47] *Shinobi* or *Kusa*. According to the *Koyogunkan* war chronicle there were variations such as *Kamari no monomi* and they were also called *Kagi-monogiki*. The skill consists in scouting close to the enemy. This form of scouting was usually undertaken by lower class people and on foot, by men such as the *Monomi-ashigaru* or 'foot soldier scouts'.

This suggests that lower ranking shinobi who held the status of *Ashigaru* were employed to undertake the position of overnight watchmen, lying in the grass watching the enemy, whilst the higher ranking shinobi considered such work *infra dignitatis*; however, this is merely speculation. One interesting anecdote that helps support this theory comes from the *Hojo Godaiki* document, which states that when a mounted warrior came to take up his position in the daytime, where a low class night watchman was situated, the night-time agent attacked and tried to kill the mounted warrior in anger.

In the Japanese language an adjective comes before the subject. So in *Shinobi-monomi* the adjective is *shinobi* and the subject is *Monomi*. The combination means a secret-scout, i.e. 'creeping in' whilst scouting. The reason for grammatical examination here is that whilst the term *shinobi-monomi* exists, there is also an example of the reverse found in the *Bansenshukai*; *Monomi-shinobi*. Here the adjective-subject argument shows that this is a ninja who is undertaking a scouting mission. So a *shinobi-monomi* is a 'secret scout' whilst a *Monomi-shinobi* is a 'ninja on a scouting mission'. Anyone can be a scout but not everyone can undertake dedicated shinobi missions. There are some people who scout in secret close to the enemy and some may go a little closer than others, to the extent of joining the enemy, making them the classic ninja.

Within the greater context of samurai warfare, the *Monomi* and the shinobi are similar, both perform scouting duties but the *Monomi* from a distance, the shinobi from within or near to the enemy. Some warriors who perform close scouting skills, such as ambush troops, may cross over into the realm of the shinobi. It may be the case that a troop of scouts would have a ninja leading them as a guide. It must be remembered that shinobi are sent to find ambush troops and hidden scouts, a constant game of cat and mouse which is played out in no-man's-land between two samurai positions.

The *Monomi* are not associated with the shinobi skills of thieving, banditry and the other 'criminal' elements.

7

Bandits, Thieves and Criminals

Certain Japanese researchers attempt to place the ninja into the criminal bracket and have history brand them as thieves, brigands and blackguards. Whilst there are cogent reasons to connect the shinobi to mere thieves, there is a more solid argument that shows that 'ninja activity' and 'theft for profit' were different sides of the same coin.

The initial step is to identify what a criminal is and how we should understand this in the context of Japanese history. *The Oxford English Dictionary* defines crime as 'an action or omission which constitutes an offence and is punishable by law'. This means that anyone who is acting against the laws of the state he resides in is a criminal. Therefore, it is difficult to accuse the ninja of being a criminal when the definition of a ninja is someone who is hired by a clan to perform espionage duties for an army in an enemy province. A man is hired to kill someone and the same man is hired by the government to shoot and kill someone, one is murder and the other is 'doing one's duty'. The argument for the ninja is eqivalent. If a shinobi is hired by an army to infiltrate the enemy, he is working for the law and not against it, yet if he is hired by a lower faction from within his domain to spy against the government or another person, he is then a criminal. If hired officially by one clan and sent to spy on another clan, he is acting within the laws of his domain, yet whilst he is in enemy territory he is in fact a criminal in that domain, making him both legal and illegal and the same time. This renders the tag of 'criminal' redundant, as it is impossible for a shinobi to be a criminal if he is performing espionage for the ruling military elite.

Medieval Japan was not unified as today, and the enemies over the mountains were not your countrymen, they were not the same people, you did not enjoy a national bond. The samurai of the Sengoku period were constantly at war, making the ninja a legitimate entity. All historical references mention the ninja in a functional context and not in a legalistic or condemnatory way. The charge of illegal shinobi activity does not come into Japanese court systems as it is logged as *Nusubito*. The samurai themselves participated in stealth raids, all people dealt in slavery, they burnt and killed and raped and stole, all of which are illegal in our eyes but were commonplace actions in the Sengoku period.

Theft is certainly a crime, as is killing, but only if done within your own state or to an individual who is under the laws of that province. If shinobi activity is sanctioned by the ruling family, it is legal, however if it is unsanctioned and the ninja is working within his own province and stealing or killing for his own personal gain or the gain of an employer who is not the ruling family, he is a criminal. Of course a shinobi who is employed by a clan for a period may in fact undertake ninjutsu legally yet when unemployed he may use his skills to work illegally for gain.

When talking of Iga and Koka warriors in particular, it is essential to understand that these men were hired by and attached to very powerful families, linking them to the samurai class, who were in many cases land owners, and also sophisticated and culturally advanced. (The idea that Iga and Koka were backward, hidden villages with peasants working in unity against the mighty samurai is fictitious.) In short, any ninja who is hired is a fully lawful and sanctioned individual who is working for a ruling body. There are numerous warnings in ninja manuals against using the skills within the texts for theft for personal gain (which implies that the shinobi did just that!). The military documents consider the shinobi a military threat and not a criminal one. Finally, the simple fact that shinobi are hired to capture criminals dispels the ninja-criminal myth.

The *Dakko Shinobi Nomachi Ryaku Chu* ninja scroll states: 'Shinobi and *Tozoku* [thieves] are different … *Tozoku* 'steal in' and steal people's belongings, whereas shinobi simply just 'steal in' [for various reasons].'

Interestingly, the word *Tozuku* has connotations of bands of thieves and brings images of rough gangs breaking and entering homes, much less subtle than the image of the creeping ninja in the night. The *Shoninki* states:

[The name] ninja refers to Japanese spies; they never feel hesitant about their business, they spy whether it is daytime or at night. They are the same as *Nusubito* thieves in skill, however a ninja does not steal [for profit].

A group of *Tozoku* thieves pillaging a house. (Courtesy of Peter Brown)

Among the alternative names for the ninja, given by certain scholars you find terms like *Akuto* 悪党 – evil bands, *Nusubito* 盗人 – thieves and mountain bandits 山賊 and others. Often, these become interchangeable or hold the same connotations as the ninja. Of all the above, only the *Nusubito* 盗人 are actually listed as being akin to ninja, and this comes from the *Shinobi-uta*, the 100 ninja poems of Yoshimori, where *Nusubito* is interchangeable with shinobi.[48] However the others, at present have no direct connection apart from geographical location.

The *Akuto* 悪党 or evil bands were written of in the records of Toidaji Temple (twelfth century) being both demonised and incorrectly given the honour of being the originators of ninjutsu. The Toidaji Temple is close to the lands of Iga and Koka in Nara and was a dominant centre, having control over the whole area. Kusunoki Masashige and others in the area rebelled against the power of the Temple and this led to them being labelled *Akuto* or evil bands by the Temple (for obvious reasons). This rebellion, coupled with Kusunoki Masashige's connection to the ninja, has given rise to the theory that the *Akuto* were the originators of ninjutsu. Whilst there is no doubt that Masashige did influence ninjutsu he cannot be attributed with its invention, as this would leave out the entire Yoshimori and Chinese chapters of the ninja story. In reality it is most likely that constant warfare in that area helped hone skills that were all ready in existence, it forged the ninja and their skills but did not create the shinobi themselves.

In summary, a ninja is a person whose primary purpose is to perform what we would see as criminal actions; however he is employed (or retained) by others to perform his skills in war. When the ninja is hired by a private individual or takes it upon himself to use ninjutsu for personal gain, he then becomes a criminal; it is then questionable if he is still a shinobi or if he is a *Nusubito*-thief by definition – a distinction that was most likely very blurred during the Sengoku period.

8

The Chinese Connection

Jiang Ziya, who was Prime Minister to King Wen of the Zhou state, wrote 71 chapters [*The Six Secret Teachings*] on shinobi ways.

The origin of ninjutsu, taken from the *Shinobi Hiden,* 1560

The Sengoku period in China (403–221BC) witnessed the development and expansion of espionage and clandestine warfare. However, unorthodox combat and intelligence gathering are not fundamentally Chinese, nor are they considered to have solely originated in China. Nevertheless the ninja of Japan are thought to have a Chinese root or connection. The aim of this chapter is to identify any relationship and look for evidence of an antecedent in the military writings of China that influenced the Japanese ninja of a later period.

It is a common myth that the ninja were Chinese immigrants who fled the horrors of their homeland and took root in Iga and thus gave birth to the ninja. This in itself is unfounded, and it is unknown if ninjutsu even began in Iga, and whilst there were Chinese immigrants or colonists who reached the shores of Japan, the beginnings of the ninja, as discussed earlier, are simply not known. It is only by a comparison of military literature that we may get an inkling of any factual connection between Chinese and Japanese spies.

As we have seen in the chapter on the origins of the ninja, they themselves believed in a Chinese connection. To prove it we need to find linguistic similarities, shared skill sets and tactics. The main argument against this form of analysis is of course that espionage and clandestine warfare have existed since time immemorial and all must contain similarities. The counter is to compare the number and the quality of the similarities between the two nations. If the comparisons are vague, universal and logical in all warfare, then it can be concluded that ninjutsu originated in Japan, without Chinese influence. However, as will be seen, the comparisons are detailed and numerous, which argues a strong case for China and the Asian mainland as the parent of ninjutsu. That leaves the mystery of its more specific origins.

The Linguistic Connections between the Chinese and Japanese Manuals

Possibly the most dominant linguistic connection between ninjutsu and the Chinese methods of spying is the use of the names *Yutei* 游偵 (playing/roving agent) and *Yushi* 遊士 (playing/roving warrior/officer). The *Bansenshukai* uses the term *Yutei* in its introduction, where it explains the origin of the shinobi. The base ideogram of 游 which is 'playing' or 'roving' also forms the basis of the word *Yushi* 遊士. Fujibayashi in the *Bansenshukai* talks of *Yushi* as an origin for, or Chinese example of, the ninja and refers to the *Ta'i Kungs,* The Six Secret Teachings as his example. In this Chinese manual we do find that the description of *Yushi* rings true to our image of certain part of the ninja's role, as can be seen in the following quote from The Six Secret Teachings:

> 'Yushi 遊士, eight of: Responsible for spying on the enemy's licentiousness and observing their changes, manipulating their emotions and observing the enemy's thoughts in order to act as spies.

The *Bansenshukai*:

> In The Six Secret Teachings it is referred to as Yushi 遊士 'playing warrior' and in the Yin Jing 陰経 manual written by Risen it is known as Koujin 行人. As seen in these, it has been described in many different ways according to the period, or the lord's intention. It is quite similar in our country, as we call it shinobi, *Yato, Suppa, Nokizaaru, Mitsumono, Kyoudan,* etc.

Without becoming laborious, there are multiple names given to spies throughout Chinese history and whilst noting that the Japanese shinobi had access to the Chinese classics, it must be concluded that certain basic names and linguistic roots do cross over, whilst a certain number do not. On its own this does not confirm a relationship between the two and still leaves the possibility that the Japanese ninja obtained some of their arts from investigating the manuals, as opposed to bringing them with them. A further look at linguistics and then the shared skill sets will help form an impression of the events of the ninja 'Dark Ages' and the birth of the ninja.

As we have seen, the shinobi themselves believed that their origins lay in China and that these skills were imported in some fashion. The origins of the ninja are discussed

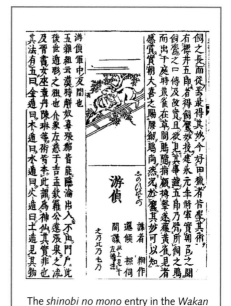

The *shinobi no mono* entry in the *Wakan Sunsaizuai* encyclopaedia of 1712.

in the 1712 document *Wakan Sunsaizuai,* which is an encyclopaedia that encompasses the curious and the mundane in Edo period Japan and is similar in approach to the *Encyclopaedia Britannica.* The commentator describes a Chinese origin for the ninja and quotes from Chinese manuals to support his theory. The most interesting aspect of this document is the reference to the five famous skills of hiding, the *Gotonpo,* a skill set which is attributed solely to the ninja but which have its origins elsewhere (and to date cannot be found in any ninja manual). The entry and descriptions of the skills themselves are fantastical and supernatural and show a belief in the shinobi as 'masters of the mysterious'. However, this belief in the supernatural is tempered by the comment that the ninja are an essential part of any army and are a pragmatic part of warfare. That the commentator believes that those ninja of Koka are the premier ninja of the day is interesting, as supremacy often changes between Iga and Koka. The encyclopaedia entry translates as follows:

Shinobi No Mono 游偵[49]

[Alternative list of names given]
Shinobi no mono 謀者[50]
Saisaku 細作
Rako 邏候
[Unknown reading] 探伺
Kancho 間諜

The Kanja is a required member of the army, the [Chinese] manual Wu-za-zu states that 'in the time of the Han Dynasty Kaidoko and Chohyo were both very skilled at hiding and that they never came in or out through doors, these two were the forerunners of the skills of hiding.'

介象 Kaisho
左慈 Saji
于吉 Ukitsu
孟欽 Moukin
羅公遠 Rakoen
張果　 Choka
女巫 [unknown]
章丹　 Shotan
陳琳　 Chinrin
These listed people were known as supernatural beings [skilled in hiding].

There are five methods called the Gotonpo[51] found within the skill of hiding:
Kinton – the skill of metal hiding.
Mokuton – the skill of wood hiding.
Suiton – the skill of water hiding.
Katon – the skill of fire hiding.
Doton – the skill of earth hiding.

You can hide using any of these elements, but of them all, earth hiding is quickest because there is nowhere that earth is not. Furthermore, to acquire these skills of hiding you can train yourself in the mountains where nobody goes, do this for 49 days and sit alone in meditation. Also, you can use talismans or spells and ask the 100 gods to help you, but remember if your concentration 一念 goes then you need to train more.[52]

There was a man called Raiken in the Ming Dynasty and he led a group who stole into a large warehouse, however they were detected and arrested. The leader then asked for water [for his men] and when it came he jumped into the container and broke it, he then disappeared within the shattered pieces. This is the skill of hiding in water. During the sixteenth century there was an old man who used to be a eunuch and an official but became a bandit. This bandit collected the top knots of men and rubbed soil on them with in his hand and thus disappeared, this is the skill of earth hiding.

I think that the *shinobi no mono* are an essential part of any army and in these modern times the people from Koka of Koshu are the best trained in this art and they still pass these traditions down through their families.

Searching the Chinese Manuals

The *Shoninki* and the *Bansenshukai* directly attribute some of their knowledge to these ancient Chinese masters and some of the lesser scrolls show an understanding of Chinese literature. However, whilst this connection is irrefutable there is still the problem of what ninjutsu is and what could be considered the art of warfare common to all armies of the world. Therefore, we need to detect where the ninja scrolls use information from Chinese manuals that are more specific than descriptions of skills as used in all espionage.

Of all the Chinese classics, Sun Tzu's *The Art of War* is without doubt the most influential and famous and was well known in feudal Japan as well as in Asia. The military elite of Japan, including such families as the Natori and Fujibayashi would have had, and we know that they did have, access to this text. Both Natori and Fujibayashi directly refer to Sun Tzu by name, showing (perhaps intentionally) that they are well read and educated. Nowhere is this more obvious than with Natori's discussion of 'Employing Spies' and his five types of agent.

The Five Types of Spy were first recorded by Sun Tzu and they have been discussed, annotated, extended and refined throughout Asian history. They consist of:

- The local spy – for knowledge of the local area.
- The internal spy – those within the enemy army.
- The turned spy – those of the enemy whom you bring to your side.
- The doomed spy – those who are expendable in use.
- The living spy – those who infiltrate and return.

Considering that Natori is consciously saying that all ninja fit into one of these categories and that all ninja are used in the same way as the Chinese version, we can identify a solid comparison between China and Japan, which is also reflected in the *Bansenshukai*, albeit not so directly. The connections with the five types of spy are numerous and are found in other lesser scrolls, making the fundamental base of the Japanese ninja, in the eyes of the ninja themselves, a Chinese art.

The following sections show a very strong link between the Chinese and Japanese descriptions, one that starts to move beyond coincidence.

Death to Anyone that Talks

Sun Tzu, amongst other Chinese writers, recommends killing anyone who either unwittingly or intentionally releases information on a clan's spying activities. The punishment for even knowing or distributing information about spies is death.

> When espionage activities and secret operations have been leaked before their implementation, then the agents concerned and those whom they are in contact with must be put to death.
>
> ...If before the mission has begun it has already been exposed, the spy and those he informed should be put to death.

The sentence of death is echoed in the *Bansenshukai*. Was this advice from Fujibayashi based on his knowledge of *The Art of War*, or was it independent and standard practice in real life? Fujibayashi writes:

> Those who are found to talk about any plans concerning the shinobi should be sent to their death immediately, as well as those who should not know about it by right. Any who take part in such secret conversations about the said shinobi and then speak to someone else, giving the information away, should also be executed at once together with the one who has heard it, according to the laws.
>
> Even when universal peace has come in the country, there is still the law of keeping it secret and not divulging to anyone that there is a shinobi in use. It is even more so when in a state of war and thus the time when shinobi are about.

Occasionally a Chinese classic will discuss shinobi-like activity. Sun Tzu says:

> Someone unfamiliar with the mountains and forests, gorges and defiles, the shape of marches and wetlands cannot advance the army. One who does not employ local guides cannot gain advantages.

This could be from the *Bansenshukai* and other ninja manuals. There are various shinobi ways to report on mountains, forests and wetlands, well documented in shinobi literature and other writings on Japanese warfare. The great disappointment and frustration is that the skills are not decribed in detail in the Chinese classics, so we cannot compare them with shinobi arts.

The Substantial and the Insubstantial

Chinese military thought is saturated in the idea of 実 and 虚, two terms which have been translated as 'Form and No Form, Substantial and Insubstantial' and 'Vacuous and Substantial'. They represent the solid and the illusion of the solid. Sun Tzu dedicates an entire chapter of *The Art of War* to this idea and the concept goes on to saturate all of Chinese military practice thereafter. The *Hu-ch'ien Ching* states: 'We should raise dust and our enemy will not know our vacuity and substance.' Wei Liao-Tzu states: '"Vacuous and substantial" are the embodiment of warfare.'

The idea is that a military strategy can be in one of two forms. It can be a solid form, when what is displayed on the surface is in fact the truth of the matter. A battle formation can be just that; a general intends to fight in that position and with the forces he has deployed. In contrast, the same position may not be the real intent and the deployment is undertaken to provoke a response from the enemy. The formation is insubstantial and of no value, save for the reaction it evokes.

A shinobi must have the ability to understand if a plan, a conversation, a troop movement or anything they encounter in their spying is 'Form' or 'No Form'. Knowing what is true and what is deceptive is fundamental to the ninja arts, be it vast army formations or a conversation in a bar.

This concept of 'Substantial and Insubstantial' appears in a selection of ninja manuals and is another example of shinobi tactics taken from, and sometimes directly quoted from, Chinese military philosophy.

The Famous Ship Analogy

The *Onmitsuhiji Shinobi-dai* ninja scroll clearly displays the influence of Chinese thought in the well known analogy of spies being akin to water, good to have but potentially disastrous if misused:

> Generally the commander [of the group] should be a shinobi and the primary aim is to make the enemy confused. The Chinese classics say that an army is like a ship and spies are like water. A ship without water will not float but also too much water can overturn a ship. If you are not a sage you cannot use spies. Every general, both new and old, should understand this principle.

The above selection of examples of Chinese thought in shinobi writings is by no means comprehensive, though they should be enough to establish the Chinese connection.[53] Arguably, most of Japanese culture was an import from mainland Asia. We therefore move on to the skill sets that the two nations shared.

Sharing China's Skills

To formalise a connection between the two nations, a shared skill set needs to be found. Having seen linguistic connections, it is now time to compare the 'field skills' of the Chinese agents and the ninja. If a varied and extensive use of identical or close to matching skills can be found, then there is a strong argument that the skills of the ninja were in fact Chinese imports.

The first section perhaps belongs by rights to the linguistic discussion, though it does define the skills of the spy. The Chinese ideogram *Kan* 間 means 'to spy' and has an interesting etymology. Firstly, the ideogram for gate is *Mon* 門 and is considered to be the gateway or gatehouse to a residence, whilst ideogram for sun[54] is 日. As can be seen, *Kan* is made up of the sun coming through a gateway. The concept here is that the moment you open a gap, even just a fraction, the light will infiltrate. This ideogram is also found later with the following variation 瞷 which has the symbol for eye next to the original spying, meaning to look through the gap. Whilst the ideogram is not actually used in the following excerpt, Natori in his *Shoninki* quotes what he calls 'an old verse', a rhyme that clearly links the Chinese ideogram and the ideology of the shinobi. 'As a matter of course you may be certain of your victory with the coming of dawn but the moment that you open the door, a ray of the moon will get in through it.'

There is a difference between the Chinese spy agents and the Japanese ninja. The Chinese *Hsin-ling Chun* manual states that they use 'dog thieves', whilst some manuals use the term '*Hsing-jen*' spies (and their complex subsections), and this manual has the addition of 'incendiary thieves', people who start fires. As discussed at the start of this book, the concept of ninja is hard to pinpoint but can be generally accepted as one whose skills include:

1 Espionage
2 Thieving and infiltration
3 Clandestine and incendiary warfare

These three specialisations being performed by one individual is what separates the shinobi agent from all other spies worldwide, including Chinese. Whilst it cannot be claimed with utmost confidence, it appears that the Chinese had specialists who were highly trained in the individual elements above or a combination of two of them, who were equal to the shinobi in their own specialisation. But the Japanese combined the three separate specialist areas and produced the characteristic ninja figure. If this theory holds, it would mean that one would see Chinese agents in ninja-like situations, such as creeping into thieve, or elite troops infiltrating with the intent of arson, but by far the most numerous accounts of the three activities in Chinese manuals are of an agent disguising himself and infiltrating the ranks of the enemy as a soldier or as an agent-spy. Of course there are examples of Chinese agents performing more than one of the skills, however it appears only ever to be two out of the three activities, such as an agent in disguise who may also set fire to a city, yet does not, say, display the creeping in of a ninja to listen. Hsu Tung hints at this possible specialisation. 'The fluent and loquacious should be employed to work as spies, [whilst] those good at filching things like rats and snatching things like dogs should be dispatched to steal the enemy signals and investigate them.'

So the Chinese tended to use people in one main application; however, there is evidence to suggest that there is also a difference in the types of Japanese shinobi. The writings of Kimura and Chikamatsu, translated at the end of this book, talk of how tacticians in their time – the end of the seventeenth century – do not understand the difference between the types of shinobi, implying that the shinobi sub-specialised into spies and 'stealers in'. Also, Fujibayashi states that *In-nin* or unseen infiltration is the skill of lower people, whereas the five types of spy or *Yo-nin* is the work of the more educated samurai. This is further supported by other writings that claim that there is a distinction between the types of shinobi. If this is the case, then the shinobi is even closer to his Chinese counterpart.

The Art of Estrangement

Infiltrating the ranks of other forces, normally other 'Houses' or clans, is not a factor that can contribute to the establishment of a connection between Chinese spies and the ninja. Espionage and estrangement is present in both Japanese and Chinese texts but it is also a logical skill of espionage all over the world. However, its usage by both nations as a fundamental spying skill must be noted and the following is an example that shows how the ninja were used.

This quote comes from the *Mikawafudoki* document, in a dialogue that was supposed to have taken place between Tokugawa Ieyasu and a samurai called Ii (pronounced 'E'):

> Tokugawa Ieyasu asked Ii, 'Have we planted shinobi in the enemy ranks?' Ii replied, 'Yes we have, we planted three inside of [your enemy] the Lord Ishida's forces the other day.' However, Lord Tokugawa then replied, 'You should send them not only to Lord Ishida, but also to other generals, including Ukita, and thus obtain what you need about the enemy's tactics. Or you can make [the shinobi] spread disinformation to cause confusion among the enemy, as this is the first priority of warfare. Therefore, be sure not to let even your allies know of this arrangement [that you have with your ninja]'. Next, Lord Ieyasu and Ii chose dozens of people from Iga and Koka who were older and more experienced and sent them to those enemy Daimyo to spread disinformation.
>
> They [the people of Iga and Koka] went to the enemy area and spread rumours, saying that some people had betrayed their Lords. Also, they 'hung around' in and on the outside of castle [boundaries], and went to the Lords of the west and informed the people that certain Lords would betray Lord Ishida and they would allow the Kanto east armies into their castles when they came. Also, they accused some people who [were loyal retainers] in the castle of being long term spies and said that they were reporting everything to the eastern side. In this manner, the people of the castles were confused by this disinformation.

We have to eliminate the obvious shared skill sets, which are common to all forms of spying, such as the work of double agents. The next step is to investigate the topics which appear to have too many identical details to be simply coincidence and that show the same skills shared by Japan and China.

The Art of Assassination

Whilst ninja are not primarily assassins, they were called upon to assassinate at times. Assassination is not a medieval concept of course and is as old as man. But it is important to note that the subject is discussed in more detail in Chinese texts and it is possible that this art of assassination was a stand-alone profession, outside of spying. The ninja on the other hand, without doubt killed during their missions but it is not clear if the killing was the primary aim and stealing a by-product or if the theft was the primary goal and the killing was ancillary. The thirteenth chapter of the *Bansenshukai* goes into detail about infiltrating a house and most of the examples given require killing the occupants; however it is not clear why the shinobi is entering the house. In contrast, a ninja when infiltrating a castle appears not to kill people, making his main role that of information gatherer or arsonist. When infiltrating a house, killing seems to have been the norm. Therefore, calling shinobi 'assassins' is potentially misleading, as they did perform assassinations but it does not appear to have been their primary role. Remembering that killing was a fundamental part of life in the Sengoku period and killing is not necessarily assassination, Fujibayashi's silence on *why* a ninja should kill means we do not know if they went to assassinate, or if they went to steal.[55]

The Art of Physiognomy

The 'skill' of understanding a man's character by his features was a mixture of pseudo-science and mysticism. This 'art' enjoyed an extensive period of popularity in both the east and west. However, here it truly lights a path of dissemination of information from China to Japan. China's physiognomic analysis predates that of Japan and was used as part of Chinese espionage. The *Natori-ryu* of Japan includes this art in their curriculum as a part of their ninja way, showing a real connection between Chinese and Japanese intelligence skills.

The Art of Transformation and Mutation – Bakemono-jutsu

This quite specific skill is often translated as ghost-skill, however, the western and eastern concepts of 'ghost' differ. *Bakemono* can have connotations of invisibility and transformation, which better fits the skill description. The idea is to become the enemy, to don his clothes, to use his speech and thus to infiltrate. The Chinese manuals echo this skill: 'Disguising some men as enemy emissaries is the means by which to sever their supply lines.'

The Art of the Thief

In China, the art of the thief appears to be separate from the art of the spy and is less frequently discussed. The art of thieving is clearly considered a skill, yet it is associated with brigands and bandits (not spies) as it was in Japan – remembering that in Japan the art of the shinobi and the *Nusubito* thief were close, if not identical on occasion.

A leader of Ch'u in China sent out a request for anyone who was skilled in the art of theft: 'One man in Ch'u who excelled in thieving came to see him and said to his attendants "I heard that my lord is seeking men skilled in the Way, I am a thief who would like to offer my skill as one of your followers."' The leader from Ch'u sent this thief to the enemy army of Ch'i, who were camped close by. The first night the thief stole the general's war curtain,[56] which was taken to the Ch'u side the next morning. On the second night, the thief took the general's pillow. On the third night the thief stole the general's hair pin. As a result of this the general of the army of Ch'i broke camp and left, saying that if he stayed a third night, then it would be his head that was stolen. The general's ministers ask why he shows the thief such respect, hinting at a difference in understanding of the relative standing of the arts of thieving and spying.

According to Sawyer in his extensive work on the Chinese classics, some ancient Chinese considered a man who could sneak into a complex unnoticed, a 'Dog-thief'. This is a small but invaluable piece of evidence. The Japanese *Gokuhi Gunpo Hidensho* manual discusses 'Dogs' in terms of defence against intruders and states:

> How to know if a 'Dog' has infiltrated:
> On the external side of a fence, dig a ditch three feet deep and three and a half meters wide, then place a layer of sand at the base, which measures around eight centimetres in depth. Do this so you can see the footprints of any 'Dog' which infiltrates [your position]. Remember, 'Dogs' are clever and they will hide their footprints, therefore you should neatly rake the sand into patterns[57] and observe [the sand] carefully.

The same manual also states: 'In ancient China, the people there used to check ahead for ambushes by sending their Dogs to detect them.'[58]

Thus in ancient China and Sengoku-period Japan, people who infiltrated your position were known as 'Dogs' and generally fulfilled the role of shinobi as one who creeps in. This puts the 'Dog-thief' in both counties and with identical skills. From the *Bansenshukai* we get confirmation that 'Dogs' are in fact high level performers of silent infiltration or *In-nin*: 'At the time of the attack, send Meakashi scouts or "Dogs" to see how numerous the enemy are or if they are asleep or not.'

A section of the *Bansenshukai* dedicated to burglary talks of big 'Dogs', and of small 'Dogs', and 'how to open the doors'.

> Question: Granted, now it is understood that watchmen should be selected with special care, but can we use those who are restless and impatient for other jobs instead of watchmen?
> Answer: It goes without saying that proper selection is the same for Meakashi scouts, Oinu big 'Dogs' and Koinu small 'Dogs', Fire Performers, Fire Assistants and other such jobs, but only watchmen are mentioned specially, because as watchmen remain outside and people of this world think that it is an easy job and do not select people carefully but use even cowards without due care and attention, this often ends in a catastrophe. Therefore, I have given emphasis to watchmen here.

The difference between big and small 'Dog' is not fully understood and could mean leader and support thief. Whilst thieves are universal, through linguistic similarities and actual usage we can see that Japanese ninja thieving arts were influenced by and descended from the earlier Chinese 'Dog-thieves'.

This image is taken from a ninja scroll in the private collection of Dr Nakashima Atsumi and is concerned with infiltration into a mansion. The script at the top describes the use of 'dogs' as infiltration agents.

Gauging the Economic State of the Enemy

A small, yet interesting connection can be seen between the *Shoninki* ninja manual and a statement from the Chinese *Kuan Tzu*. The latter states that Kuan Chung dispatches 80 people to go all over the country as merchants and sell items to people of all provinces. They do this to collate information on all the provinces and to note the wealth of those investigated, and who is 'dissolute and discontented'. The overall aim was to identify those areas that were in a chaotic state and attack them. This actually helps identify the meaning of a skill described in the *Shoninki*. Natori describes the stratagem and how to defend against it; however he does not state why the people wish to know the financial situation of others. This lack of additional information is a typical Natori trait. Through the Chinese description, we now know they were collecting information on the enemy's economic status in preparation for an attack.

'Fattening up' the Servants

One tactic found in Natori's writings is the idea of setting up a visit to an enemy residence and distributing gifts to the servants. At this point the ninja, having pleased the enemy, will be in a position to start probing for information. The *Ts'ao-lu Ching-lueh* warns against this ploy: 'Those who provide generous gifts to your attendants want to ferret out secret plans.' As with the previous example, this is a perfect illustration of Chinese espionage skills in the shinobi repertoire that are too specific to be a coincidence.

The Art of Assembling Data to Form a Greater Picture

Manuals such as the *Shinobi Hiden* expand on collation of information, as does the Chinese *Ts'ao-lu Ching-lueh*: 'When the five types of agents are employed, you must invariably assemble all the data and probe for similarities.'

The *Shinobi Hiden* and others discuss this, and recommend that when controlling agents, one must check their information individually, root out any double agents and fully investigate if one's own spies are lying.

The Skill of Finding the Disillusioned

Ninja manuals instruct on how to find the disillusioned in an enemy camp and bring them to your side, more often then not with the promise of gold. This is reflected in the Chinese manuals:

> Internal spies – Relying on those among the enemy who have lost their government positions, such as sons and grandsons of those who suffered corporal punishment and families who have been fined [excessively].

It is as important to find information on 'stable' people and a stable area: 'Have our roving agents [*Yushi*] observe the enemy's ruler and ministers, attendants and officials, noting who is worthy.' The Six Secret Teachings says:

> Ears and Eyes – Seven of. Responsible for going about everywhere, listening to what people are saying; seeing the changes; and observing the officers in all four directions and the army's true situation.

The Art of Secret Communications

One definite sharing of skills can be found in the form of secret letters, as a shinobi is responsible for such communication, as described by the shinobi section of the *Gunpo Jiyoshu* manual:

> Secret communication is a job that a shinobi should undertake. A secret letter should not be normally intelligible if dropped or exposed to others' eyes. In ancient times, there was a way of writing a secret message with tangerine juice.

Both the Chinese classics and the *Bansenshukai* talk of dividing letters so that if any sections are found or intercepted the contents will not be known. The *Bansenshukai* states:

> The written secret agreement should be cut into three so three people can keep it separately and it will make sense only when the general and the ninja combine it together, this is because the characters are divided, further details to be orally transmitted.

The Six Secret Teachings states:

> The letters are composed in one unit, then divided. They are sent out in three parts with only one person knowing [the full] contents.

> Secret Signals Officers – Three of; Responsible for the pennants and drums, for clearly signalling to the eyes and ears; for creating deceptive signs and seals and for issuing false

designations and orders; and for stealthily and hastily moving back and forth, going in and out like sprits and ghosts.[59]

The *Ping-fa pai-yen* states: 'Establish clandestine watchwords … an invisible writing.' These watchwords are described in the *Bansenshukai*, which also explains their usage. They are a simple call and response, such as Mount Fuji/snow or tree/forest. They are to be changed daily and have to be easy to remember and are sometimes accompanied by physical gestures.

The Art of Ladders

A further connection that can be identified between the two countries in the use of the Cloud Ladder 雲梯. The linguistic and descriptive similarities show that China should be considered as the originator of this tool.

The Cloud Ladder's use in ninjutsu literature is also found in The Six Secret Teachings: 'For seeing inside the walls [of the enemy] there are cloud ladders.' The Chinese document in question then goes on to tell of a new skill, which is to observe the enemy

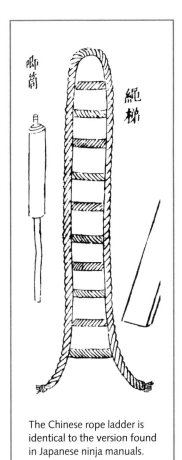

The Chinese rope ladder is identical to the version found in Japanese ninja manuals.

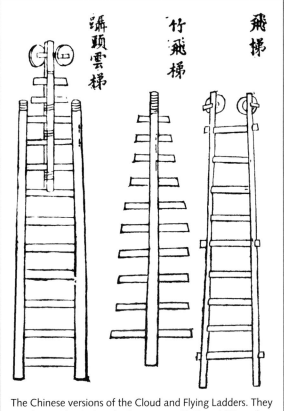

The Chinese versions of the Cloud and Flying Ladders. They are almost identical to the Japanese, with the addition of a wheel at the top of the Cloud Ladder.

at a distance by climbing this ladder, a tactic which could be possibly used by the shinobi. 'In the daytime, climb the Cloud Ladders and look off into the distance.'

One further usage can be found from the same manual, for when the enemy are using *Jiyaki* or ground burning – that is to burn the grass around enemy troops – then this ladder should be used to observe what is going on in the distance, presumably above the smoke: 'Under such circumstances use the cloud ladders and flying towers to look far out to the left and right.'

The Art of Towers

A minor puzzle presented in the *Gunpo Jiyoshu* manual is that the author places portable watch towers in the ninja section. The question is, were these towers used by the shinobi or used against them? The answer is found in the *Hu-ling Ching* where it states that 'you should use watch towers and capture living agents.' This would mean that these portable watchtowers were positioned along army lines and used to search for movements of the shinobi as they tried to pass through enemy lines. Of course, this is only a daytime measure and that there was a need for listening scouts at night. However, it is an art used in Chinese warfare, and interestingly, both are connected with the 'living agent'. In the *Shoninki* a 'living agent' is a ninja, thus making the skill set and linguistics identical in both countries.

The Art of Floating in Pots and on Rafts

Not only shinobi manuals, but also other Japanese documents talk of using pots, barrels and flotation devices to cross water, and whilst this may be universal, it does appear in the Chinese texts: 'Use bamboo and rope and pass over water in pots.'

However, both Chinese and Japanese manuals share a selection of complex water bridging tools, some of which are ninja and some of which are more common military practice. Shinobi bridges tend to be smaller than their Chinese counterparts, even if they share a linguistic connection. *The Six Secret Teachings* says: 'Unorthodox technical skills are the means by which to cross deep waters and to ford rivers. For crossing moats and ditches, there is the flying bridge. One section is fifteen feet wide and more than 20 feet long.'

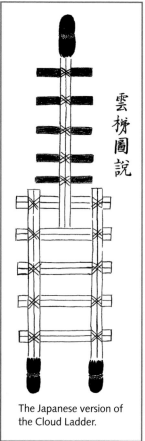

The Japanese version of the Cloud Ladder.

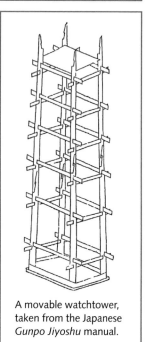

A movable watchtower, taken from the Japanese *Gunpo Jiyoshu* manual.

The Chinese art of using pots to float across rivers.

The use of inflatable leather floats is shared by the Chinese and Japanese.

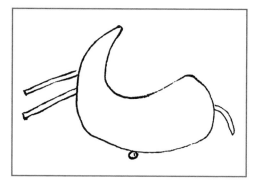

Left: The leather floating aid in the Japanese *Shinobi Hiden* manual and which can be found in other ninja manuals.

Below left: The Chinese version of the cat-tail raft.

Below right: As can be seen, the cat-tail raft which appears in the *Bansenshukai* ninja manual is identical to its Chinese counterpart.

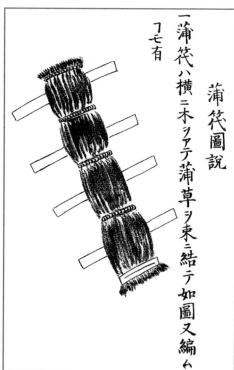

The Japanese and the Chinese also share the skill of using animal skins as flotation buoys, and whilst this skill is a worldwide phenomenon, the similarities between the Chinese manuals and the ninja scrolls cannot be ignored.

Sharing China's Fire Skills

Sun Tzu's chapter 'Incendiary Attacks' can be seen as the foundation of the understanding of the use of conflagration in the ancient eastern world. It spawned multiple written expansions on the use of fire tools and their development, some of which were produced by active generals and some of which were produced by theorists. Chinese fire skills without doubt came to Japan, as China is the source of all explosive warfare skills. How much did the Chinese influence the Japanese ninja?

Ninja-like Fire Assaults in China

Whilst ninja-like stealthy infiltrations in China do not prove a direct connection with the ninja, the methods and tactics used by both the Chinese and the Japanese are very similar. The *Ts'ui-wei Pei-cheng-lu* describes a form of agent known as the *Yu Ping* and instructs that they should 'steal enemy foodstuffs and burn provisions but should not get bogged down in combat'. The *Koa Chiung* advises the secret despatch of agents 'to exploit favourable winds to set fires and then wait until they rebuild their structures and we burn them again…'

Perhaps the earliest entry of ninja-like figures in Chinese history are the *T'ai-pai Yin-ching's* 'Incendiary Thieves' or *Huo Tao*. The resemblance to the ninja borders on the identical:

> Pick a man who is courageous and nimble, whose speech and clothes are the same as the enemy. After filching their passwords, he should be dispatched to sneak into the enemy's encampment bearing fire and burn their stores and provisions. When the fire starts he can then exploit the confusion and get out.

The only difference to this in the *Bansenshukai* is that the ninja should attempt to stay hidden during the confusion so he is not killed by his own side on exit. The *Ts'ao-lu Ching-lueh* again:

> Select clever, skilled warriors who are strong enough to oppose 100 men, have them pretend to be merchants or traders and enter the city long before any action develops. Then when your own soldiers reach the city walls, they [the agents] can respond by burning the people's dwellings in the middle of the night. When the flames illuminate the entire area, they should falsely yell out that the enemy has penetrated the city. The people and the soldiers will be totally confused and you can exploit the opportunity and achieve your objective.

The 'false cry' is a common feature in shinobi manuals. A shinobi might infiltrate a house and cry 'thief' simply to see the enemy's reactions and defence methods. Misdirection was often used by the shinobi. The *Bansenshukai* talks of sending troops to fight and cause distraction whilst individuals or teams of shinobi use the diversion to infiltrate a position. Its mirror can be found in Sung's use of shinobi-like troops in ancient China: 'Sung had his soldiers ascend the city walls carrying burning torches and his elite troops secretly worked their way out through the siege line to set fire to the enemy's encampment.'

Of all the ninja manuals, it is the *Shoninki* that most clearly quotes from *The Art of War* in relation to fire. The first of these connections is the use of the 'Lunar Lodges' or 'Mansions', which famously originated with Sun Tzu. Lunar Lodges or Mansions are 28 theoretical divisions in the night sky along the Elliptic Plane stretching from pole to pole. These divisions are not equal and the origin of their names has been lost. However, the Chinese (and the rest of Asia) used this division of 28 to map the moon's progress through the lunar month. As we can see from Fujibayashi and Natori's use of Sun Tzu's incendiary advice, a ninja would have to understand when the moon was in each lodge. The Lunar Lodges were used to understand dates, direction and time, a skill which a shinobi required. *The Art of War*:

> As for the day [to set ablaze], it is when the moon is in the lunar lodges of chi, pi, yi, or chen. When it is in these four lunar lodges/mansions wind will arise [therefore it is good to set a fire].

The *Shoninki* ninja manual states that tradition says:

> It is said when the moon crosses the mansion lines of the following:

> 1   Ki 箕 the Winnowing Basket.
> 2   Heki 壁 the Wall.
> 3   Yoku 翼 the Wings.
> 4   Shin 軫 the Chariot

> That when it does cross these lines, then it is always windy.

The Art of War continues: 'Launching an incendiary attack has its appropriate seasons, igniting the fire has its proper days, as for the seasons then it is the time of the dry spell [to ignite fires].'

The *shinobi-uta* or ninja poems attributed to the famous Yoshimori appear to emulate this:

> 四季の火はならひの道のある物を　しらで立るはあやうかりけり
> To make fire you should learn the way in accordance with the four seasons. It is inadvisable if you make fire without this knowledge.

Sun Tzu says: 'Winds that arise in the daytime and those that arise at night will stop.' The *shinobi-uta* poems state:

> 城や陣に火をつけぬべき時はただ　あかつき方の風を待つべし
> When you intend to set fire to the castle or camp, you should wait for a wind just before dawn.

Sawyer states that in ancient China, if a fire was to start, then only those people allotted the task of fire control could respond to it, to maintain defences. The ninja section of the *Gunpo Jiyoshu* has the following similar command:

> In the case of a fire, send four or five foot soldiers to notify others of the fire; let those with Tobikuchi or Kumade rakes stay there, but the leader should go around patrolling, this is done to watch out for enemy [attacks]. If you find the enemy on a secret night attack, hiding

behind the wall or fence, you should get your shooting weapons armed or beat a drum or something similar.

Animal Fire Delivery Systems

The Chinese manuals are full of animal delivery systems that use nature's fear of fire to encourage an animal to take fire to the enemy and burn their positions. Of these the most well know are the 'Fire Oxen', which included elaborate dummies packed with explosives and other ingenious devices. The use of animals and fire on the battlefield was not a secret weapon, these animals would have been 'decorated' and 'dressed up' to arouse fear. The shinobi scrolls of the *Gunpo Jiyoshu* reference a 'Heat Horse' which is used to incite fear and confusion in the enemy troops:

> On a night attack you can place torches on horseback and drive the horse into the enemy.
> Attaching the torches upside down is also a good method. The amount is dependent upon
> the enemy. The horse should be a packhorse. The torches should be tied up with a short
> rope, with a single loop, to a packsaddle so that it will burn up in a short time.

The *Izu-ryu Kohi no Furoku*, a scroll of unknown date and reliability, displays the image of the 'Fire Horse', with the torches attached to the sides of the animal.

The use of animals to launch incendiary attacks is not limited to driving pack animals into the enemy. Whilst the following is only a theory, it is a possible connection between Chinese warfare and the ninja skills of the Hattori family of Iga. The *Shinobi*

The Fire Horse of the *Izu-ryu* school.

Hiden manual lists *Kotori No Koto* or 'The Art of Small Birds' yet does not explain the skill nor its application and neither does it list it in the fire section, but it appears in a section of mixed skills. However, it is still of major interest to find a skill utilising small birds. Many Chinese manuals contain the art of using birds as a fire delivery system. The *T'ai-pai Yin-ching* states: 'Hollow out apricot cores and stuff them with burning moxa, and tie them to the feet of [small] birds.[60] Toward dusk, release the flock so that they will fly into the city to roost for the night.'

Some manuals claim (unsurprisingly) that this is impractical and would need to be tested!

The Land Mine

The *Uzumihi* or landmine appears in the *Bansenshukai*, the *Gunpo Jiyoshu* and the *Shinobi Hiden* and is regarded as highly secret. The concept itself is simple and pragmatic, the only problem with this weapon is the trigger mechanism. To trigger the landmine, live embers are needed, which creates two problems, first, keeping the embers live and second, not discharging the weapon prematurely. This is most definitely a Chinese weapon and exists in a few versions, both subterranean and sub-aquatic, and contemporary Chinese writers showed the problematic nature of keeping the fuse burning. The *Bansenshukai* version contains fuses held within bamboo tubes that would break when an enemy stepped upon them; this method appears simplistic next to Chinese examples. One ingenious Chinese method was a cog mechanism that when pulled would create a spark and detonate the mine, however it required a man on constant standby in hiding with a long length of string.

The landmine shown is similar to the ones in the ninja manuals and *Sung Ying-hsing* states that the fuse is possibly bamboo containing

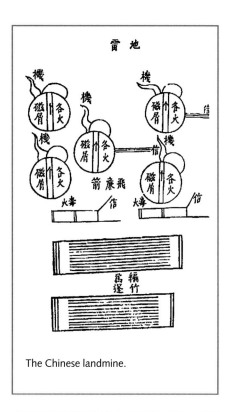

The Chinese landmine.

A Chinese sub-aquatic mine.

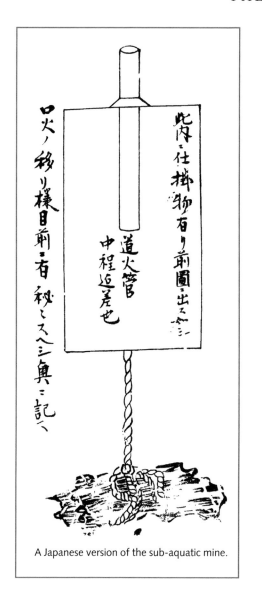

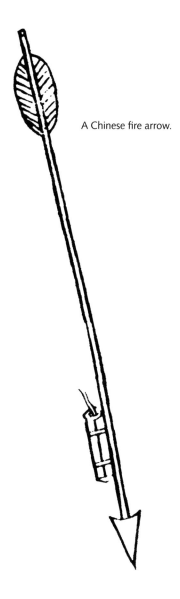

A Chinese fire arrow.

A Japanese version of the sub-aquatic mine.

embers and bitumen, similar to the Japanese version. Japanese fire skill manuals show in detail sub-aquatic mines that are used to destroy enemy ships.

Fire Arrows and Rockets

Author and academic Joseph Needham's extensive work catalogues the common use of rockets and incendiary projectiles and establishes their prevalent employment in Chinese warfare. The use of these weapons was well known to the ninja. The shinobi arrows closely match those of the Chinese military.

Fire arrows in the *Bansenshukai* and the *Shinobi Hiden's Youchi Tenmon Hi* exactly match the Chinese description from the *T'ai-pai Yin-ching*: 'Take small gourds full of oil, affix them to the tips of arrows and shoot them onto the roof of towers and turrets.'

The Fire Rats

The concept of 'fire rat' can be found in both Chinese warfare and entertainment. A fire rat (*Huo lao shu*)[61] is a small incendiary 'rocket' or firecracker that jumps around the floor in a rat-like fashion. This has been used as both a weapon and a child's toy and is still in use in China and Japan today. As a weapon, it is a small cylinder with hooks embedded in the sides and the aim is to put several in a container and throw them at the enemy, so that the fire rats shoot out and attach themselves via their hooks to enemy troops and buildings, causing fires and distractions.

In the shinobi sections of the *Gunpo Jiyoshu* manual a form of explosive hand-thrown arrow is described and illustrated. It is accompanied by an intriguing quote: 'This should be used just as the name implies '*Nezumihi*, or Rat Fire'. The connection does not stop there; the ideograms themselves are identical to the Chinese and the Japanese description fits entirely with their use.

The weapon in the manual may be the container that housed these fire rats, as stated in the Chinese manuals, or a larger single fire rat. The latter is probably more likely as the conical end of the weapon is not designed to penetrate (like others in the manual) but would aid a spinning motion. It has to be imagined that a good quantity of these were thrown during a night attack.

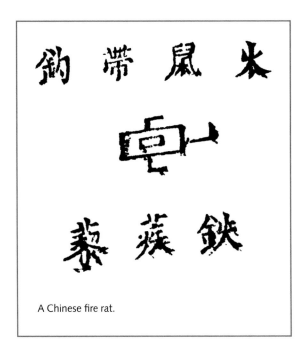

A Chinese fire rat.

The Art of Ground Burning

The *Shoninki* adds to its instruction on tools for carrying embers the statement 'This [tool] is also good for *Jiyaki*.' The meaning of *Jiyaki* when literally translated is 'ground burning' and is relatively difficult to find in Japanese. *Jiyaki* is burning the ground around an army, paying attention to the wind, making use of dry grassy areas. The counter to this was to identify areas which would be open to *Jiyaki* attacks and pre-burn them, or if a *Jiyaki* attack was initiated, then to set a fire behind the troops to allow for open ground to form before the enemy fire reached your own troops – a dangerous gamble. Remembering that this was only done in dry seasons and on massive scales, it would only take the wind to shift or a miscalculation for utter disaster to hit. The *Ts'ao-lu Ching-Lueh* shows how to defend against this ground burning skill: 'Should you happen to encounter fire, cut down grass and reeds to the side of the army and in accordance with the wind, burn them in advance [of the approaching fire].'

All of these examples show without doubt that there is a shared understanding of espionage methods between Japan and China. All of the Chinese references predate the ninja, some by a considerable amount of time, showing that China influenced Japan, not only in literature, art, architecture and religion, but also warfare and as a part of that warfare, the secret agent. What we cannot know is how that information came to Japan, whether carried by trained combatants or tacticians who took it over and taught the skills to the Japanese, or through literature.

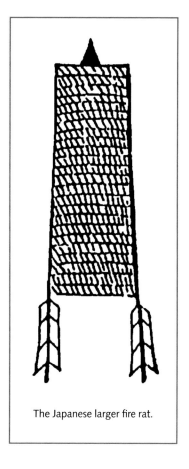

The Japanese larger fire rat.

It is most likely that the Chinese information came gradually to Japanese shores in various forms, where it was adapted to create the ninja, a Japanese product in its own right.

9

Unknown Ninja Skills

Do not fire guns from your castle at night because the birds will take flight and a shinobi will get in.[62]

Medieval War Poem

he Historical Ninjutsu Research Team have, whilst investigating and translating historical manuals, come across various skills that were not within the general public understanding of the ninja. The following selections are examples of ninja skills that are not fully represented in the manuals or are only mentioned in passing, with little or no explanation or in an indirect manner.

The Art of Spying

The ninja spy concentrated on imitating the lesser roles in life. Many people consider that there are a limited number of disguises for the ninja; examples like the *Shoninki's* 'Seven Disguises' help promote this idea. However, nearly all ninja manuals that deal with this spying element say these disguises are not fixed and are in fact only a guideline. A shinobi would take on the guise of a trader, a (low ranking) samurai, a street performer, a servant, a beggar, a pilgrim, any form of monk or priest, or any other required masquerade. He would adopt the guise of someone of a low level and normally someone who would have a reason for travelling. We often forget that in a bustling city of maybe tens or even hundreds of thousands of people, a shinobi would be hard to find amongst all the beggars and travellers.

A ninja must know the job and background of anyone he wishes to emulate, if he is a fortune teller, he must be able to tell people's fortunes in the way people expect, or if a monk, he must have a solid knowledge, including a temple to support his claims.

The 'Five Types of Spy' from the *Shoninki* were discussed earlier, however, they should be reiterated here to reinforce the idea that ninjutsu was highly involved in the area of undercover espionage. To show further examples (out of the many) the *Koka Ryu Densho* lists the following selections:

The Five Types of Practical[63] Training [Required For Infiltration in *Koka Ryu Ninjutsu*]

1   Of Gods and of Buddhism [and all required sections religious training]

2   Medicinal Training[64]

3   Craftsmanship and the Arts of the Merchant

4   Sake Manufacture and Farming[65]

5   The 'Arts' [including, dance, theatre, street performance]

The Seven Forms of Infiltration[66]

1   Through Temples and Shrines

2   As a Medicine Peddler

3   As a Craftsman or Merchant

4   As a Sake [merchant or] Farmer

5   Through exploiting the Arts and Performance

6   [Damaged Text]

7   Through Greed or Desire

The above systems and selections are mainly what we would consider 'short term' spying but we do in fact find a selection of 'long term' spies in use. What is often overlooked is the idea of 'sleeper agents' within the enemy, from low-level serving maids used for collecting information and opening doors and locks when required, to traders that have been established for many years with shops and clientele or even 'hermit samurai' who live on the outskirts of a town but are known to the townsfolk. It is these long-term established spies who act as a network to be used by the ninja. Information about this network is scarce and hard to come by and it is only identified through subtle hints given in various texts. The *Bansenshukai* is one of the only manuals (to date) to talk of this network directly and advises that people should be sent out years in advance to set up such positions and to wait for times of war. The *Shoninki* also talks of visiting shinobi in the area you infiltrate. A few manuals talk of getting to a form of safe house when you get to an area and meeting up with the 'correct people' when you arrive at your destination. This network of shinobi appears not to be bound by political shifts, it seems that shinobi of opposing sides would or could interact. We must remember that the ninja of Iga and Koka were considered the best of Japan and they were sent all over the country to serve various lords. This fact automatically creates a network of people who have shared blood relations. The people of this loose network would know of other groups or people that any ninja might need to visit, creating a larger and integrated spy network, albeit without a central command. Spying is the foundation skill of the shinobi, which all the other skills rest on.[67]

The Art of *Baiboku* 枚木 or Mouth Gags

The *Shoninki* ninja manual lists ten ancient ways of ninjutsu that are described as fundamental building blocks of the shinobi arts. The first principle of the ten is named as *Onsei-nin* and concerns sound. The word *Baiboku* emerges with regard to information gathering, music and eavesdropping. *Baiboku* was initially thought to be the concept of gagging a horse, but it was in fact also the skill of gagging humans of their own free will. Those who engaged in *Youchi* or night raids, including shinobi, would place wooden sticks in their mouths and tie them around their heads for security with the aim of the individual and the team remaining silent during their raid. Perhaps only the samurai troops were gagged and the shinobi kept their mouths free to use passwords and to talk to each other.

The ideogram for *Baiboku* is made up of 枚 – which consists of 'holding a rod' and the ideogram 木 wood, thus 'wooden gag'. It is unknown whether the *Baiboku* gag was flat or round, however it was logically a fraction wider than the mouth and has been described in modern dictionaries as having the thickness of a chopstick.

The appearance of the *Baiboku* gag in the *Shoninki* manual, though brief, shows how Natori hid his teachings. He does not describe its use, nor its construction, which fortunately can be inferred from other manuals.

The *Baiboku* can be found outside of the shinobi arts and in Chinese literature. According to Sawyer the *T'ai-pai Yin-ching* Chinese war manual contains a form of *Baiboku* used by 'Incendiary Troops' during cavalry excursions. It also states that the horses should be gagged or bound, showing a relationship to the Japanese *Otsubohon-Ryu* school of horsemanship, discussed later. *Baiboku* gags are found in T'ai Kung's Six Secret Teachings. The Tiger Secret Teachings scroll talks of raids – 'Require the soldiers to put wooden gags 枚 into their mouths, then move out at night.' According to various Japanese manuals, it was also a practice to gag a horse's mouth in a more restrictive way than a normal bit, to ensure the silence of the animal. The gags are known in Japanese as 'shinobi horse bits' and again, this appears in Chinese literature.

The author wearing the *Baiboku* gag used to keep men quiet on a night raid.

To follow on with this equestrian theme, the translation in the next skill set comes from an undated manual of the *Otsubo hon* school of horsemanship and displays how the shinobi used gagged horses as described in both Chinese war texts and Japanese manuals.

Ninja Horsemanship

The horse and the ninja appear to be an unlikely combination, as horsemanship in connection to Japanese scouting appears to be linked predominantly to *Monomi* scouts. However the *Otsubo Hon-ryu*, a prestigious school of horsemanship, has an account taken from oral traditions concerning the ninja and horses.

Preparing a horse for a *shinobi* mission from the *Otsubo Hon* school of horsemanship:

When you ride at night you should cover the eyes of your horse fully and avoid using horse shoes.[68] However if it's a horse that makes a loud stepping sound you should cover the hooves or use fur shoes. In the case that you do not have any fur, you should use normal shoes and make improvements by saturating them in water before you put them on. The details for this are secret. When applying the horse bit you need to apply wet paper [to the bit] and you should tie the tongue up with thin string before you ride out. This is called 'The Way of the Dragon's Whisper'. The string used for tying the tongue should be soaked in sparrow's blood and meat and then dried. If the horse is easily frightened by small sounds use the method called Shi'in or the paper cover, this is the idea of putting paper in the horse's ears, the details are secret.

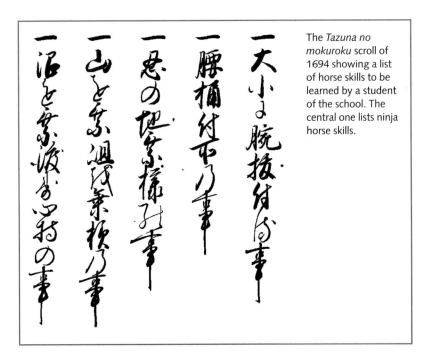

The *Tazuna no mokuroku* scroll of 1694 showing a list of horse skills to be learned by a student of the school. The central one lists ninja horse skills.

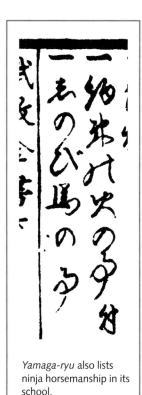

Yamaga-ryu also lists ninja horsemanship in its school.

The rider should close his eyes when he leaves the camp [to maintain his night vision]. After a whilst open your eyes and observe the way you are going so you can see the way ahead 'clearly' even in pitch darkness. This also, is secret. This is how a shinobi rides a horse.

When a shinobi rides a horse he should cover the horse's eyes because if he comes from an illuminated place into a dark one, he will be blinded. Therefore you should also cover the horse's eyes where there are lights. In this way you make it dark even where it is light. Keep the horse's eyes covered until you are outside of the bright area and keep him running for two or three *Cho* and then open his eyes, so that they can see the road clearly.

The reason you should not put shoes on the horse is that, if you are attacked by the enemy, you have to return as quickly as possible, and if you put shoes on the horse, it will not run well, therefore do not put shoes on horses. However, it is difficult not to put them on a horse whose step is loud. If the stepping is loud, the enemy will realise you are coming in advance, so, you need to be silent. Therefore, fur shoes will create a silent step. To make fur shoes you discard the sole of the normal shoes and exchange them for fur. Also you should put wet paper into the centre indents of a horse's hooves, creating a soft tread. This is the most important way of the shinobi-horse, that is, the art of paper-shoes. Some Tozoku thieves of Joshu province happened to know this skill and when they stole horses they put fur shoes on them and took them away. If you do not have fur shoes as stated, then you need to soak normal shoes in water and use them. Again this is secret. If you put wet paper onto the back of the hooves as stated above it will fill the gap in the back of the hoof and thus make less noise. Also, you should cover the joints of the horse's bit with wet paper and also apply this wet paper to the rings of horse tackle; this is done by rolling wet paper around them. In this way, the bit [and tackle] will not make any noise. This way was also written down in the Tales of the Heike and shinobi also use this way. So, if you tie the horse's tongue with string it will not neigh; remember the string should be soaked in sparrow's blood and meat. This is because sparrows are the 'fire in the south' and Suzaku controls your energy.[69] This is also called *Shinobi no ito* or the 'string of the shinobi'. Remember if you use this great skill of the dragon and tie up the tongue of your horse, then it will not even make a whisper.

Finding Kamari whilst Riding

The *Otsubo Hon* school of horsemanship makes further reference to ninja-like activities, as a horse scout searching for enemies and clearing certain areas ready for an army, establishing a safe passage. As seen in the image overleaf the manual refers to a specific route taken when searching for enemy *Kamari*, a word that is known to represent ambush troops and shinobi-like hiding.

The basic premise was to follow an undulating route and periodically stop and rear the horse and search for ambushes and *Kamari* who are lying in the grass. In the image this is displayed by the ideogram for person 人 at the points of turning.

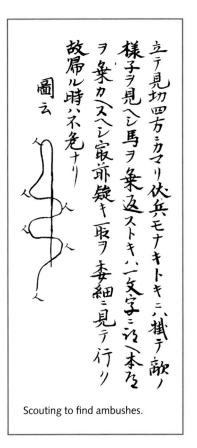

> If you venture out on mounted scouting run by yourself you should take a 'weaving' pattern and keep your posture low. Then investigate closely suspicious areas or in those places that need to be examined closely, at such places you should make your horse rear up so that you can look in all directions and if there are no *Kamari* or ambush troops you should proceed and observe the enemy's situation. When you return you should take a straight route as you have already cleared that area on your way through, thus you will be safe on the way back.

Scouting to find ambushes.

The Skill of *Dakko* 奪口

Dakko is possibly the greatest contender for a direct skill from ancient China to have reached Japan. The Chinese classics when referring to spies do so with an emphasis on the art of *Yo-nin*, that is the art of open disguise and immersion into the enemy culture as opposed to stealing in and remaining hidden from view. The art of *Dakko* is the ability to understand and merge with the enemy, to have the power to fool those of a province that you are one of them. Whilst less dramatic then other ninja skills, it is clearly a skill that can only be achieved to a high level by a select few. The rigorous training and preparation is daunting and even the ninja Natori Masatake states the difficulty in his monograph:

> Originally, the skill of *Dakko* was to imitate the dialects of more than 60 provinces with a great fluency. Those skilled knew and were aware of all the points of interest, historic spots and famous places of natural beauty within each area. Thus, it is called *Dakko* – depriving the world with your mouth.

The *Kusonoki-ryu*[70] *Ninpo Dakko Shinobi* annotated scroll discusses the three major forms of *Dakko* that a shinobi of that school would be required to know:

1. To 'deprive the world by mouth', that is to have the ability to understand multiple dialects and to move around freely in the world, gathering information by using your understanding of the local language and customs to infiltrate an area and gather what is required.

2   To 'steal from the world through the mouth', that is, to listen to the conversations of others and to go unnoticed as you gather information by allowing the conversations of others to supplement you with the information you require.

3   To 'take advantage of the way people talk and to live in lies'. This third point refers to the concept that you will use the conversations of others to take advantage of any situation and bring about your intended goal by manipulating situations and people to your own advantage, whilst you yourself live as a lie, you never reveal who you are, what you think or even your own thoughts, the aim is to remove your personality from the equation and maintain a life of lies with a final goal in mind.

Both the *Shoninki* and the *Dakko Shinobi No Maki Ryakuchu* scrolls talk about sending a shinobi as a messenger to the enemy to find out their secrets and to gather information on their formations. This is a part of the skill of *Dakko* and relies on the shinobi, no matter what his social status, appearing as a *Chu-nin* servant of an ambassador to the enemy. Once in the enemy camp he is mainly ignored as a lower person and maybe even quartered with the servants. It is clear from the writings that this 'servant' would have free rein in the public areas of the camp and be allowed to interact with the enemy.

The *Toryu Shinobi No Maki* scroll is heavily based on Chinese thought and the system of the five spies and is considered to be connected to *Natori-ryu*. The scroll itself lists the 139 ways of *Dakko*. Unfortunately this list is a selection of mnemonics or prods to be used to pass on *Kuden,* or oral tradition. The inventory includes:

*   Detaching from desire
*   Concealing the ego
*   How to use the common methods of people
*   The keeping of a calm mind
*   The art of knowing if people speak the truth
*   Shinobi used as scouts

The word *Dakko* in this scroll is used specifically to mean *shinobi no jutsu* or the art of spying but overall *Dakko* is the art of information gathering by taking advantage of other people's speech and collecting information in all the ways you can and then constructing a picture of the enemy's plans.

The Art of *Kyodo*

Kyodo is at times referred to as a skill and at other times a person. It means using a local person (or someone planted as an undercover agent) to gather information about the area you wish to infiltrate or investigate; a mundane skill perhaps, yet an important one for the shinobi when gathering information, This would constitute a high percentage of the ninja's work, listening and talking to locals as he makes his way through the enemy province. The *Heiho Nukigaki Hippu No Sho Gunshi No Maki* states:

Of Kyodo and Guidance:

This is a [person who is a] guide for you in your enemy's province. It is desirable to place one there beforehand or [at least] have one in the enemy province when needs arise.

The Art of Using Animal Skins

There are multiple references to the ninja using animal skins to help in their infiltration and are not for the squeamish. The idea is that an agent will gut a monkey, dog, fox or Japanese 'racoon' and use the striped skin and head to change his outline. It is a misconception that the ninja make a 'monkey suit' and pretend to be a monkey. The actual skill is to aid a ninja climb through trees in a garden without being noticed. The ninja of Japan were small, but even at less than five feet in stature, the monkeys of Japan are smaller. In truth, the idea is most likely that a ninja would use the skin of a monkey and drape it over his head and shoulders whilst he shimmied along branches. If this movement was seen, then the observer would in fact see a silhouette against the sky or even the shape of a monkey's head in the branches of the tree and hopefully would simply pass it off as local wildlife. In this manner other animals were used depending on the situation. Larger animals, such as smaller species of bear, were quite hefty in comparison to the medieval Japanese so a ninja would disembowel the animal and drape the entire skin over his frame and move along the edges of camps or buildings. Examples of this skill do exist outside of ninja manuals and even find their way into art, as seen here. This skill must not be confused with the art of *sounding* like a dog, which is a method to attract the attention of people inside of a house to establish their whereabouts.

The ninja image used in the *Wakan Sunsaizuai* encyclopaedia shows the skill of using an animal skin to infiltrate an area. However, this could also be a reference to specialist ninja who infiltrate being known as 'Dogs'.

Sleeping Powders

A selection of various ninja manuals talk of a form of sleeping powder, such as the *Iga Ninhi no Kan*, the *Bansenshukai*, the *Ninpo Hikan* and the *Shinobi No Maki Te Kagami*. The latter has details about the sleeping powder:

Tradition says if you inhale [sleeping medicine/powder[71]] you will become intoxicated and fall asleep. If you are going to use it [whilst stealing in] you should first burn and inhale incense at a distance from the target house, this will prevent you from succumbing to the effects of the sleeping medicine/powder.

Generally the idea is to soak paper (or material) in the blood of certain animals and add a 'secret' ingredient into the mix, which is normally a form of insect or parasite, such as the worms found in human excrement. The paper is then dried and rolled up. When this is ignited it is placed in an enclosed guardroom: 'They will become intoxicated and fall asleep.'

Some manuals discuss amphibians such as newts whilst the *Bansenshukai* recommends the blood of a brown dog. Similar potions exist in medieval European literature. Even though full experimentation has not been undertaken, a chemical analysis can be performed on the ingredients themselves.

At first glance, the ninja 'Sleeping Medicine' appears to be medieval madness, however, according to the theoretical[72] analysis by Alex Allera of the Chemistry Department of Turin University, there may be more to it.

Soaking animal[73] blood (especially blood of the liver) into paper and combusting it in an enclosed area could produce the drowsy effects described in the manuals.

A breakdown of the chemicals that could have 'drowsy effects' that are present in just the paper itself, without the other elements, produces carbon monoxide (CO), which comes from the combustion.

A breakdown of the chemicals that have drowsy or harmful effects and are present in blood and its subsequent combustion are as follows:

- ammonia (NH3) – negligible amounts
- nitrogen oxides (NOx)
- sulphur oxides (SOx)

The combustion of the amino acids present in the blood would create the following elements:

- nitric oxide (NO)
- ipoazotide or nitrogen dioxide (NO_2 or N_2O_4)
- nitrous oxide (N_2O)
- dinitrogen trioxide or nitrous anhydride (N_2O_3)
- dinitrogen pentoxide and nitric dioxide (N_2O_5)

The following chemicals are produced on combustion of the sulphur that is present in the blood:

- sulphur trioxide (SO_3)
- sulphur dioxide (SO_2)

The latter chemical, sulphur dioxide, alongside carbon monoxide, are the strongest contenders for effectiveness. Sulphur dioxide is a strong irritant to the respiratory tract and prolonged exposure to even small concentrations, measurements in the order of parts per billion (ppb), can cause sore throats, fatigue and disorders of sensory apparatus, including irritation to the eyes and nose.

The size of the paper required to succeed in creating a sleeping gas is not given, therefore the following example is based on a ten-centimetre-square of paper to gain a standard model. It is unknown if all the blood contained in the paper will produce a sulphur derivative or not (however a selection of percentages is given further on).

A square of paper, $10cm^2$ weighs approximately 2.4g and it can be assumed that after absorbing the blood, the total weight will double. Therefore, the weight of blood would be equal to half the overall weight and measure around 2.4g, which means it would contain 0.05g/ml multiplied[74] by 10ml, 0.5g of sulphur.

Assuming that the maximum amount of sulphur is transformed into SO_2, it would produce 1g of sulphur dioxide. Therefore, if the guard room was $26m^3$, then this amount of sulphur would correspond to 13.5 parts per million (ppm) in the atmosphere. The American Conference of Governmental Industrial Hygienists have set the short-term exposure limit to fifteen minutes in an environment containing SO_2 to the measurement of 0.25ppm. This means that according to modern American health standards, no one should work unprotected in air with more than this amount of sulphur dioxide. Our $10cm^2$ of paper can pump a maximum of nearly 13.5ppm into the atmosphere of a guard room, making it more than enough to affect the guards within.

Even halving that amount to allow for variation and minor ventilation in a medieval guard room, we can see that prolonged exposure to even such a small amount would cause the guards to suffer from irritation of the eyes, difficulty in breathing and possibly fatigue. Add to this the carbon monoxide and we can see that this strange tool might work – and of course we should not forget the 'secret ingredient'!

Because we are unsure of the ventilation in the room, and because it is unknown what percentage of amino acids will turn into sulphur, the following list shows the range of emissions of sulphur dioxide which would disperse into a $26m^3$ guardhouse. Remember, American health guidelines state that 0.25ppm is the maximum anyone should endure.

- 50% of the sulphur becoming SO_2 would result in 5.18ppm in the guardroom.
- 30% of the sulphur becoming SO_2 would result in 3.11ppm in the guardroom.
- 10% of the sulphur becoming SO_2 would result in 1.04ppm in the guardroom.

It appears that a ninja would creep up to a guard house and drop this lit paper into a room of guards, who may not notice the smoke due to the candles and lamps. With some ventilation, the toxic compounds might escape the room, but after an unknown time of exposure the guardsmen would most likely feel unwell, have chest pains and perhaps feel the need to sleep.

The chemical analysis was for the blood-soaked paper alone, the insects and worms that were used historically are missing and they are the main ingredient.

The Rolled Tablet Version

Other forms beside the paper version exist, and consist of charred animal matter – toad milt, latrine larvae etc – which are then powdered and rolled in thin material, which is then cut into small 'tablet' sections and burnt upwind from an enemy, placed on an open windward side window of a building or inside a hole made on the windward wall of a building. Of course, experimentation would prove or disprove effectiveness.

The 'Waking Medicine'

The *Ninpo Hikan* scroll talks of a 'medicine' to keep you awake in times of need. It is one of the more outlandish ninja schemes and potentially deadly. The translation is paraphrased below:

> To make this medicine, place mercury into a shell [and when laying down] put the mercury into your belly button and place paper on top. By doing this you will not sleep for five nights. However, if the Chi of the mercury gets into your belly it will cause you a great harm. Therefore, you should only perform this skill in dire need. If you do become ill then you should make a square of lotus leaves of 4 or 5 Sun across [approximately 15cm] and sit on it.

It is unclear whether the ninja takes the mercury out of the shell or he leaves it in the shell when he places it in his navel. Some shinobi may have contracted mercury poisoning from this venture – but did it keep them awake? The *Bansenshukai* uses the same method, however, it recommends bird excrement but without use of the shell.

Hunger Pills

Hunger Pills are 'field rations' for the ninja and consist of a selection of ingredients mixed into various size pills to be taken with a shinobi on a mission to give him energy and to keep hunger at bay.

The following table is a breakdown of the nutritional information found in one of the recipes from the *Bansenshukai* and displays the energy rates produced from each ingredient.[75]

The *Bansenshukai* Hunger Pills									
Ingredients (g)	Quantity (g)	Kilocalories	Protein (g)	Carbohydrate (g)	Fat	Fibre (g)	Iron (mg)	Calcium (mg)	Vitamin C (mg)
Asiatic ginseng (Panax ginseng)[76]	150	225	Nil	Nil.	Nil	Nil	Nil	Nil	Nil
Buckwheat flour	300	1092	0[77]	24.3	254.7	4.5	6.3	6	36
Flour	300	912	0	37.8	183.3	8.3	10.5	10.5	87
Dioscorea japonica	300	665	0	1.5	180	6	6.5	4.5	54
Glycyrrhiza glabra var. glandulifera	15	52	0	0.5	12	0.8	0.3	0	0
Coix seed[78]	150	Nil	Nil	Nil	Nil	Nil	Nil	Nil	Nil
Rice powder	300	1107	0	20.1	240	3	6.6	0	0

The chemical analysis of these pills indicates that every kilogram of the mixture produces an average output of around 2600 kilocalories,[79] and the total calorie count for the whole mixture above is approximately 4000 kilocalories.

The shinobi 'Hunger Pill' is featured in a selection of manuals in various forms and comes with information reassuring a ninja that these will help keep hunger at bay and most importantly, allow them to continue to function.

Today we are instructed that around 2000 calories are required to satisfy the needs of the average male and whilst it is tempting to try to use this number to produce a calculation to discover how many pills would be required to feed a ninja per day, there are so many variables have to be considered.

Firstly, the average Sengoku-period Japanese man may have been as small as five feet in height and will have been 'wafer thin' compared to our modern standards. This changes his nutritional needs from our point of view and by using a *standard* calorie calculator and assuming the man was engaged in light exercise, such as hiding and listening to the enemy or moving about at night, the calculation produces the figure of 1600 calories required to maintain his body weight at that size. This would require the ninja to eat just over 600 grams of the pills per day[80] to maintain his body weight.

Secondly, we don't know his energy output and exercise pattern. The ninja may have been hidden in a hole, listening to the enemy for days on end making his calorie requirements minimal, or he could be taking a high path through barren mountains where food is scarce but his energy requirements are vast.

The third variable is that his situation is not modern and a 'healthy average' is a luxury – survival is the primary objective. A man may go without food for days in a wartime situation and eat meagre rations when he can get them, allowing weeks for the body to deteriorate and finally starve. A shinobi may be on the brink of starvation, he may be at his wit's end, but still, in war some men will simply go on and on. The pills' impressive energy output of over 2500 calories per kilogram represents a ninja aid that really does work, helping the ninja to survive without real food for an unknown period of time.

The Art of the 'Nose Clock'

Two extraordinary statements are made in the *Bansenshukai* and the *Shoninki*, both of which refer to the ability to tell the time via observation of a switch between breathing through one nostril or the other. Natori states that 'some people can perform this' and Fujibayashi says 'I have not mastered this.' Unbeknownst to both of them, this skill was ahead of scientific observation by at least 200 years. What they are both referring to is in fact the biological phenomenon known as 'The Nasal Cycle'. This cycle is the unconscious tendency of the human nose to switch between a priority air intake of either the left or right nostril that switches over at regular intervals. Dr Block and academic associates describe the cycle's pattern in their research article 'Unilateral Nostril Breathing':

[The physician] Kayser first discovered a nasal cycle in 1895. Heetderks (1927) reported that the nasal cycle ranges between [a period of] 25 minutes and four hours and that it averages about two and a half hours. The autonomic nervous system probably regulates the cycle (Keuning, 1968; Stoksted, 1952, 1953). In this account, increased parasympathetic activation of a nostril causes the mucous membranes of that nostril to become engorged with blood. As a result, airflow decreases in it and the other nostril becomes more open.

What is most interesting is that the average time for the process is just above two hours but can be much less or much more. The difficulty that both Natori and Fujibayashi had is that they are trying to match the cycle to the contemporary Japanese hour system, which at the time averaged two hours but changed with the seasons. Modern research states that around 80% of the world population have an active nasal cycle and that they have variable cycle times. This means for a ninja to be able to use this skill he would have had to have had the cycle and had a similar rhythm to that of a two-hour period, around the average. Fujibayashi and Natori, if they had understood this fact, would have realised that each person has their own regular cycle and adjusted accordingly. Whilst the shinobi had this skill, they did not realise it could only work for certain people.

Appropriate Times to Infiltrate an Enemy House
There are specific times for a ninja to infiltrate a mansion.

TIme	Times to Creep In		Time	Times to Creep In
From 9pm	Positive		From 9am	Negative
From 10pm	Positive		From 10am	Negative
From 11pm	Positive		From 11am	Positive
From 12pm	Positive		From 12am	Positive
From 1am	Negative		From 1pm	Negative
From 2am	Negative		From 2pm	Negative
From 3am	Positive		From 3pm	Negative
From 4am	Positive		From 4pm	Negative
From 5am	Positive		From 5pm	Positive
From 6am	Positive		From 6pm	Positive
From 7am	Negative		From 7pm	Negative
From 8am	Negative		From 8pm	Negative

According to Fujibayashi, daytime infiltration is at times when a shinobi's movements would be ignored, when the household is waking, at midday and also at mid-evening, all of which revolve around meal times or when people are moving around.

An investigation into night-time operations displays that the times recorded in the manuals shown above do not show an early understanding of the sleep cycle[81] and are not based on when a person is most likely to be in a deep sleep.

The sleep cycle.

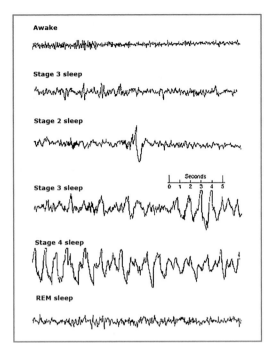

The ninja is not concerned with how the person is sleeping, only concerned with whether or not they are asleep. Natori states that most people fall asleep around 1am and that shinobi should stop infiltrating at this time and start again at 3am. In fact, research shows that the deepest sleep can happen in the first sleep cycle of the night, which according to Natori is exactly when a ninja should not infiltrate. It is advised that a ninja should infiltrate between 9pm and 11pm and the reason for this is explained in the *Bansenshukai*.

Dusk, is the time when movement and preparation in a household take place and when visibility is low, therefore, it is easy for the shinobi to walk among the people, listening to facts and carrying out fake preparation tasks making others believe he is part of the household staff. This time merges into the next positive infiltration time, between 11pm and 1am. Natori states that most people go to bed before 11pm but that they do not sleep before 1am. This would mean that people may still be walking around, making visits to the latrines or generally still in some form of movement, thus any noise or movement the ninja makes would most likely not bring any attention to him. Then at 1am a ninja is told to stop and to not infiltrate as by 1am, because most people are asleep and movement in the house has stopped. In this situation, any unusual movement would bring unwanted attention from the household or any guards. Natori then says that people wake between 5 and 6am, when again movement would occur and this is considered a positive time to infiltrate as people are again involved in preparation activities. In Japan, especially in summer it is relatively bright by this time and that it can no longer really be considered night.

Between the hours of 3am and 5am should be considered positive times to infiltrate, yet the reasons for this statement are unknown. It is possible that the ninja themselves believed that people were in a 'deeper sleep' at this point, or alternatively, this time was in fact another period of movement. Perhaps, as discussed in the *Bansenshukai*, this is the period where night-time guards are starting to let their concentration slip, because between the hours of three and five there is the end of the night watch and the rise of the household occupants. This could mean that a ninja waits for this time as the guards are becoming lax, or if the ninja's movements are heard, a guard may attribute the movement to a member of the house who has woken early, such as kitchen staff and servants.

On the whole, it appears that shinobi would infiltrate when their presence was disguised by other noises or movement from within a household compound. The result of this is that a ninja would concentrate on hiding noise or blending in with the surroundings and acting as a member of a household – hardly the stereotypical image of the figure in black.[82] It must be noted that these times are used to infiltrate a household and not a castle.

The Art of Measurement

The Chinese *Lu-shih Ch'un-ch'iu* states: 'Ching wanted to launch a surprise attack against Sung so they had scouts first chart the depth of the Young river.'

One fundamental element missing from the modern concept of the ninja is that shinobi were trained in mathematics, geometry and engineering with a focus on understanding enemy fortifications and defences. A shinobi had to have the ability to quickly calculate enemy numbers, dependent on elements such as the length of an army's marching order and the number of columns; the height of enemy fortifications, so that they could calculate the trajectory needed for a fire rocket assault; and the depth and width of water defences such as rivers and moats. A basic understanding of mathematics was a fundamental part of a ninja's arsenal.

The following translation comes from the *Chuken Jutsu Hiden* scroll, which is a collection on the art of measurement and contains a section dedicated to ninjutsu.

The Skill of Estimation [of distance] During Night Time:
Use a [distant] fire or a specific point such as a mountain as a guide and 'target' for this skill. Stand a stick of incense on a flat plate or a ruler and hold a carpenter's iron square alongside it. Next, to determine how many Cho in distance it is to the target you should trap a Hinawa burning fuse in the gap of a partially split bamboo and make sure you know the distance between the two people [marked by 人 on the drawing], then look to the target [fire or point] in front of you and use *Kokogen no jutsu* which is Pythagorean theorem. This is *shinobi no jutsu*.

How to Calculate Distance Beyond a Mountain:[83]
If there is a mountain in front and it is hard for you to look out across it, pick a point on the mountain top, such as a tree or a rock, as a reference. Next turn to the base of the mountain [where the person 人 in the diagram is] then look out to target [which is beyond the mountain] and use the art of *Mikaeshi no jutsu*.[84]

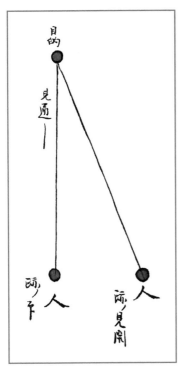

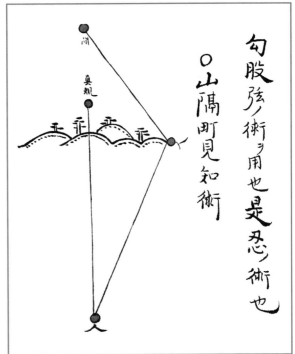

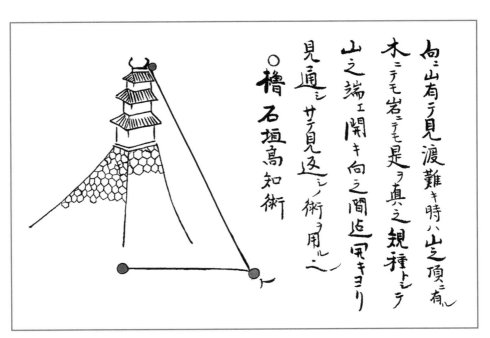

Estimating the Height of a Turret or Stone Wall:

Take the top of the turret or wall as a reference and mark it, then using the bottom [measurement and the angle between the ground and the turret] you can use *Kokogen no jutsu,* which is Pythagorean theorem.

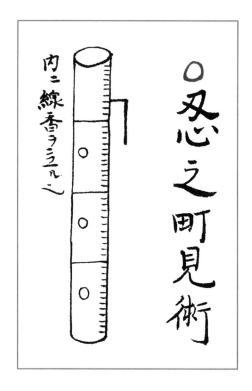

The Shinobi Way of Knowing Distance: Stand a stick of incense inside this bamboo tube. On a bamboo cylinder of seven or eight Sun in length, make a mark for every five Bu and drill holes through which you can see the incense burning down. Make sure the holes are large enough to see through.

In preparation for this skill, you must record how many of these marks a single incense stick will burn past for the distance of one Cho of average travel. Once you know this number, then walk with this cylinder on your waist and with an incense stick burning in it. This way you can measure the distance that you travel with this skill. Also, for the sea or a river, you can estimate the distance you have travelled with this skill. However, you need to consider the speed of the boat.

The 'Water Spider' Mistake

Often when people contest the validity of the ninja and the recorded skills that they, the shinobi, attribute to themselves, people point to the 'Water-Spider' tool or 'shoes for floating on water', attempting to discredit the writings of the shinobi as fantasy. Ironically, this highly publicised mistake was introduced and promoted by the ninja-supportive researcher Fujita Seiko and the mistake has even made it as far as popular television in the programme *Mythbusters*.

People believe that the 'Water-Spider' tool is supposed to be a pair of shoes that a ninja would use to 'float' across water and get to the other side. In reality it is not a pair of 'Water-Spiders' but a single ring used as a flotation device.

The middle platform is made of leather and is used as a seat. The ninja puts his legs on either side and uses wooden flippers to propel himself forward. The whole apparatus is leather-covered, sealed and collapsible. Interestingly, the Momochi 'ninja house' of Koka has been displaying this information for many years, yet the tool's proper use continues to be ignored.

In 1963 the researcher Mr Okuse claimed that the tool is borrowed from the Chinese document the *Bubishi*, yet fails to mention that the *Bansenshukai* shows an alternative version and that other scrolls, including the *Shinobi Hiden,* show examples of flotation devices that anchor at the waist. We see the same mistake in the 1959 book *Hidden Ninjutsu*, which appears to stem from the original mistake made in a 1936 publication by Fujita Seiko, where he shows his attempt to use these 'shoes' – and claims they do not

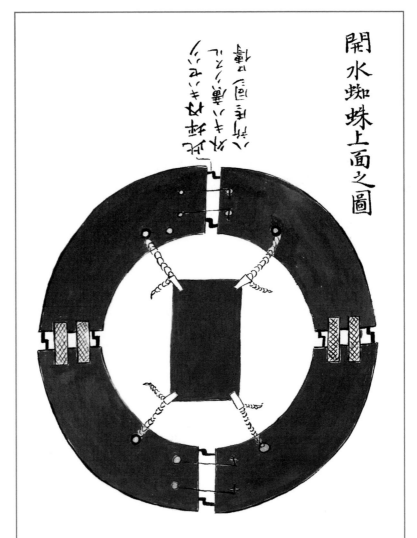

The Water Spider float from the *Ohara* version of the *Bansenshukai* kept in the National Archives.

The display at the Momochi ninja house.

This image of the Water Spider in action is a depiction given by the late ninja researcher Yumio Nawa, a contemporary of Fujita Seiko. Unlike Seiko, he described the Water Spider correctly.

A fifteenth-century German version of the ninja 'Water Spider' floating seat.

Daniel Schwenter's 'Water Spider'.

work! Fujita Seiko claimed to be the inheritor of the last line of Koka ninjutsu (amongst other people). His mistake was probably based on the mention of 'water shoes' in several manuals, tools similar to the Water Spider which are in fact lifejackets.

The 'Water Spider' tool was also a concept of western medieval warfare. The German fight master Hans Talhoffer, who was influenced by the war manual *Bellifortis* written by Konrad Kyeser, shows a version of the floating ring.

Apparently,[85] Daniel Schwenter, the seventeenth-century German mathematician, claimed to have seen a version of this tool in action and recorded it in his *Deliciae Physico-Mathematicae*. Notice (previous page) the identical use of fins attached to the feet or legs which have a one-way hinge, a system reminiscent of the *Bansenshukai* 'flippers'.

Ninjas at Sea

One often overlooked part of ninjutsu is the art of the shinobi on open water. Whilst not a central theme to *shinobi no jutsu* there is evidence of the use of ninja during naval battles.

As discussed at the start of this book, simply having the term shinobi in a title does not make the object a ninja or ninja-related. *The Warship Account* manual talks of how to use a 'shinobi-ship' and states that a boat should be rigged in the form of a merchant or fishing vessel and made to go amongst the enemy ships, listening to conversations, noting orders and flag commands, and basically doing everything a shinobi would do on land. It talks of stealth and infiltration amongst enemy shipping lines, which most probably was undertaken at night and with the aim of arson.

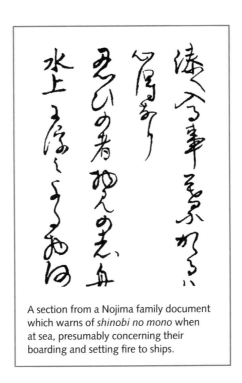

A section from a Nojima family document which warns of *shinobi no mono* when at sea, presumably concerning their boarding and setting fire to ships.

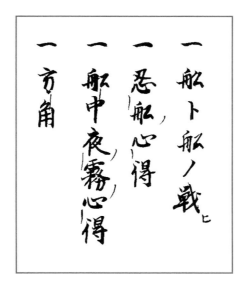

Keeping Ninja out of Your Night Raiding Squad

> If the lord of the enemy castle is inexperienced, try to goad and lure them out of the castle,
> so that you can follow them secretly back into the fortress [when they retreat].
> Medieval War Poem

The *Onmitsuhiji shinobi-dai* ninja manual states: 'Make sure no one gets mixed in with your squad.' One major task of the shinobi was to conduct, or at least lead, night attacks on enemy encampments. A constant game of cat and mouse was being played, as shinobi from the enemy side tried to infiltrate the attacking force, with the intention of joining their night raid squads so that when the attack was over they could return with the raiders and be guided directly into their encampment. Each army had methods to keep enemy shinobi out, from passwords to ribbons on helmets, even identification by underwear.

No-man's-land between two encamped samurai armies was a hive of night-time activity, where scouts would fight and blockades and alarm relay systems were set in motion. Feints and repeated night attacks would be mounted to wear down the enemy morale. The fake night raids would be conducted with the intent of drawing enemy shinobi into their group to lead them to a naturally fortified area where they could be butchered. Fire signals, flares, explosions and musical instruments would fill the night air with secret signals.

The Art of Stealth Walking

The shinobi had two main categories of walking; those that disguise one's own natural walk and sound of one's footsteps, such as walking as a cripple, and stealth walks, the art of walking quietly when infiltrating. The latter is of course simply the art of 'tip-toeing' with subtle variations. However, the ninja researcher Steven Nojiri has put forward a theory concernig the steps presented in the *Bansenshukai* manual and he believes that the 'four steps' written by Fujibayashi represent the stages of infiltration into a building. The four steps of the *Bansenshukai*:

1 *Nukiashi,* or steps where the toe is pulled directly out of water and vertical. Alongside this and used as an alternative, Fujibayashi says use 'Board Shoes' for marshy areas. These board shoes are square sections of wood akin to snow shoes.
2 *Ukiashi* or light and swift footsteps, these should be nimble, like a dog running or a monkey swinging through the trees.
3 The 'Rabbit Steps' (discussed below) or 'Secret Silent Sandals': this is for walking through house interiors, along corridors and on wooden floored areas.
4 Walking and probing the room with a sword. When in an enemy room the sword is held out in front in the scabbard with only three to six[86] centimetres of the blade out of the scabbard to form a temporary probe.

Nojiri proposes that these four walks actually represent the stages that a ninja would have to go through to infiltrate a house.

Stage One
A ninja would approach a house through the marshy area outside the walls, probably through rice paddies or even a moat. Here the ninja uses *Nukiashi* or steps where he pulls the foot out of the water vertically to avoid a splashing sound. Or he uses board-like sandals as worn by farmers in marshy areas.

Stage Two
After crossing the marshy area outside of a house the ninja climbs the outer wall and now finds himself between the wall and an open area of land, which he has to cross to get to the house. Here a ninja uses *Ukiashi* or speed running, which is light and darting.

Stage Three
Once the ninja has broken into the house, he walks along the outer wooden platforms or inner corridors of the building, using padded sandals, rabbit fur or a specialised form of walking to creep around the edges of the house in silence.

Stage Four
Having moved around the outer sections of the house, the ninja finds the required room he is searching for and gains entrance. It is here he pulls out his sword and points it in front of him, checking for people and objects in the dark.

The Infamous 'Rabbit Step'

The following problem is caused by researchers and ninjutsu practitioners mixing up two separate and special ways of walking.

The 'Deep Grass Rabbit Step' is famous in the world of ninjutsu and poses the largest problem. In modern times[87] it have been interpreted as a form of silent walking, where a ninja places his hands underneath each respective foot, left hand under left foot and right hand under right foot, at which point the ninja in a couched position, shuffles forward. A similar form of this crouched walk exists in the *Shinobi Hiden* but in this version a ninja alternates his steps, placing his left foot on his right hand and then moving forward and placing his right foot on his left hand. He crouches and moves forward placing each hand forward and then stepping on it with the opposite foot. However, this is *not* called 'Rabbit Stepping' in the *Shinobi Hiden* manual and there was no association with the 'Rabbit Step' until the researcher Yumio Nawa made an unfounded connection in the twentieth century.

The original description of the unnamed walk in the *Shinobi Hiden* manual states: 'Place your left hand [forward] and then place your right foot on it and then put down your left hand and put your left foot on it.' As can be seen there is a transcription error here as the walk would be impossible. There is a strange use of two versions of the ideogram for left – this use of alternative ideograms and the flow of the original writing has led the Historical Ninjutsu Research Team to conclude that the original walk was opposite hand to opposite foot (but the same hand same foot method has not been discarded), making

The opposite hand on opposite foot original version in the *Shinobi Hiden* manual by Hattori Hanzo, 1560.

The same unnamed step which occurs in the much later and changed version of the *Shinobi Hiden* manual in the Nagata family (1843), which is now the popular and probably incorrect version misnamed the Rabbit Step.

the translation as follows: 'Place your left hand [forward] and then place your right foot on it and then put down your right hand and put your left foot on it.'

The later nineteenth-century *Nagata* transcription of the *Shinobi Hiden* manual changes the method of the unnamed walk, from the above to the same hand/same foot method. This is a change 250 years after the event.

Returning to the 'Rabbit Step' in the *Bansenshukai* and the modern idea that a ninja steps on each respective hand, it is *possible* that this skill of walking on same hand same foot is authentic, however the *Bansenshukai* itself never explains how to perform the 'Rabbit Steps', it simply states that a ninja should use *Shinso no Uho*[88] *Jutsu* which translates as 'the art of regular or make shift Uho-rabbit steps'. His instructions also state that a ninja should use these steps (including the use of the cotton padded silent sandals) like a 'leaf floating on water', i.e. the foot does not leave the ground, it 'floats' along in a sliding pattern. The now modern form of standing on the respective hands is never shown with this 'floating' movement and is usually done in a form of short stepping or shuffling motion, where the foot leaves the floor.[89] The Rabbit Step so named in the *Bansenshukai* and the Unnamed Step in the *Shinobi Hiden* appear to have been mixed together by modern researchers incorrectly.

Alternatively, I and team mate Yoshie Minami favour another method which can be found documented, a step called 'Uho' (sometimes 'Ufu') which exists outside of ninjutsu documentation.

This Uho step is found in the Chinese ritual 'magic' art of Omyodo where the Uho[90] (Henbai) or 'Emperor's Step' is used in ritual ceremonies in Japan. One steps and slides one foot forward, doing the same with the alternate foot and bringing the feet together, side by side as each step continues. Slide forward with the left, then bring the right foot to meet it, then slide forward with the right foot and bring the left to meet it so that they are side by side again, akin to skating.

The name of both the Chinese magical step and the Bansenshukai step can be read as Uho:

禹歩 – Uho or the 'U' dynasty step (meaning the Emperor of)
兎歩 – Uho rabbit step taken from the Bansenshukai

It is possible that Fujibayashi is referring to this 'ritual' step and that his instructions about doing it 'like a leaf on water' is an instruction to not raise the foot. The step itself is named after a Chinese Emperor of the 禹 dynasty and as is often found in Japanese manuals, an ideogram is chosen for its phonetic sound and not its meaning. This step with the sound of Uho would have been understood by Fujibayashi's contemporaries and the phonetic use would not have been an issue, which may be why he never describes its actual method. It must be remembered that often in the Bansenshukai alternative ideograms are used simply for their sound and not their meaning. To further support this theory of the sliding side-by-side step we can see that the Shoninki manual shares some of the 'ninja' steps used in the Bansenshukai and also that the Shoninki uses the Suriashi step, a form of 'sliding' step. To further associate this Uho step with the Suriashi or sliding step we can turn to the document Sho Henbai Saho Narabini Goshinho written in 1154 by the Wakasugi clan, who served the Tsuchimikado clan. The Tsuchimikados were the official head family of the Chinese art of Onmyodo and approved by the imperial court. According to this document, the Uho or Ufu step is as follows:

Whilst chanting the nine stars of the Tonko Shikisen, step forward from with left foot with the Suriashi sliding step and continue as follows:

Left foot chant	'Tenpo'
Right foot chant	'Tendai'
Left foot	'Tensho'
Right foot	'Tenpo'
Left foot	'Tenkin'
Right foot	'Tenshin'
Left foot	'Tenchu'
Right foot	'Tennin'
Left foot	'Tenei'

The *Uho* step performed like a leaf on water in the *Bansenshukai* may actually be a variation on the *Suriashi* or sliding step. And whilst it seems likely, there is no mention of chanting the name of the stars whilst infiltrating, which is maybe why Fujibayashi says perform a 'modified' version.

The prefix to the word *Uho* is the word *Shinso*. If all the above mistakes by Japanese researchers were not enough to cause trouble, then this final section is the nail in the coffin. People in the past translated the term *Shinso no Toho (Uho)* 深草兎歩 to mean 'Deep Grass Rabbit Step', which is a problem, because the *Bansenshukai* never says this. The *Bansenshukai* says 真草兎歩 which translates as 'use normal or make shift *Uho* steps' The term 'Deep Grass' was added in the twentieth century, because the researchers at the time did not understand that the term '*Shinso*' meant modified steps. Fujibayashi does use this word in other parts of the *Bansenshukai* to mean 'use the original or the modified version'. In summary, using the original manual only, the art of the *Uho* step is a form of sliding *Suriashi* walk, a sliding step to move silently down corridors.

The Unnamed Step in the *Shinobi Hiden*

Using the original 1560 version only, this is the art of crouching and walking on the tops of your hands, left hand to right foot, right hand to left foot. Are you confused yet? I will now list the evolution of this misunderstood yet important 'ninja' step. Be aware that the manuals listed below are in their transcription order, that is the physical date that they were actually produced, not the date of the original writings they were copied from.

- Seventeenth century: the *Bansenshukai* names the 'Rabbit Step' for the first time but does not describe the process in any way and simply states 'use normal or makeshift *Uho* steps like a leaf on water.'
- 1731: The *Okimori* version of the *Shinobi Hiden* manual describes an unnamed step where the left hand goes under the right foot and the right hand goes under the left foot. This original version of the step comes from 1560 and remains unchanged until the mid-nineteenth century – which still leaves the issue of the transcription error in this edition, which uses two versions for left – the original manual is now lost.
- 1843: The *Nagata* version of the *Shinobi Hiden* manual knowingly changes the above unnamed walk to left hand to left foot and right hand to right foot but without explanation for the alteration.
- 1972: Nawa claims that the 'Rabbit Step' found in the *Bansenshukai* is actually the unnamed step in the *Shinobi Hiden*, without any explanation as to why he believes they are connected.
- Around the same time, researchers start to change the term *Shinso*, meaning 'normal' or 'makeshift' to 'Deep Grass', most likely to make sense of the use of the rabbit ideogram.

The modern ninjutsu community has adopted only the same-hand same-foot version which as can be seen, can only be dated as far as the late 1800s and has no connection to the *Bansenshukai's* 'Rabbit Step'.

Therefore, without solid proof, such as an alternative manual[91] (if one exists) which describes this same hand to same foot 'Rabbit Step' mix in detail, then it is possible that this step could be one of the following. We favour option one.

1   A variation on the *Omyodo Uho* or 'Emperor's Step' making the 'Rabbit Step' a form of sliding walk, similar to the *Suriashi* in the *Shoninki*.
2   The use of rabbit fur shoes.
3   The real name for the unnamed step in the *Shinobi Hiden* (however, to date no historical connection has been made).
4   An unknown alternative yet to be discovered in an undiscovered or revealed manual.

10

Similar yet Dissimilar

Are the ninja manuals genuine? During the Edo period of peace the samurai looked back and reflected on the Sengoku period in a romanticised way. However, some documentation of the Edo period intended to save the military knowledge for future generations is an invaluable historical source.

Apart from a very select few manuals that were penned at the end of the Sengoku period or a minority that were written at the start of the Edo period, nearly all ninja manuals are written by those who never saw combat in warfare. The further the date of a manual gets from 1603, the more questionable its content. These problems have led academics in Japan to keep ninjutsu at arm's length and in some cases to bring even the core manuals, such as the *Bansenshukai, Shoninki* and *Shinobi Hiden,* into question. However, a high percentage of researchers do not question the validity of the information provided by the *Bansenshukai* and the *Shoninki* (especially the latter). There are a few points that raise concern. Why, for example, has the author of the *Bansenshukai* taken so much information from external manuals, some of which were in the public domain; and why does Fujibayashi quote so heavily from the Chinese classics? In fact, these two questions are easily answered and reflect positively on the author. The issue of using other ninja manuals is explained in the text as an attempt to unify ninjutsu and bring about not only a record for future generations, but to establish a curriculum and to reject that which is not needed. Fujibayashi's use of *Gunpo Densho,* or war manuals, such as the *Gunpo Jiyoshu*, is evident. It is known that the *Gunpo Jiyoshu* manual itself was published at least 20 years before the writing of the *Bansenshukai;* but the shinobi information from that manual is in fact Hattori information and has its origins in Iga. So we have an Iga manual – the *Bansenshukai* – referring to a published work that is a copy of Ninja information from Iga. Some have claimed that references to Chinese classics were an attempt to look 'worthy' and 'educated', as an understanding of the Chinese classics and Chinese culture was deemed highly desirable at this time in Japan. This is true, but we must not forget that Fujibayashi was of samurai status (at some level) and was indeed educated. He is not pretending to be cultured. It is only the inclusion of ninjutsu that make people raise the point in the first place, implying that his ninjutsu is fake and the classics are there to give it credibility. Other contemporary manuals refer to Chinese culture and style, other samurai of the time did look to China and use Chinese literature as a foundation for their instruction. Therefore, Fujibayashi, whilst a shinobi, was samurai and was in fact simply following in the footsteps of his peers. This does not undermine the credibility of his instruction on ninjutsu in itself.

Having answered these two criticisms of the *Bansenshukai*, we must investigate its overall authenticity. Firstly, its contents beyond the Chinese link display a vast amount of understanding and knowledge of the shinobi arts, skills which ring true with the architecture of the time and contemporary military procedures. To make all this up would take an eccentric yet brilliant mind; or Fujibayashi was in fact acquainted with the Iga *shinobi* ways, which is of course backed up by the fact that he was born in Iga. Secondly, the *Bansenshukai* was clearly adopted by many (if not all) of the families of both Koka and Iga, families with hundreds of years of ninjutsu experience who were not likely to be duped by a forgery. To help save the traditions of Koka, copies of the *Bansenshukai* were distributed amongst them in an attempt to retain the correct skills of the ninja within the respective families. Lastly, there are the three *Koka Koshi,* or 'displaced warriors of Koka', who presented the *Bansenshukai* to the Shogun's Magistrate to support their formal request for employment. The Ohara document names three warriors, Ohara Kazuma, Ueno Hachizaemon and Oki Moriichiro, who requested government sponsorship and employment for the Koka families who could no longer afford to train shinobi. They expressed concern for the future of their arts – whilst also trying to place the Ohara family at the top of the hierarchy. This was not the first attempt to gain government support, it was tried at various points. The frequently missed point here is that the *Bansenshukai* was presented as an official document to the Shogunate; this indirectly confirms the authenticity of the document. It is almost impossible that the combined families of Koka would petition the supreme ruler of Japan, with their future at stake, with a falsified document, a simple fact that has gone unremarked for years.

Another, not so well known factor is that one year before the *Bansenshukai* (1676), another ninja manual called the *Tsugeke Shinobi no Jutsu Hidensho* was written that was kept in the Inamasu family, who claimed to have been given ninjutsu by the Fujibayashi family. It is recorded that Inamasu Jirozaemon (who recived a Menkyo Kaiden certificate from a Fujibayashi member) taught ninjutsu in the Todo clan of Iga and their manual reflects Fujibayashi teachings. This confirms that the Fujibayashi family were practising shinobi. The ninjutsu in the *Bansenshukai* clearly reflects the ninjutsu as described in the manual preceding it. The following is a list of skills taken from the *Tsugeke Ninjutsu Hidensho* manual (1675) displaying similarities with the *Bansenshukai*.

- The art of the 'Tono' Fire
- The art of the Attack Torch
- The art of the 'Pulling' Rope
- The art of 'Osei' Gunnery
- The art of the [Grapple[92]] and Rope
- The art of the Extending Key
- The art of Drills [for infiltration]
- The art of Saws [for infiltration]

- The art of the Kunai [digging tool]
- The art of Crossing Moats
- The art of Illusion Fire
- The art of Yoshitune's Torch
- The art of the Palm Torch
- The art of the Shinobi Torch
- The art of the Night Attack Rocket
- The art of the Greater Rainproof Battle Camp Torch

The *Murasami Diahi No Maki* manual shows how even smaller manuals truly reflect real *shinobi no jutsu* and deal with similar themes. The short table of contents is as follows:

- Concerning Gunpowder
- The Fire [Cylinder]
- The Water [Torch]
- [illegible text – probably a recipe for an explosive]
- Murasami Powder
- Concerning Medicines [or Powders]
- The Art of the Hinawa Fuse [for guns and explosives]
- Concerning the Cord Attached to Swords

The similarities to the *Bansenshukai* help to confirm it as a treasure trove of ninjutsu knowledge, written by an educated warrior of Iga who was an adept.

The *Shoninki* is also well established as an authentic ninja manual, as it was written by the head of a secret *Gunpo* war school under one of the most powerful families in Japan and has possible origins in the Takeda clan. It was of course kept secret until well after the author's death, which, along with his social station, gives it an almost unshakable position when the question of legitimacy arises. Therefore, the litmus test for the legitimacy of any manual are the *Shoninki* and the *Bansenshukai*. It was impossible for Fujibayashi to copy Natori's *Shoninki* as the *Bansenshukai* was written five years prior to the *Shoninki*, which would mean that only Natori could have plagiarised Fujibayashi. However, the dissimilarities are far too apparent. Natori writes with a note book approach, that is, the *Shoninki* is a working manual, it lists skills and ideas yet does not expand on them, whilst the *Bansenshukai* is heavy with detail. Thus, if it was the case that Natori got hold of a copy of Fujibayashi's work, why did he not steal the factual sections to support his writings? Furthermore, the *Natori-ryu* document is full of original terminology and ideas, showing it is not plagiarised. At the same time, there are enough similarities, such as ideogram origins and terminology, to show a shared body of knowledge: examples such as 'ninjas need a silver tongue,' or identical recommended times for infiltration.

Often manuals are simply copied from older ones and information is repeated. Yet, at times you find manuals that use a similar vocabulary, syntax, root word connections, linguistics and shared skill sets but are not direct copies. This points to a shared origin and yet displays evolution in the dissimilarities. This is where fake ninja schools can be discovered, as they directly quote from historical ninjutsu manuals and their dissimilarity is not in linguistics or subtle points, but in wholly new skills that seem contradictory to ninjutsu when compared to the authentic examples: ninja as a martial art system for example, or the description of 'secret weapons' that are actually common knowledge. Comparing in this way highlights where historical manuals have simply been arranged from earlier sources. It also helps identify if a manual has any new and valid information. The excitement of such a discovery is muted by the enormous task of attempting to trace the history and 'journey' of such a document, yet amidst the dross, diamonds do appear.

We will now explore some of the major similarities and dissimilarities between certain manuals; it is by no means a complete picture but it helps us to identify historically authentic information, that which is suspicious, and that which is copied.[93]

Linguistic Similarities

As Japanese is based on ideograms it is relatively easy to identify connections as both phonetic and pictorial representations are displayed. As discussed it is impossible for the author of the *Bansenshukai* to have taken anything from the *Shoninki*, as it postdates the writing. The *Shoninki* talks of the 'Ten Ancient Ways of Ninjutsu' that flow through all of the ninja skills. Remembering that the *Shoninki* has *Koshu* and *Kusonoki* origins and that the *Bansenshukai* is from Iga/Koka, we see multiple links. One stands out above all.

Number five of the ten basic ninja skills is '*Joei* – 如影' or 'shadow-like ninjutsu'. The *Shoninki* says very little and says it meant staying near people, or using the shadows. The *Bansenshukai* talks of '*Jokei* – 如景' or the art of the shadow – as he uses the suffix of *no jutsu*. Whilst the two second halves of the ideogram look dissimilar – 影 and 景 – they are created with the same meaning. 景 *Kei*, has the same meaning as 影 *Ei*, which is 'shadow' and 如 which is 'like'. The two ideograms were interchangeable in the early Edo period. The *Bansenshukai* then goes on to talk of this 'shadow-like art' as the ability to get people into position before a war starts and observe them at a close distance. So both manuals use an ideogram which has a shared origin and use that ideogram to mean the same skill set, yet they are not identical. This continues to help establish that ninjutsu had some point of origin.

A Ninja Should Look Stupid

Both the *Bansenshukai* and the *Shoninki* ninja manuals promote the concept of appearing stupid to go unnoticed as a ninja agent. Remembering that these two manuals were kept secret within the ninja community for a long time, it would be almost impossible for two samurai[94] simultaneously to write of this same skill by coincidence. Here is what they say:

> *Bansenshukai*
> Similarly, the wisdom of a competent ninja 能キ忍者 is as vast as heaven, so that no human being can know it exactly. A ninja should look as stupid, whilst their strategies are as profound and deep as the earth or an abyss and beyond mere human knowledge.

Shoninki

This section is about the advantage of making people think that they are smarter then you are, with the aim to glean information indirectly from them. You should never divulge your true capabilities for any reason, ever.

To make people reveal their opinions, you should pretend to be too stupid to think reasonably and ask someone to tell you what they think about a certain subject you wish to know about.

People wish to show how intelligent they are and they want to see you as more stupid; therefore you should just disguise your own reasoning power and gain information through listening.

Part of a shinobi's skill set is to be careful and not show your true intelligence at any time.

A well-trained shinobi looks like a very stupid man. It is a core principle to praise others as much as possible to keep them carrying on about a subject at their own leisure, this skill is called *Hito ni Kuruma wo Kakeru* 人に車をかける

Weapons not to be Used During *Shinobi* Night Attacks

Whilst cross-referencing ninja manuals helps to dispel doubts about the authenticity of the skills described, finding references from texts that are external to the world of the shinobi and can have no agenda at all is more satisfying. Returning to the manuals of the *Otsubo Hon* school of horsemanship, we can start to find correlations not only in the words used to describe shinobi, such as the name *Kamari* and its connections to the ninja, but also in the instructions themselves. The school teaches that when adventuring out on a shinobi mission, you should refrain from taking long weapons such as spears and halberds. The *Bansenshukai* in the section makes the same point: 'Do not take any long weapons such as spears [on shinobi night attacks]'. Simple instructions such as this help to authenticate the writings of certain shinobi masters. Most attempts at counterfeiting ninjutsu tend to aim at the more dramatic and mystical elements and neglect such apparently mundane matters. Through such relatively unimportant connections we build a more solid argument for the validity of writings such as the *Bansenshukai* and the *Shoninki*.

The *Otsubo Hon* school talking of shinobi raids.

Echoes of the *Shoninki*

For those familiar with the teachings of the *Shoninki* the following extracts will certainly ring bells. The similarities imply connection between the two documents. The manual in question is the *Dakko Shinobi No Maki Ryakuchu*, a monograph that offers an exciting visual window into the world of the ninja: It may simply be a list of Natori-ryu skills and so closely associated with the *Shoninki* manual, or if external to Natori-ryu, then both documents spring from the same sources.

> In Relation to Wind and Rain
> It is beneficial to steal in when it is windy; however it is not so beneficial when it rains as you will leave footprints.
>
> **The 'Black Board'**
> When you 'steal in' and your [presence] has been detected, you should hide under a window, this is because [if someone] examines the outside from a window, they seldom look downwards, so you should carry a 'black board' [to cover you][95] called 'the window lid' and thus you will not be found. A shinobi should first of all think of windows [when he infiltrates].
>
> **The Pipe[96] Ladder**
> Place sections of bamboo like that of a smoking pipe onto a rope with a hook on the end, this is called the *Kudanawa Bashigo* or the Pipe Ladder.
>
> **The Sword Ladder**
> When crossing a fence, place your sword against the fence and use the hilt (*tsuba*) as a foot hold so you can climb over the wall.
>
> **Iron Spike Steps**
> The *Kogai Bashigo*: Place iron spikes [*kogai*] into a wall to make footholds so that you can climb up them.
>
> **The Collapsible Hook and Rod**
> *Kaginawa Bashigo*: As with the Pipe Ladder above you put bamboo pipes onto a rope with a hook, with this version you can pull the rope [to give it tension].
>
> **Securing Doors and Gates**
> Some gatehouse doors can be opened by [removing] the bar[97] or by keys, therefore tie a rope to the [illegible text] and then secure it to the bottom [to hold fast the door and to stop people entering].

The connections to individual ninja schools and the *Shoninki* manual do not stop there, the ninja manual *Ninpo Mizukagami* written by Fujita Ungyoanryo of Kaga discusses the skill of identifying if an enemy light is approaching or not, at night. The *Shoninki* states that if you place your sword on the ground and use a fan as an upper cross bar and then get a line of sight to the light in question, you can use these as 'cross hairs' to see if the light goes up or down, left or right and you can thus determine if the enemy is advancing or not. This is echoed in Fujita's manual, even though the two schools are over 300km apart:

> If you put a paper handkerchief or your sleeve across your eyes and look at the light ahead [you can determine a direction]. If they are moving away from you, you will see the light retreat, however, if they are advancing the light will move down and out of your vision. If the actual distance [of the enemy] is one Cho away it will be in reality three Cho.

The manual continues with a 'recipe' for a *Donohi* body warmer, which is a utensil to carry fire or more accurately smouldering embers to start a fire and keep a ninja warm. Whilst the concept is the same in both manuals, the difference in ingredients shows that one is not copied from the other, they are independent during at least the early Edo period.

The *Ninpo Mizukagami* ninja manual held at the Iga Ueno Museum is a document of the *Muhyoshi* school and was passed down in Kaga and Ichizen and consists of two volumes that are dedicated to the shinobi arts, declaring that a *Bushi* (samurai) should know such things, another counter to the samurai versus ninja myth. It is believed that *Muhyoshi-ryu* was an offshoot of a martial school called *Shinjin-ryu* founded by the swordsman Kusabuka Jinshiro Tokinobu of the Kaga domain. The school *Muhyoshi-ryu* appears to have been founded by a man named Niki Shinjuro who was a *Yorikigumi*[98] and a disciple of the swordsman. It appears he took the school of *Shinjin-ryu* and mixed it with others to form the *Muhyoshi-ryu*, which ended up containing this ninja information. It is unknown how the ninja information entered this school of military arts:

> I have collected various kinds of deception and recorded them to aid future generations [in any time of need].
> If you have a mighty enemy and you need to make a night attack on your own, you should attack with these shinobi ways.

The concept of using *shinobi no jutsu* or the arts of the ninja for defence is a common theme in ninja writing. It could be the case that these are genuine instructions to future generations, or they might be self-justification by the author who uses what are considered unorthodox strategies including theft; or a mix of the two.

The *Ninpo Sho Ka-zamurai Techo* ninja scroll also strongly echoes the *Bansenshukai* but lists more tools:

The Kurorokagi Latch Finder
This tool is used as a sickle saw. It is made of iron and should be thin, place it between the gap in sliding doors and probe upward, thus finding the lock. This it is called a *Toigaki*.[99] However, it has a second use, it can be used as a latch probe, to find the Kuroro latch and open it.

The Saw

This is a *sotogiri* and *uchigiri* – that is an outside and inside cutter.[100] Put the blade into the [unknown text][101] and cut a wider whole.

The Sound Amplifier

Hang this sound amplifier up like a weight and scales. Next place a plate underneath it with a gap of five Rin [1.5 mm]. With this you can know if those inside are asleep or not and if they are the bell will drop down on to the plate.

Caltrops

Spread or scatter these at every exit when you infiltrate, so that the enemy may not follow. Also on your way out leave them behind you as you retreat.

The 'snorkel'

Make this of tanned leather and use when you travel underwater – this allows you to breathe.

One superb link between other manuals and ninja lore is this sound amplifier. First the concept of amplifying sound is in the *Shinobi Hiden* and its mentions the use of the shell of the sea usrchin to do the same job, (discussed later). However more interestingly, it is a duplication of ninja folklore, first expressed by Natori in the *Shoninki*. Natori states that if you attach a weight on a thread held just off the floor in an old building, then when the occupants of the house fall asleep, the stone will touch the floor. This is nearly the same description.[102]

The only even remotely logical interpetation for this folklore is that the wood of the house contracts as the night gets colder, allowing the weight to hit the floor.

Listening was an important skill in both using ninjutsu and defending against it. The

Caltrops are a worldwide phenomenon; however a possible ninja connection can be seen with this image from the Chinese manual.

sounds of insects, the behaviour of dogs and frogs, the sound of opening doors, squeaky floorboards and the direction of the wind were taken into account when using ninjutsu. The 'Listening Cylinder' came in two basic forms, firstly as an 'ear trumpet'. This could have been a metal flared cylinder or even the shell of a sea urchin, as described in the *Shinobi Hiden* manual and was used by pushing it through holes in walls or through lattice work. The second version consisted of a cylinder open at only one end on a string, as illustrated right. A shinobi would hold it next to an open window or next to a hole he had scraped out of a clay wall so that he conversation of the people in the room might be heard. Both of these examples show how close a ninja had to approach an enemy.

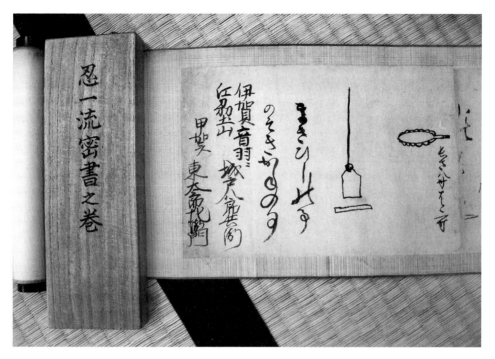

'The Sound Amplifier' (Courtesy of Nakashima Atsumi)

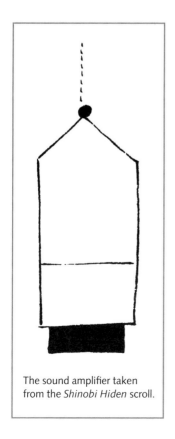

The sound amplifier taken from the *Shinobi Hiden* scroll.

A fifteenth-century German snorkel.

一隱眥之事

一言語相通之事

口傳

右之條々雖為秘事貴

殿依信望令授與訖奴

々不可輕忽云々

The scroll does not explain the method of secret signalling; however it talks of secret ways to communicate with conch shells, which were passed down in oral form.

A typical Japanese compound, where a shinobi might be hiding.

Looking at the snorkel in the *Ninpo Sho Ka-zamurai Techo*, we can see that the *shinobi* used these tools to hide in water and that snorkelling is not a modern concept. A shinobi could only move around using the snorkel if it was raining, so that it did not matter if the ninja left wet footprints. Or he could use it if spotted by the enemy by dashing into the water to hide.

Western European war manuals also contain snorkelling as can be seen in the fifteenth-century image on page 121; note the bowl to aid air intake, common with longer pipes.

It is well documented that the ninja used secret codes and hidden writings to convey messages in a warring situation. The *shinobi* also had to become proficient in the arts of signalling to the unseen. The *Bansenshukai* states that the ninja must be set up around a defensive position and that they should signal with sound and fire. Again linked to this central text, several manuals talk about the use of conch shells, bells, whistles, clappers and flutes to send messages. Of course, there was no standard message and each system had to be constructed between people, but elements such as vibrations and length of note were used to differentiate between meanings. The *Bansenshukai* even goes as far as to say a person well versed in this can hold a 'conversation' in much the same way as with Morse code.

A traditional gate, which a shinobi would have had to infiltrate.

The outer shutter on a Japanese window.

A Japanese locking bar.

Thatched roofs were easy targets for arson.

The shinobi would hide under bridges and listen to conversations in order to obtain information.

11

Ninja Magic

he ninja left us with only a small selection of spells from the ritual magic component of their art. The authors of the *Shoninki* and the *Bansenshukai* warn that *ninjutsu* is not 'magic' and is in fact a practical art, devoid of mysticism, yet both still include ritual magic. On the other hand, the Koka ninja named Kimura informs us that the deepest arts of ninjutsu are esoteric and 'magical' but become true and practical if understood. Natori Masatake also warns us not to throw away ritual magic or dismiss it, as some things do hold power. When dealing with the ninja and magic, a few considerations must be at the forefront. Firstly, ninja magic leans towards 'psychological magic', that is, talismans and rituals of hiding, or things that could be considered to give a ninja the psychological strength to progress. Secondly, magic was learned so that it could be used against the enemy and *his* belief in magic (Fujibayashi is clear on this point). We must remember that the ninja were from a medieval world, at a time when magic was taken for granted as a reality by many and that Japan at the time was heavily influenced by Buddhism and other creeds that were associated with esoteric magical practices. Here we encounter 'fake ninja magic', that is, ninja magic that was written down years later and does not comply with the feeling of the original manuals, where spells are numerous and practical ninjutsu is lacking.[103] The *Shinobi Densho* (1827) ninja scroll is concerned entirely with magic. It has reams of magical examples, some of which can be found in other ninja manuals, some of

The *Koka-ryu Ninjutsu No Ikkan Goshinho* manual displays magic found in many non-Ninja scrolls, and is considered dubious.

which are not, such as using the bones of rats to keep one awake for over 100 days. The authentic Koka ninja, Kimura of the Owari-Tokugawa clan, assures us that esoteric methods, such as the arts of 'Toothpick Hiding' or 'Fingernail Catching', are true and deep ninja secrets, and these do appear in the scroll.

There is a sad tale to be told in the world of ninja research. The epic manual, the *Bansenshukai* lists a chapter heading in its table of contents, in book five of the collection, 'Secret Writings with Occult Powers'. The tragedy is that the text is missing and what could have been the greatest find in the world of the ninja and magic has been lost to us, unless it is retained in a private collection in Japan.

Ninja Protection

The protection spell found within the undated ninja scroll *Iga-ryu Kanpo Mizukagami No Maki*[104] closely resembles the protection spell found within the *Shoninki* manual. Whilst the origin of the *Iga-ryu* scroll is dubious, it does contain elements consistent with ninjutsu from a 'magic' perspective.

The spell can be considered as a full spell of protection as in the Natori school or it can be broken up in the following manner to protect sections of the body.

The Right Hand Line
Jōryakuhō 上略法: or Upper Strategy
This spell should be written on paper and inserted into a helmet or head-ware to protect your upper parts.

The Centre Line
Chūryakuhō 中略法: or Middle Strategy
This spell should be written on paper and placed on the inside of your belt or around your waist, this protects the lower sections of your body.

The Left Hand Line
Karyaku 下略法: or Lower Strategy
This spell should be written on paper and swallowed; this will protect the trunk of your body.

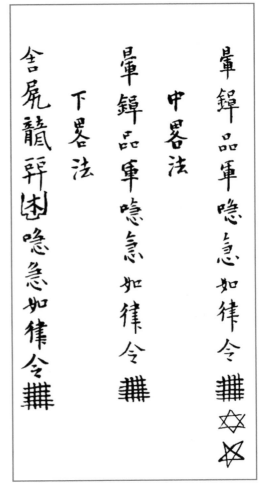

Ninja Hiding Magic

The ninja curriculum includes a minute amount of magic to enhance the ability to hide. The shinobi pride themselves on practicality, therefore it has been postulated that these spells were developed to help calm the nerves of ninja under threat, giving them a psychological edge, however, it is impossible to tell how far contemporary superstition found its way into the world of the shinobi, or how much they believed compared to how much they understood that the skill was psychological.

The *Bansenshukai* holds a fascinating magic spell which gives us a view of the world of the ninja and the daring behind his infiltration tactics.

When you happen to meet an enemy patrol, you should not be upset but hide yourself by staying by the side of a wall, fence, shrubbery, some lumber, a pile of firewood or anything like this and without making any noise. You should cover your face with your sleeve and only expose your eyes, make no breathing sound and be careful not to make the enemy feel your breath, stay standing and be completely still and then chant the mantra of Ongyo hiding magic [in your mind][105] – '*On A Ni Chi Marishi Ei Sowaka*' and shape your hands in the mudra of Hokyo.[106]

Or you can turn your back to the enemy whilst standing if needs be. If you perform this you will not be detected in most cases. There have been many examples of this spell's success.

Those who do not know this method tend to lose their head and rush to seek a place to hide when they realise that the enemy is coming, so that they will often make the sound of footsteps or audibly breathe, hit something, tread in dust and end up being found out because of this.

Further to this, the *Koka Ryu Ninjutsu Densho,* combined with clarification from the *Koyogunkan Tekito* manual, display another form of ninja hiding magic called *Shinden Yaguruma no Ho,* which translates as 'The Arts of the Divine Arrow Windmill'. The shinobi uses a popular Japanese charm called a *Yaguruma,* which is a collection of eight arrows pointing inwards making a circle, with their heads at the centre. Whilst the *Koka Ryu Densho* gives the spell for this, the second manual, the *Koyogunkan Tekito* explains that when trying to hide, a person uses this arrow windmill and places a mirror over the top of it and then buries the arrows and mirror in leaves and soil. The mirror is thought to contain the reflection of the person in it and supposedly hides the form of the infiltrator from his enemy.

Magical Ninja Hiding Hair Pins or Talismans

The *Gunpo Jiyoshu* manual discusses the art of invisibility when attempting night raids or shinobi missions.

> [To become invisible to the enemy] take the fangs from a live [venomous] Mamushi pit viper, and put them into your topknot, in the case of an emergency. If the captain of a shinobi night attack or scout carries this [in his hair], then they will not be seen by the eyes of the enemy. However, if they have doubts or use this skill for their own evil desires, they will meet their nemesis and will be discovered by the enemy and be seen more than they usually would.

An extremely interesting confirmation of this magic is given in the *Koka Ryu Densho*. The version found is similar yet dissimilar enough to show development of or variation in the spell. In this version of *Ongyo jutsu* (hiding), a ninja would wait for a lunar eclipse and then make a hairpin talisman for hiding. On the lunar eclipse the ninja would carve a wooden *Kanzashi* hair pin and chant the spell of concealment as he waited for the eclipse to finish. It is possible that the shinobi was trying to 'capture the darkness' of the eclipse and contain it within the pin. The manual teaches that a ninja should chant a similar spell to the one found in the *Bansenshukai* as quoted above, however this time the words were '*Rai de seishin kou ten kou setsu*'. Also, finally, the manual says that a ninja should envisage black clouds around him, concentrating on making him blend in with the darkness.

The *Gunpo Jiyoshu* then goes on to describe 'a secret method to stop a person', magic that helps protect against a ninja:

> To stop someone [infiltrating], make a brush of Muku wood (Aphananthe aspera) on the day of Kanoe when it also corresponds with the day of the Monkey and write the spell below, on all four sides on the inside face of a gate (lintel, sides and threshold).

Also when you search for shinobi or a suspicious person, first write the spell as above and put it on each exit, so that the person will not be able to go out. It is said this talisman was passed down by Nichirin Shonin Hakone Gongen.

The *Gunpo Jiyoshu* manual does not stop there with its instructions on defending against an enemy shinobi through magic. Both Chinese and Japanese armies relied on the skill of seeing *Chi* to understand the nature and status of the enemy army. This skill of understanding and reading *Chi* was extended to buildings and their occupants. This skill could enable a commander to prevent an enemy ninja from performing an incendiary attack. The skill is under the title '*Chi* of a *Yato*' which is an alternative name for ninja.

Chi of a ninja.

The *Chi* you see as trailing smoke as in the picture is a sign of an enemy coming to conduct a night attack or of a shinobi coming to set a fire. Therefore, this is called the *Chi* of the *Yato*. The attack will take place within three days if it can be seen from the direction of the Chicken and is heading towards the Rat. If it is from the Ox to the Monkey, then watch out for the attack that night. The same holds true all through the seasons. The colour of the *Chi* should be a yellowish black. If it is blue, red or white, be careful for the next fifteen days of the month.

The next example is a perfect illustration of the difficulty in understanding if a text means a ninja or if it is simply someone sneaking in to a residence. The manual is undated, with this insert being the only '*nin*' character found in the book, and also lacks any military instructions, which points to a non-ninja content, however the actions are still the same. The instructions in the text say that when you infiltrate (shinobi) into a house, you should write the name of the house master on a wooden bucket and then turn that bucket upside down. The house master will fall asleep, allowing you to enter.

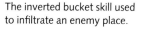

The inverted bucket skill used to infiltrate an enemy place.

The Way of the God Izuna-gongen

The eighteenth-century Koka ninja, Ohara Kazuma, wrote down a selection of his family's esoteric practices with a connection to ninjutsu. Based in Shugendo and dedicated to the god Izuna-gongen this spell is not for the faint of heart. It possibly displays the harsh world of ancient Japan and the lengths people would go to in order attain knowledge; or it is designed to emphasise the inestimable value of ninja secrets.

- Catch a mating pair of deer and skin them alive, then dry and tan them in the shade.
- Catch a pond turtle and put it in a tub of clean water and then place the plant *Cleyara Japonica* around the outside of the bucket.
- For three days feed the turtle a small amount of alcohol.
- Remove the shell of the turtle whilst it is alive with a knife. Whilst doing this you must say: 'I am not doing this to you to wrong you, I am doing this to help the world and its people, to build a fruitful future, please forgive me.'
- To bury the flesh and organs of the turtle you should use divination to guide you to a pure place. Here you must build a small shrine in secret and dedicate it to the god Izuna-gongen.
- Dry roast the shell in a lidded earthware pot and include some *Rhus Javanica* wood. When this has blackened grind this down into a powder.
- Cut the male deer skin into a rectangle of 84cm long by 9cm in width.
- Cut the female deer into a rectangle of 78cm long by 9cm in width.
- Mix the burnt shell powder from above with glutinous rice powder to make glue.
- Apply this glue to the back of the skin to make a single talisman.
- Now as it is made of male and female it is now both male and female, that is In-Yo, and next, install it on the shrine that you have created. Pray each day at this shrine from 3 March to 5 May. This is the period between the festival for girls and the festival for boys. When you are praying you should say this spell:
- '*Takamagahara ni kami todomarimasu kami no manako no konoizuna kikitomete haraetamae kiyometamou*' ['Izuna and the realm of the gods, hear my prayer and fulfil my wish and purify'].
- When you have chanted this spell, you should make your wish and ask the god Izuna-gongen to fulfil your wish and show you the secrets of the ninja.
- After the last day of the above mentioned period you should take the talisman and carry it with you.

Other Magical Spells

The above spell is from the *Inko-ryu* which, along with *Fukushima-ryu,* show a heavy slant towards magical skills, alongside historical ninjutsu. The *Fukushima-ryu* is thought to have been passed down in the family of Fukushima Saemon Dayu and to have been connected to the Nojiri family through Nojiri Jiroemon Narimasa. The *Fukushima-ryu* manual deals with some very esoteric areas, some of which are not fully understood, as seen below:

- The subtitles [of ninjutsu?]
- The spider hand
- Dream and fantasy [ninjutsu?]
- 'The pulling of your body'[107]
- Attacking and defending
- Defence against Juji magic[108]

The *Koka Ryu Bujutsu* manual also includes magical spells among its lists. Samples from the document:

- Explosives
- Magical spells
- Medicines
- Signals
- Torches
- Sleeping powders
- How to identify secret letters
- How to get water from sea water
- Charms and talismans
- Sea sickness cures

The *Inko-ryu* document contains the following list:

- Of breathing
- The art of whistles
- Seeing at night
- Skills and tools of the shinobi
- Poisons
- Removing poisons
- Important points to be used at night
- Things to do in the dark without a light
- Magical spells

The Fukushima document has some interesting melding of the esoteric and the practical. Here is how to 'defend' your saw or drill against sound by magical means. Whilst possibly symbolic or considered magical, the mixture would in fact work as a lubricant to reduce noise, just as the 'oil of toad' would for the saws in the *Shinobi Hiden* manual. 'If you apply a mixture of newt and owl blood mixed in with sake, and apply it to your saw, you will cut without noise or if applied to a drill it will become a magical drill.'

The *Fukushima-ryu* also holds a spell of hiding, the 'Spell of the Blind Buddha': 'Write the spell [overleaf] on the belly of a Buddha [statue] and write the Sanskrit image found below on its back. When you write this, do it in the blood of a weasel.'

The *Shinobi No Maki Te Kagami* describes a poem that is said to entice your enemies into the open. The explanation is not extensive and it is presumed to be a form of mantra

to bring your enemy into a position that you would want them in. '*Ken no to chigiri shuto o wasurete kazoo no ineshie no bushi no hito moto.*'

Sometimes, the esoteric elements of ninja manuals sound outrageous but it has to be remembered that most of these scrolls are from a time of widespread superstition. The *Shinobi No Maki Te Kagami* ninja scroll even claims to hold the key to seeing the dead and spiritual beings. The instructions are ambiguous, however, the general procedure is as follows: dry a red (possibly brown/red) cat and take ointment from it and then apply it to the edges of one's eyes. The 'magician' should dry bat's eyeballs in the shade. The manual then becomes almost incomprehensible. He should perform an unknown action to a beehive, possibly create a hole or taking a section and, along with the bat's eyes, add the extract to the edges of his eyes. The dead or those things that are part of the supernatural world are then made visible.

Rather than be surprised by such superstition, the modern reader should be more shocked by the shinobi's theme of *non-reliance* on magic, one which flows through the main manuals. The 'psychological' magic mainly found in the true ninja manuals contrasts with the the more outlandish magic found in the less historically authentic manuals.

12

Oral Traditions – The Ninja Way of Kuden

How to construct useful tools should be passed down by 'hand to hand' transmission, such things as fire arrows, torches, watch-fires etc, should not be gained without direct teaching.

Taken from the *Onmitsuhiji shinobi-daii*

Embedded in the way of Japanese arts, be it the martial arts or other skills and especially in *shinobi no jutsu*, the term '*Kuden*' is bandied around in conversation and is half understood. *Kuden* is oral tradition and that which is passed on by teacher to student alone. It is made up of two ideograms, *Ku* 口 or 'mouth' and *Den* 伝 for 'transmission'. Also, this alternative ideogram for *Kuden* was sometimes used: 口傳.

Many people hold the misconception that ninja manuals are written in code, with the encryption passed on by word of mouth. This is incorrect with the exception of a few examples, such as the ingredients for some explosives. Most manuals have explanatory details with some further skills to be passed on by mouth, or a list of skills used as mnemonics for practising ninja.

The only real contender for the full oral transmission of tradition comes from the *Ogiden* manual, one of the oldest in existence (1586):

Of Heart and Mind:

Do not forget; Righteousness, Fidelity and Loyalty and remember, only through prayer will you achieve the truly wondrous.

Of the Body:

The conduct of *shinobi no jutsu* is found in the seven 'ways[109] and they are what you should know.

These next five sentences are word of mouth secrets:

Of army conduct or ways
The scroll of In (Yin) and of tools
The scroll of the army at night
The scroll of the ways of the shinobi
The scroll of water and fire

These five 'scrolls' above are not passed down in writing but only by *Kuden* which is by word of mouth.

[Omitted text]

Written on the seventh day of the eleventh lunar month in 1586 by the descendant of Koka Saburo Kaneie, Mochizuki Shigeie.

In the main, a ninja manual is informative, with little hidden meaning or secret subtext. Anything that is considered too secret to write down is marked with the above ideogram and labelled *Kuden*. Sometimes ninja scrolls are comprised of a list of skills or tools where only the titles are present. This gives the illusion of code, however this may not be so, what each title meant may have been general knowledge to anyone who had been involved in military action. Simply because we no longer understand the names does not make them a secret at the time. Writing the word *Kuden* next to some points probably makes the ones without the word attached general knowledge, or at least understood to the people of the school. Some elements would only be understood by the school themselves, thus a list of skills would be written and anyone of that school would have understood its meaning; some may have had deeper *Kuden* teachings on finer points.

With these above points understood, ninjutsu can be broken down into three basic kinds of secrecy:

1   Skills and information that are known by most people who have taken part in military operations and who have dealt with a shinobi or are in fact shinobi themselves. Skill sets such as scouting and information retrieval, measurement skills and elements that are observable by the entire army.
2   Skills the effects of which are understood by all, such as explosives and night raiding techniques but where the precise details are not commonly understood, thus the way of the skills (and not the outcome) are *Kuden* and are only known by a select number.
3   Those elements which are deep secrets and only passed between a few members and down through the schools. Those who are subject to their effects are unaware of their application, such as a shinobi listening to conversations from within an enemy castle and without detection, infiltrating spies and sleeper agents and never having them revealed to the enemy, or magical elements retained for higher students.

Ninjutsu was not in itself a secret, as simply paying a local inhabitant for information was considered ninjutsu, as was sending a man to look at the banners of an army, these are both forms of ninjutsu and are not secret. The deeper into ninjutsu a person went, the more concealed the details of the art were. Ninjutsu is a series of levels with no strictly defined boundaries, becoming more and more secret as one gets closer to the head of the school. Some tricks were known by many but the closer you get to the head of a system then the closer to the deeper secrets you were. This might mean sharing a school's deepest secrets with only one person. But ninjutsu was not always only given to one individual a generation; men of Iga were hired to teach others the arts of the ninja across most Japanese armies and up to 50 ninja were hired by each domain, which would make hundreds if not thousands of schools a requirement to fill the needs of the country if only one man per generation held the knowledge, an absurdity. Both the *Shinobi Hiden* and the *Shoninki* talk of sharing the deepest secrets with only a single person, and this does not have to mean between family members, but should be with those who are most suitable for the job.

Kuden did not refer to to the ninja alone, even the art of acting held deep secrets that were considered fit to be divulged only to a single person in each generation. The *Ogiden* ninja manual states:

> If you have children or grandchildren who are not able enough or of the correct mind, then they should not use these traditions [of ninjutsu] and also, the arts should be kept secret and only given to one person [in full].

The *Shoninki* ninja manual states:

> This Shoninki is the pure and supreme secret of the shinobi arts of this, our school. Though since the time of our old and previous master, this book and the arts written within has been inherited exclusively by none but only one person and now upon the request of my son [or apprentice] I hereby give all of this, in its entirety, to you. You should master it gracefully with due respect and never show it to anybody!
> Seiryūken Natori Hyōzaemon, 1743

The *Fushikaden* 'acting manual' translated by William Scot Wilson, states:

> This separate oral teaching concerning our art is extraordinarily important to our clan, and should be conferred to only one person every generation. It should not be given to someone without talent, even if he is your child. As the saying goes, 'a birthright is not the clan. The clan is the handing down of the arts.'
> Zeami, 1418

We do not find whole schools passed on in secret or whole schools based on oral tradition alone (with the exception of the comments of the *Ogiden* mentioned previously), but elements of the inner mechanisms are only passed on to one person per generation. Only a small percentage of a school's curriculum was secret to its members.

The *Fushikaden* manual quoted above is passed over by most students of ninjutsu. The manual itself has no connection to the ninja, it is a manual on the art of *Dengaku* acting, which became Japanese *Noh* theatre. *Dengaku* and travelling acting arts were practised by the ninja and they would use these skills to travel the country incognito and to perform in towns and villages, recording information as they went. This manual is actually an acting school of Iga, the 'centre' of *ninjutsu* and gives us a direct window into the world of the acting skills used by the men of Iga when they toured the country in disguise. Furthermore, the manual's author is thought by some scholars to be connected to both the Ueshima and Hattori clans of Iga and that there is a distant relationship to the famous Kusunoki family, all of whom are connected to ninjutsu; though no direct connection between the author and ninjutsu can be made.

Overall, *Kuden* appears in most of Japanese culture, is a massive part of ninjutsu and is also the reason for the loss of some of the finer points of the art, as all lines have died out and we no longer have a living oral tradition with a verifiable background.[110] For a western reader, the best advice is to view *Kuden* as oral transmission which may hold a secret, or it simply indicates something too complex to write down.

13

The Famous Ninja Families of Hattori and Natori

The next step is to take a brief look into the history of two of Japan's most famous ninja families. Neither should be seen as *primus inter pares,* better than other families. It is just that their their manuals survived.

The Hattori Ninja

One name that is always used next to the word ninja is Hattori; in plays, films and games, Hattori, or in particular Hattori Hanzo, is associated with the ninja. This has led to some strain in the academic and modern ninjutsu community, as some take for granted the connection, whilst others state that the Hattori family has no connection to the shinobi. However, actual investigation is seldom undertaken.

The germane document is the *Shinobi-hiden,* also commonly known as the *Ninpiden* ninja manual, written by an author who called himself Hattori Hanzo. The original manual is missing and that the oldest copy is an early eighteenth-century transcription. It must be pointed out at this stage that the *Shinobi Hiden* is considered by this research team to be a collection of four separate ninja documents penned by various authors, one of whom is probably the father of the famous Hattori Hanzo II or Devil-Hanzo. It can be argued that Hattori Hanzo II, or Devil-Hanzo as he is known, was socially too elevated to be shinobi as he was a tactical commander and that his name was attached to the *Shinobi Hiden* manual to give it credibility. However, Hattori Hanzo II was the son of a hired *Iga no mono,* Hattori Hanzo I, who was retained in Mikawa province. The social position of this retainer was in all likelihood not that high, and his father's station in Mikawa was in all probability lower than the leading member of the Iga Hattori branch from where they originally came. The Iga branch members of the Hattori family were an elite and had an hereditary heir in Iga, making the father of the famous Hattori Hanzo lower in the chain, which could be a possible reason for his employment outside of Iga. This would exclude the now famous Hattori Hanzo II from the upper echelons. It appears that Devil-Hanzo made his mark in the world through a mixture of social poistion and his actions, swiftly

The original Demon Killing Spear of Hattori Hanzo, now located in Shinjuku Japan.

taking him up the ladder in the Tokugawa forces. So those arguing against Hanzo as a shinobi are forgetting that his father was a man of Iga and that the Hattori branch from Iga was heavily involved with ninjutsu; and that by tradition he would have assumed his father's role as a retainer. The *Hattori Hanzo Shoyou Yari Onikirimaru Zu* document claims that Hattori Hanzo II was given his 'Demon Killing Spear' as a result of his achievements at Udo Castle, where he is said to have led a large group of shinobi on a night infiltration mission at the age of sixteen.

There are contradictions in this document, such as some clashes of dates. At the supposed time of the attack, Tokugawa Ieyasu was imprisoned and could not have given the spear to Hattori. Therefore, it is assumed that the raid was later than stated, making Hattori older than sixteen. However, the fact still stands that Hattori was given this spear for his achievements and that the Edo period document considers that his job was to lead shinobi in night raids. Hanzo was the person who organised Ieyasu's escape through Iga with the help of *Iga no mono* and the Hattori Family. Because of this, Hattori Hanzo II was given the command (not ownership) of 200 Iga men, who were retained by Ieyasu, the Shogun.

In short, Hattori is the son of a man hired from Iga in the Sengoku period, which is a position normally associated with the ninja, he is from one of the Iga families who were heavily associated with ninjutsu, he led ninja in war, he was the leader of a band of 200 ninja and has one of the three major ninja manuals attributed to him. It is difficult therefore to see how Hattori Hanzo is not connected to the shinobi. In all probability, Hattori Hanzo was an *Iga no mono*, born in Mikawa, who was taught by his father in ninjutsu and given the *Shinobi Hiden* manual. He then distinguished himself as a good tactician and leader, bringing him promotion to commander of Iga ninja.

徳川様はよい人もちよ服部半蔵は鬼半蔵　渡辺半蔵は鑓半蔵　渥美源五は首取
源五

Lord Tokugawa has good men. Hattori Hanzo is the Devil Hanzo, Watanabe Hanzo is the Spear Hanzo and Atsumi Gengo is called the 'Head Taker' Gengo.

The 'Hanzo' poem

The author at the grave of Hattori Hanzo II, the Shinobi leader for Tokugawa Ieyasu.

Move evidence for a ninja connection to the Hattori family comes from the *Iga Zukesashidashi Cho,* which is a directory of Iga men and lists those available for service to their 'parent' domain of Tsu under the Todo family. By the time this document was written in 1636, the province of Iga had been under the control of the Damiyo regime and the Todo family for more than 50 years. The document lists those outside of the regular army who can be called upon for service if the ruling family so wishes. In one section it lists the following four groups:

- *Horo*[111] *Gumi-shu* (warriors of the cloak)
- *Teppo-gashira gumi* (rifle – or more accurately musket – squad captains)
- *Rusui-shu* (castle defence force for when the lord is absent)
- *Shinobi no shu* (ninja squads)

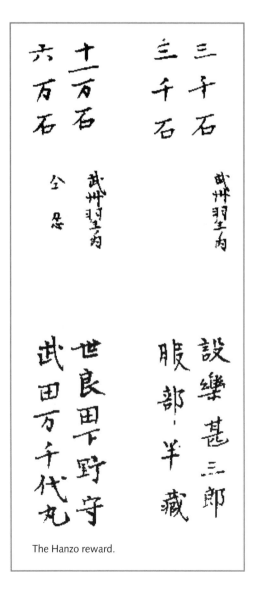

The Hanzo reward.

The document then goes on to say: 'In October of the year 1636 the lord of Todo hired 20 people as a shinobi group. Within the list of 20 the name Hattori is given three times: Hattori Shichiuemon, Hattori Mozaimon and Hattori Bunzaimon. The name Hattori Mozaimon reappears, but we do not know if it is the same man or a descendant, as in the 1680s he is listed in the *Toshukai* document alongside another Hattori ninja, Hattori Gohei.

The *Iga Ninhi no Kan* manual was written by Hattori Yasumasa in 1624 and transcribed by Nakakura Munefumi in 1672. The manual talks of the fire skills of the ninja and most of the mixes of gunpowder are the same as described in *Bansenshukai*, which is thought to be an Iga manual. The *Iga-ryu Ninpo Gokuhi No Maki,* a manual of secret ninja skills, also mentions the Hattori family.

A strong connection of the Hattori to the ninja comes from the *Gunpo Jiyoshu* manual, as all of its contents relating to the ninja are said to have come from 'Hattori Jibuemon and other warriors', which the author uses in context with *Iga no mono,* implying that this Hattori is of the Iga branch.

Another interesting reference to the Hattori family can be seen in the image opposite. This is a list of battle spoils given out after the Battle of Sekigahara. On the lower row on the right hand side we see the name Hattori Hanzo, who is given 3000 Koku for his part in the war. Whilst it does not directly mention shinobi, we do know that at this time, Hattori Hanzo was the leader of a group of approximately 200 *Iga no mono*. However, this Hattori Hanzo is actually the son of Hattori Hanzo II (Devil Hanzo). The son was disliked by the *Iga no Mono* of his group. Perhaps he was the cause of the first strike in Japan, as those *Iga no mono* under him supposedly refused to remain under his command. He must have been a huge disappointment to the famous Devil Hanzo, his father.

It can be concluded that the Hattori are not only connected to the ninja, but are also a powerful family. They were well known in their own time, leaving us with little doubt of their involvement in Sengoku period shinobi activities, affirming their position as ninja in our modern understanding. This leads to another 'ninja family', not quite as prestigious in the eyes of modern readers or as well known as the Hattori but one which has come to prominence since the publication of *True Path of the Ninja*.

The Natori Ninja

If it were not for a single word in the inscription attached to the ninja manual the *Shoninki,* the world would never have known that this manual was a record of the Natori family's shinobi tactics.

The *Record of the History of the Kishu-Tokugawa Clan* or the *Nanki Tokugawa Shi* document from the early Meiji Restoration was compiled from 1888–1901 and used original documents of the Kishu-Tokugawa clan (1602–1869). Whilst produced much later than the events themselves, it is an official document of the Tokugawa and should be considered as a highly reliable source, owing to its purpose and access to primary documentation. It states:

The Natori family gravestone. The head stone was used for the entire family clan. This is a smaller version dated 1809.

Their ancestor was a Koshu warrior, therefore they used Koshu military ways and it was named Natori-ryu. From generation to generation they were a master family of the military arts and recruited disciples; the things they did were secret, therefore the way of their school is unknown.

Now we do know the way of their school, as their secret arts have been translated into English and they have given the world an insight into Japanese espionage. It is best to start with the founding of the school. The popular theory that *Natori-ryu* was born of an Iga school is wrong.

The Founding

The military arts of the Natori family 名取 are based on the tactics derived from Koshu, the homeland of the famous tactician Takeda Shingen, who was a genius on the field of battle and who is strongly associated with the ninja. The origins of the skills themselves cannot be accounted for but the skills of *Natori-ryu* reach into the Sengoku period, something that many ninja schools cannot claim with certainty. What we do know is that the school was a *Gunpo* or military arts school and by the time of Natori Masatake, *Natori-ryu* was considered the third best ranking school inside the Kishu-Tokugawa clan, who were one of the three great houses of the Tokugawa regime. The order of status of the clan's military schools is as follows:

1	*Usami-ryu*	high tactics
2	*Hashizume-ryu*	manners and ways
3	*Natori-ryu*	secret military arts

Interestingly all three founders of each of the traditions originated from the Koshu domain, which means they were employed by the Takeda clan before the Edo period. Tokugawa Ieyasu had a great respect for the warriors of Koshu under the Takeda clan; to be a school under Takeda was a highly prestigious historical claim. It is highly likely that the Natori military arts were founded in the tradition of the Takeda clan, making the *Shoninki* a detailed historical account of Takeda ninja skills. Whilst the origins can be located in the Takeda tradition, there is also the possibility that some of the shinobi skills would have come from a Kusunoki line.

Wakayama Castle was burnt down in the Second World War and reconstructed. This is where the Natori family served the Tokugawa.

Natori Yoichinojo Masatoshi (?–1619)

Masatoshi was the grandfather of the now famous ninja author and was a military man and samurai in the Sengoku period. Records of this Natori member are scant, however it is known that he served the Takeda clan from an unknown date until 1582/3 where his position within the Takeda clan was in the *Sakite*[112] or in the vanguard, making him a front-line samurai of the Sengoku period. As his age is unknown it is difficult to determine what date he started his service, or more importantly if he served under the famous warlord Takeda Shingen himself. It is certain that this Natori served Shingen's son Takeda Katsunori and was thus involved with the conflicts with Tokugawa Ieyasu, which led to the defeat of the Takeda clan and the death of Katsunori.

With the fall of their lord and the Takeda family, the Koshu warriors were now at the mercy of the Tokugawa war engine. Luckily, with Tokugawa Ieyasu having such a high respect for Takeda and the warriors of Koshu, he travelled to the Takeda domain to personally retain sections of the Takeda force. In 1582/3 Tokugawa met with these warriors and instructed them on their future service. We do know that Tokugawa Ieyasu spoke to and directed Natori Masatoshi on his future service to the Tokugawa family,[113] which confirms he was a samurai.

Natori was instructed to serve Yoshiwara Matabei, who was one of the *Anegawa Shichi Hon Yari* or the 'Seven Spears of the Battle of Anegawa', a battle where Yoshiwara Matabei earned respect with an unknown but formidable deed. It is here that information becomes limited.

The last piece of information we have is that Natori Masatoshi retired from Tokugawa service and became a *Ronin* or samurai for hire, a job he carried out in the domain of the Sanada clan. Natori died in Sanada in 1619, having never met his grandson, the author of the *Shoninki*.

For those not intimately familiar with Japanese history, it is important to realise how significant Natori's life is when looked at from a shinobi perspective in terms of location, occupation and chronology. As we do not know his age at death or birth date, speculation will have to play a part. If Natori was 60 at the time of his final illness then that would mean he was born around 1560. If so, he grew up amidst the territorial expansions of Takeda Shingen. If born earlier, then he would have been a front line warrior at the important battles, making him a shinobi of the Takeda golden years. Even if this is not the case, he did serve Takeda's son, which was still a time of war, making him a shinobi of the Sengoku period.

There appears to be no record of why he moved from serving as a confidant of the Tokugawa clan to becoming a *Ronin*. There could be many reasons for this move from trusted samurai to wandering mercenary. Because of what we know of ninjutsu his move to *Ronin* starts to raise questions. Natori served the Tokugawa clan in the time leading up to the famous Battle of Sekigahara, a battle at which the Sanada clan was divided. Therefore it is possible that Natori was a shinobi for the Tokugawa clan and that the Tokugawa clan had a vested interest in the actions of the Sanada clan. This respected Koshu warrior could have been working indirectly for Tokugawa Ieyasu, as a shinobi during his years as a *Ronin* in Sanada lands, though we cannot know this.

Natori Yajiemo Masatomi (?–1648)

Son to the above and father to the famous Natori Masatake, Natori Yajiemo is the second grandmaster of the *Natori-ryu* and the head of the family. Whilst not much is known about his life, it is known that he was a samurai worth 250 Koku at the point he was employed by the Shogunate. Early on he served Suwa Inaba no Kami, presumably of the *Suwa* clan. His next lord was recorded simply as Kazusa Sama, but his final destination, at the level of 250 Koku, was the newly formed Kishu-Tokugawa clan, recommended to them by Matodaira Osumi No Kami Meakei Genzaimon. His position within the clan was that of *Oban*, or 'Great Guard'. This could mean either guarding the imperial homeland or, according to Dr Turnbull, being one a group of 'elite' mounted troops, who could be sent anywhere the Shogun needed them at speed. The latter is more probable. All we can tell from the listings is that 308 people were in the *Oban* and they were divided into eight groups. This Natori was in *Goban,* or group number five.

Returning to Dr Turnbull's research, a samurai of 250 Koku had some standing. According to the *Bansenshukai*, a mounted samurai, which Natori would have been at such a pay grade, would have had with him four retainers when going into battle. Natori would have ridden out with:

1 A lower ranking samurai
2 A squire for his armour
3 A squire for his spear
4 A groom

So this Natori was alive when the Kishu-Tokugawa clan was established and he served the first Kishu-Tokugawa lord, Lord Tokugawa Yorinobu, who ruled the clan between 1619 and 1667 and would have been the lord's grandmaster of secret military tactics. He died at an unknown age in 1648, which provides the latest possible date of birth for Natori Masatake, the author of the *Shoninki* ninja manual and other military texts.

Natori Sanjuro Masazumi (?–1708)

The author of the *Shoninki* and the ninja master – officially his name is Natori Sanjuro Masazumi (hereafter known as Masatake)[114] was a fourth son. This Natori was *not* the head of the family, that privilege goes to the first son by right, therefore Natori Rokudayu (his eldest brother) was given 200 Koku as the successor and the rest of the family income was shared amongst the remaining three brothers. This left Natori Masatake with a modest income of 25 Koku, making him a samurai on foot. However, Natori Masatake was the head of the family military school and appears to have been a very military-orientated man. He started his service to the first Kishu-Tokugawa lord in 1654 as a *Chukoshu* or 'page boy'. His service would have started at around the age of eleven to fifteen and he would have served either the lord or his family. We can see Natori's abilities in his acceleration through the ranks. Whilst it is believed his income did not increase, his positions were of some military importance to the Kishu-Tokugawa family. After his role as page, he became a *Goshoinban* or 'Defender of the Writing Room', which appears to have been the duty of protecting the inner confines of the castle. From here, Natori became a *Gokinjusume*, which translates as 'a close and permanent retainer'. Whilst it is unknown what this entailed, the *Monumenta Nipponica* (Volume 56) explains that this could have been a position as a medical physician, which is a possibility as the Natori family are believed to have been involved with medicine and that they had a famous remedy for sword wounds and bruises. This is, however, speculation. From here, Natori's final position was that of *Ogoban,* which, according to the eighteenth-century commentator Ogyu Sorai, is 'The Great Guard'. What is not known is which member of the Kishu-Tokugawa family Natori guarded; it is tempting to hope he guarded the main lord of the clan.

So Natori eventually became perhaps an important guard to the lord himself or the family of the Kishu-Tokugawa clan, but also the grandmaster of their secret military tactics and presumably parts of their spy network, which in the end became a part of the infamous *Oniwaba,* or secret police. Alongside this knowledge of *shinobi no jutsu*, we know that Natori was a military strategist and author of some splendid military treatises.

If this Natori was a personal servant to the main lord he would have served three Kishu-Tokugawa lords, Tokugawa Yorinobu, Tokugawa Mitsusada and Tokugawa Tsunanori. Natori retired from active service to the countryside, where he died in 1708. He probably did not serve the fourth lord, who came to power in 1705, at which point Natori will have most likely have been retired.

Natori Sanjuro Masatake's bloodline continued with Natori Hyozaemon Kuninori, the fourth grandmaster of the Natori-ryu, with a salary of 25 Koku. The next,

The death entry for Natori Sanjuro (Masazumi) who wrote the *Shoninki* manual. (Photo by Juho Yamamoto)

Natori Shirosaburo Takanobu (?–1794) was an interesting character as he was supposed to succeed as the next grandmaster but his father requested that it go to Unobe Matasaburo. It is unknown why. What is known is that this Natori started life as his father and grandfather on 25 Koku, however he appeared to gain favour with the lord and was given the spectacular retainer of 600 Koku for some unknown reason. The position of shinobi or secret military strategist may have been two low for such a highly paid samurai. The name of his son is unknown and a gap appears in Natori Masatake's linage, which then continues with Natori Hyozaemon Masanao, who was father to Natori Takenosuke Masakuni (?–1863) who inherited 500 Koku and adopted (Natori) Kamegusu Masakane.

One thing that this family story does prove beyond doubt is that the Natori family were samurai worth 250–500 Koku; these were no peasant ninja.

The Shinobi Writings of the Natori Clan

The *Shoninki*, which translates as 'True Ninja Account', was written in 1681 and is unsigned and does not reveal anything about the school to which it belongs, it simply states 'Our School or Touryu'. The introduction written by the samurai Katsuda states

The death tablet for Natori Hyozaemon (Fujiwara Kuninori) who wrote the inscription at the back of the *Shoninki* manual.

the author is Toissuishi[115] Masatake and records his request for a preface. However, the surname given here is not a family one and was given, as sometimes was the case in old Japan, as a salute to the nature of the author, making it more of a title than a name. The suffix of 子 which is *Shi* here means 'educated one' and denotes accomplishment. This leaves only the first name, Masatake. The manual was passed down in the clan and came to the samurai Natori Hyozaemon, who in his inscription passes a copy to a man named Watanabe in 1743.

Upon investigation, the listings for the Kishu–Tokugawa clan only have one Natori who fits the description of the author and that is Natori Sanjoro Masazumi or Natori Masazumi for short. The ideogram for *Masa* in both names is the same, so the only person to fit the bill as author of the Natori secret document was the grandmaster at that time, Natori Sanjoro Masazumi.

A version of the *Shoninki* document is found in the private collection of Dr Nakashima Atsumi, a stolen version. The inscription of 1716 in his edition reads:

> The above [Shoninki] is what I copied and stole in stealth from a secret writing of the New-Kusunoki school of military warfare, therefore it is not my own work, however I will now pass it down for generations to sons and grandsons to use and practise with.

> Inaba Tango no Kami[116] Michihisa, 67 years old. The tenth day of the sixth lunar month, the month of no water in the year 1716

He believes that the Natori–ryu is a new version of *Kusonoki-ryu*, the association with Kusunoki is complex but the name 'shin-kusunoki' was given to the school by the lord at that time. What is not known is how it was transcribed in secret. Was this man a student of the *Natori-ryu* or was he in the castle for an extended period? Natori Masatake was dead at this point and it was his son who allowed the manuscript to be stolen in such a manner.

The Natori-Ryu Grandmasters

When the history of the Kishu–Tokugawa clan was recorded, as described at the start of this chapter, the compilers were working in the early stages of the Meiji Restoration and had the opportunity to talk with and record the words of the last grandmaster of the *Natori-ryu*. That man was Yabutani Yoichiro, the apparent tenth grandmaster who was the stepson of Yabutani Yoichi, (the eighth grandmaster) and over 80 years old at the time of the interview. This shows that the *Natori-ryu* continued as a ninja school and its members were employed as such up until the end of the Edo period. What is highly interesting is that he, along with the grandmasters of the other two tactics schools of the clan, were in attendance at the second *Choshu* expedition, a battle in which the Shogunate forces, including the *Natori-ryu,* were defeated by a technically superior and modern Japanese army. Upon seeing this defeat, the grandmaster Yabutani Yoichiro reported to the compilers that he considered the old military ways to be outdated and of little use. He said that no one has since inherited the arts, effectively killing the *Natori-ryu* after more than 250 years of existence. This interesting episode postdates the now famous episode of a ninja who boarded Commodore Perry's ship by over a decade, usually seen as the last ninja action. Whilst we do not know exactly what the *Natori-ryu's* position was at the *Choshu* expedition, they were a shinobi school and the shinobi role in the Shogunate's army is clear.

Problems with the Grandmaster List

The first problem is that of of Natori Sanjiro Masazumi being employed by the Tokugawa clan when he was just six years old after his father had died. There must be a missing grandmaster between the author of the *Shoninki* and his father. Or was the position held by Natori's older brother until Masazumi came of age? Secondly, the record of the Kishu-Tokugawa states that the seventh grandmaster was the uncle of the fourth grandmaster, which would make him the brother of Natori Sanjuro Masazumi and over 100 years old, which leads to the probability that he was in fact the nephew and that it was a mistake in the recording. The current list of *Natori-ryu* grandmasters[117] is not is not perfect but it is the best we have to date:

The author with Yamamoto Juho, the priest of Eiunji Temple with the local records of deaths that include Natori Masazumi's death certificate.

1 Natori Yoichinojo Masatoshi
2 Natori Yajiemo Masatomi
3 Natori Sanjuro Masazumi (also Masatake)
4 Natori Hyozaemon Kuninori
5 Natori (Unobe) Matasaburo (adopted and given 20 Koku)
6 Ohata Kihachiro (passed it back to the Natori family)
7 Natori Nanjuro
8 Yabutani Yoichi
9 Tomiyama Umon
10 Yabutani Yoichiro

After the feudal domains were abolished, all the secret writings about the traditions of the *Natori-ryu* were dedicated to a shrine in Kii province and no one else inherited the school, bringing a Takeda (or *Shin-Kusunoki*) shinobi school, which passed through Tokugawa hands, to an end.

One final piece of information about the lineage helps in understanding the process of inheritance within ninja schools. The inscription in the *Shoninki* states that the fourth grandmaster passed the *Shoninki* document on to Watanabe Rokurozaemon, which some have taken to mean[118] that the school itself was passed on to the above man. However, on inspection and with the support of the above list, it is thought that Watanabe was simply given the secrets of the art and a transcription of the *Shoninki* itself.

The *Natori-ryu* served the Takeda and then the Kishu–Tokugawa clan for hundreds of years until its demise at the Meiji Restoration. It was a military art that was based on the unorthodox and the secret; no one knows how much of the school was dedicated to the ninja arts and how much to other forms of warfare.

14

The Prowess of the Men of Iga and Koka

J ust how renowned the men of Iga and Koka were in military Japan is shown in the following examples.

The *Sokokushi* document declares: 'I hear that those called *Iga no Mono* are in great demand by other clans.' The *Mikawa Gofudoki* document states:

The first time Tokugawa Ieyasu used people from Koka he had them attack a castle to put those inside into confusion and to take advantage of any gaps. As a result 70 people died, he was much impressed and chose to use them thereafter.

The Battle of Fushimi Castle in 1600 was the first action in a series of events that led to the greatest 'internal' conflict in Japanese history, the Battle of Sekigahara. Tokugawa Ieyasu had 60 Koka men stationed in the castle for its defence, a number which increased. The overall number of defenders in the castle was 1800 whilst the besieging army was upwards of 40,000. The castle's defence was part of the stategy leading up to the Battle of Sekigahara. All 1800 men were expected to die and apparently they knew it. However, the castle was not succumbing to the onslaught of the western forces and its defence held out. To counter this, the besieging forces sent some *Yabumi* or secret letters in arrows to the defending men of Koka. It said that the men of Koka should set fire to their own castle so that it would fall; if they did not comply then the besiegers would execute and crucify their wives and children. To support this they had some of their families brought from Koka and made to enact a mock crucifixion. An unknown amount of *Koka no mono* gave in and set fire to the castle, however other *Koka no mono* stayed true. The castle fell and many were slain including the Koka defenders. Tokugawa Ieyasu was so impressed by the defence put up by some of the loyal Koka people that he then hired 10 *Yoriki* samurai and 100 *Doushin,* or displaced samurai, making 110 *Koka no mono* under Tokugawa employment. These were known as the *Koka Gumi* and were led by a man named Doami, the brother of a warrior who had died in the castle. These were the same men who took it in turns with the *Iga no mono* to guard the main castle in Edo, now the imperial palace where the One Hundred Guard Hut can still be seen to this day.

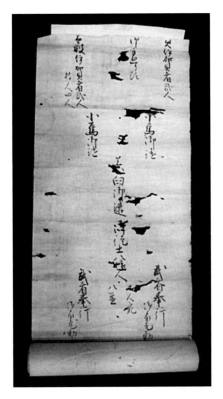

Iga no Mono parade guards. (Courtesy of Dr Nakashima Atsumi)

Crossroads. A point of danger for a lord on the move, which must be scouted.

The prestige of the *Iga no mono* can also be identified in documentation which is not directly concerned with them. The image shown is of a warlord's (*Daimiyo*) parade, showing the order of his guards. The two men at the front are '*Iga no mono*' and are positioned at the head. There is no explanation for their position but there is a cogent theory. The *Taiheiki* war chronicle states that men are sent ahead to wait at crossroads to guard the passing of a lord. Some gunnery and fire skills manuals explain the dangers of passing through crossroads, as can be seen in the Edo period manual shown.

Perhaps these *Iga no Mono* were sent ahead of the line of march to check crossroads for explosives and ambushes, as would befit their skills. They were advanced troops who helped clear the way of any threats, a suitable task considering that their history is so deeply rooted in scouting.

The following example comes from the *Keicho Kenmonshu*[119] document from before 1650, which records government matters. The account pertains to the hiring of Iga men after Tokugawa Ieyasu's now famous flight across Iga itself when Lord Nobunaga was assassinated, which left Ieyasu in peril. The account shows how, during Lord Nobunaga's war, the social structure of Iga was falling apart:

Lo, when Lord Nobunaga was killed and Lord Ieyasu had to pass through Iga, there was a hostage offered to Lord Ieyasu [to guarantee his safety] and he was thus guarded through to where he wanted to go, which allowed Lord Ieyasu to get back home and afterwards the country came to peace. [For this] 200 people where hired and later came under Hanzo III and these [Iga] men were all Hyakso-samurai or peasant samurai. This was also the rank of

Hanzo's grandfather[120] but he had moved out of Iga and left his hometown at an earlier point and had come to the Mikawa clan, where he performed several great deeds and thus came up through the ranks [of the samurai]. But others [from Iga] stayed in their homeland, and subsequently the Iga people, those of samurai class, were devastated by Lord Nobunaga and were reduced in status down to peasants.

After Ieyasu's crossing of Iga [the samurai] Miyata Gonemon,[121] Yoneji Hansuke and others were hired and also other men of Iga wanted to serve Lord Ieyasu and thus gained employment [as described above]. However, the crossing of Iga by Ieyasu soon faded from his mind, so he made [the Iga] men on foot *Doushin* [which is a rank slightly lower than samurai], but [this did not sit well with them] because some of them were of good samurai stock back in their hometown. This was a problem because Iwami-dono [Hanzo III] was from a lower class Hattori line, a line lower than their own ancestors and therefore Hanzo's men rebelled, they said that Hanzo III was of a lower class, the Hattori family had come to Mikawa earlier and were given large fief and it was only in this manner that he took control of the Iga people under him, who were [once samurai] but were treated now as low people [*genin*].

This a great insight in to workings of the Iga men employed under Ieyasu and the Tokugawa clan and a good example of the problematic nature of the class upheaval in this period, especially in Iga. The author is writing in a post-Sengoku period and as a third party. He uses the word *Hyakusho-samurai*, which is a form of peasant-samurai, on the border between the samurai class and those who are not, but still samurai. This is not an official term and holds derogatory connotations, showing that the Iga people did not perceive themselves in this way. Further on the text describes the higher samurai of Iga as *Kuni-samurai,* or provincial samurai. It reaffirms the fact that *Iga no mono* or *Iga shinobi* were predominantly lower level samurai who lost their status in the war with Oda Nobunaga in the late sixteenth century.

15

the Female Ninja

O ne word has become mainstream in the ninja world and has been taken up by many female martial artists around the globe; the word is *Kunoichi* or 'female ninja'. To some extent, it has become adopted by females who wish to identify themselves as followers of the path of ninjutsu and wish to connect with a strong female character from history. This sentiment is a positive one and meaningful, however, the story of the female ninja or *Kunoichi* is often misunderstood.

The image of the *Kunoichi* female ninja agent was mainly created in the mid-twentieth century. The researcher Yumio Nawa did much to create this *Kunoichi* female ninja, a seductive counterpart to the male infiltration agent.

The primary concern when dealing with the *Kunoichi* is the fact that only a single ninja manual (to date) uses this term, the *Bansenshukai*. This would suggest that the title originated with the author Fujibayashi in an attempt to codify the differences between male and female agents. The Chinese ideogram for woman is 女 and is made up of three parts when broken down – く 'Ku' ノ 'No' and 一 'Ichi' which make the symbol for woman 女. Many people consider the ideogram 女 to read as '*Kunoichi*', however this is not the case, as when the three components are put together in this manner it cannot be read this way and simply means 'woman' or 'female'. The *Bansenshukai* manual never uses the single ideogram 女 at any point in its description of the female ninja, nor does it use the modern breakdown as displayed above. The actual writing in the manual is 久ノ一, here Fujibayashi uses the older version of 久 instead of く. What does this

A female model posing for one of Yumio Nawa's books, portraying the romanticised *Kunoichi* figure.

mean? It means that from a native speaker's point of view he never actually says female; but it is obvious from the use of the phonetic spelling of *Kunoichi* that it is a reference to the ideogram for woman and it can be considered that the word *Kunoichi* is actually a codeword for undercover female agent. Interestingly, a second 'codeword' appears but this time for male ninja, this is *Tajikara,* this is made up of 田 'Ta' and 力 making 'Chikara' which when put together form the ideogram for man – 男. This is Fujibayashi's way of explaining the secret use of both male and female operatives in the context of ninjutsu.

Kunoichi is both a skill and a name. *Kunochi no jutsu,* 'the art of the female agent', consists of placing a *Kunoichi* female agent into an enemy stronghold to work from the inside, normally in tandem with a male shinobi, who will infiltrate at a later date. This was not a glamorous position and would involve sexual exploitation, slavery and possibly death for the female, depending on circumstance. Remembering that Fujibayashi is the author that brought the concept of the *Kunoichi* ninja to the world, it is relevant that he himself denigrates the female role and sees the *Kunoichi* simply as a tool. The following quote is the *Kunoichi's* first appearance in the *Bansenshukai* and in history:

> *Kunoichi no Jutsu* is to send a shinobi who is represented by one ideogram which consists of three letters combined.[122] When it seems difficult for Tajikara or male ninja to infiltrate, use this art. In general, Kunoichi have a twisted and inferior mind, shallow intelligence and poor speech, so for example [Text deleted with the number 'two' left exposed][123] – you should not use those you cannot follow up.[124] If you have someone you have checked out, make her take a strict oath, educate her thoroughly and specifically about the signals or promises so that you can send her deep into the enemy by taking the appropriate measures. If you make her a servant accompanying someone who is getting embedded with the enemy or anybody like that, [her infiltration] will be successful.

Fujibayashi's contempt is unsurprising at a time when education of women was rare.

Fujibayashi discusses the tendency for those in power to indulge in sexual adventures, so setting a *Kunoichi* in place to be the target's *inamorata* is a way of getting an operative on the inside.

Whilst ambiguous, the *Bansenshukai* talks about the horrible plan of including a mock wife and mock child into one's plans. Often, it was the case that the family of a retainer would be held by the lord as hostages to ensure loyalty, especially from ninja! Many historical references pertaining to the ninja, written by others and the ninja themselves, talk of the need to force a shinobi to leave guarantees of his loyalty. Therefore, Fujibayashi states that a ninja in this situation should prepare a fake wife and child to establish as hostages whilst he is working with the enemy lord in question. Once the rival lord has his trust and believes he has guaranteed the ninja's loyalty, the shinobi will carry out his true mission and help bring down that lord, at which point the shinobi obviously returns to his real master. What happens to the fake wife and child? The defeated lord is not going to show mercy to the fake family who have obviously lied about their connection to the ninja. The woman and child are put to death; before this, as they have been fed with false information by the original lord who sent them, when they break down and confess they unconsciously work as doomed agents, feeding the enemy with misinformation.

Such exploitation of women and children shows the ruthlessness of the times and the inaccuracy of the modern interpretation of the *Kunoichi* as some form of heroine. Were any of the female agents and their children given escape routes? Who are these people and where did they come from? It is doubtful that any family of status would give up their own children for such a ruse, so did they take the fake family from the peasant class or were they taken and trained from youth, or simply slaves? Questions such as these will be hard for any historian to answer due to a lack of records.

In stark contrast, there is a single case of a female ninja agent with the skills of her male counterpart. The *Iga-ryu Kako Ryu Shinobi Hiden* manual talks of the extraordinary case of a female taking over a ninja school or at least holding the knowledge of the school until she could pass it on to a male. In the Matsushiro Domain of Shinshu province at some point in the Edo period, a woman, described as a saint named Umemura Sawano, was given the secrets of the school as she had exceptional skill and no suitable male could be found. She latter passed this skill onto Matsumoto Jirozaemon, who in turn passed it on to Sasaki Yasuke, both of whom were of course male. This shows that whilst it is not impossible to find a female trained in the ninja ways, it was a man's world and it was very rare.

16

The Gateless Gate

A n overlooked aspect of ninjutsu and one of its fundamentals is the art of spying.
Within this art, the ninja attempted to understand the human mind and the
truth behind illusory social structure. Ethics and the law change through time
and across borders. Hitting a child with a cane in 1950s England was a daily
occurrence, whilst now such an act would carry a prison sentence, a change put
into effect within one generation. There are two worlds that exist at the same time, the
unchanging physical world we live in, which includes the generally suppressed emotions
of the people who outwardly do what is considered correct – and the world created by
our group morality and laws.

The ninja were well aware of this duality and understood how to manipulate it, how to
identify and interact with people's inner desires as opposed to their externally constructed
codes of behaviour. The greatest example of this is the *Natori-ryu* concept and skill of
Mumon no Ikkan or the 'Gateless Gate'.

The *Mumon no Ikkan* is an annotated thirteenth-century Zen document[125] that
is a collection of Zen *Koans* or 'riddles' designed to bring an individual closer to
enlightenment. It is a staple text in the Zen Buddhism canon. The term 'Gateless Gate' is
perhaps not as correct as the translation 'a checkpoint without a barrier'.

From a (simplified) Zen angle, the 'Gateless Gate' is an imaginary barrier inside your
mind, a grand checkpoint with truth and enlightenment on the far side and normal
constructed human existence on the side the average person stands. The checkpoint itself
has no barrier and it is possible to walk through it at any time, however to pass through
it, a person has to understand the difference between 'truth' and 'intelligence'. Once a
person is enlightened and they can see through the illusions of self-identity and the
network of the human ethical societal web, the gate, and the concept of the gate, will
dissolve and the person will stand in the realm of truth, free of the burden of the ego. The
enlightened person does not allow the ebb and flow of the human condition to control
his or her thoughts, actions or metal state.

The Gateless Gate document is a series of ancient riddles that help direct a student
of Zen to this position, breaking through the illusions and showing the student the
truth behind why humans do what they do, a concept that the ninja Natori Masatake
appropriated with the aim of aiding the ninja in his work. Natori places a great deal of

trust in the idea[126] of *The Gateless Gate* but with a slight twist on its use. He names the skill of entering a man's mind after it – *Mumon no Ikkan Shinchi no Ho*.

According to Buddhist thought, humans are made up of seven emotions in different states of balance and a human's true emotion is hidden by 'social masking'. Everything that is said by someone is generally a projection of the image they wish the world to see of them, which does not always correspond to their 'true' self. An apparently noble and courageous person may be so because they are in fact vain, whereas a quiet and polite person may be repressing anger and hate and the quietness masks the rage inside. In this way a ninja, according to *Natori-ryu* must identify the 'construct' and then identify the 'truth' of a person's personality. It would be useless for a ninja to give praise and to highlight the deeds of someone who had the *true* nature of humility, and at the same time it would be wrong for a ninja to ignore a quiet person when deep down inside they wanted respect and recognition. It is in this way that a ninja must break through the *Gateless Gate*, not for self improvement, (whilst that may also be a motivation) but to gain an understanding of the patterns that appear in human behaviour and to manipulate them to gain an advantage. The *Shinobi Hiden*, considered a Sengoku period manual,[127] gives a more direct approach. The author advises causing panic and distress, such as burning down a house, or letting a group of horses escape or even calling out an intruder alarm whilst a ninja is still hidden in a castle. The idea is that in true emergencies, the veil of the 'constructed' world falls away, even if for a short time and that a human will revert back to their 'true' state until they can regain composure and thus continue to project what they wish people to see. During the hiatus, a ninja can 'enter' into their minds and discover the true human behind the veil.

All in all, a ninja was predominantly a spy and his job was to creep into human minds as much as it was to creep into castles, and the idea of the two worlds is fundamental to understanding the art of manipulation in a world of espionage, leaving a ninja standing at the Gateless Gate, one foot in the 'constructed' world and one foot in the realm of 'truth'.

17

The Fringes of Ninjutsu

There are certain elements of study that the Research Team has unearthed that do not fit with ease into any of the previous categories, yet they are important. Therefore, they have been included here as a kind of concordance of ninjutsu.

The Christian Rebellion

Ninja were employed in the 1637 Shimabara Christian rebellion at Hara castle, one of the last major military campaigns before prolonged peace. The rebels – many of them Catholic Christian peasants, some leaderless samurai – held out against the vastly superior numbers of Shogunate forces (some 125,000) for months, before running out of food and gunpowder. After the castle fell, an estimated 35,000 rebels and sympathisers were beheaded and the ban on Christianity already in place was strictly enforced.

Poison

Killing people by this means is nothing new to the world of espionage and it is without doubt that the shinobi would have utilised poison. However, poison itself is not mentioned as often as one might expect in the ninja manuals, a reminder that ninja are not, by definition, assassins. Poisons were readily available in medieval Japan and some documents in private collections in Koka talk about their use. Interestingly, some poisons were distributed as powder on the air, showing they had no particular target but rather the death or incapacitation of troops.

The scroll pictured overleaf is dated the first day of the ninth lunar month in the year 1686 and is signed by Tango Izu. It has no title. It is not aimed at the ninja, nor does it mention shinobi. The document is an outline for the regulation of poisons and fake or bogus medicines and is believed to be an attempt at controlling poison and its distribution. If there was a need for a form of regulation of dangerous substances, then poison was widely available and not a hidden weapon of the ninja. A shinobi would use strychnine as a digested poison and various poison gases based on arsenic, white lead and mercury. It is known that some shinobi would have had access to and been proficient at snake handling so they would have had the ability to utilise snake venom, if they so desired.

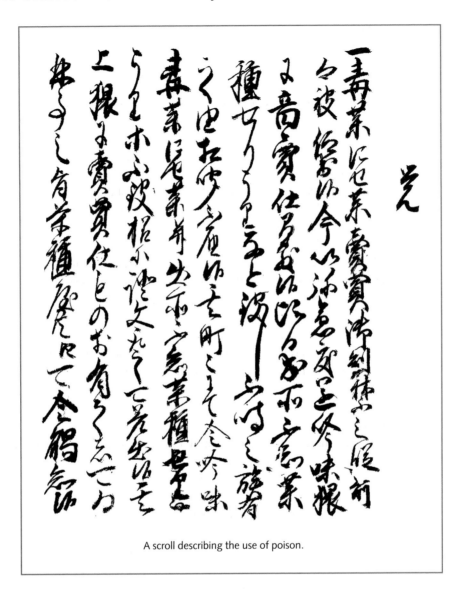

A scroll describing the use of poison.

The *Ninpo Gyokan* manual, now in a private collection, talks of *Emyousan* or 'well poisoning', using a poison based on crushed insects and the puffer-fish. 'This is a poison to kill a number of people by stealthily putting poison in a well.'

Manuals mention poison muskets, where shots are fired into a castle and a crowd of troops, killing 'hundreds'. Perhaps this was a form of shaft with a poison package fired from a musket. Lastly, an ointment to stop poison killing a person – presumably an airborne irritant – is red monoxide and asiatic ginseng mixed with oil and applied to the skin.

The Hidden Pistol

A selection of scrolls talk of a pistol triggered from and hidden within the sleeve of a ninja's jacket. This is done whilst they are using the skill of *Yo-nin* or open disguise, as they would not need to hide a weapon if the ninja themselves were hiding. Further manuals also allude to this weapon with tantalising clues, like 'the inside of the sleeve weapon' which can only be presumed to be the same weapon or a variant, such as a form of hand-held flame thrower, hidden in the sleeve of the kimono.

Where are all the Shuriken?

In popular imagery, a ninja leaps out from the darkness, blades flashing in the moonlight as darts of light leave his hands, throwing the legendary *Shuriken* or 'Ninja Throwing Stars'. *Shuriken* are not ninja weapons, in fact they are used by the samurai and are weapons that belong to many schools of the warrior arts that exist today in Japan. It may surprise many that the *Shuriken* fail to appear in any of the main ninja manuals, the *Bansenshukai*, the *Shinobi Hiden*, the *Gunpo Jiyoshu* and the *Shoninki*. The *Bansenshukai* is a manual epic in scale and content, and lists even the smallest of points, and most likely encompasses more knowledge that the average ninja had, as its purpose was to bring the fragments of ninjutsu together. Yet the *shuriken* throwing star is not described. The only mention of *shuriken* in any of the manuals is with reference to a throwing torch with a nail attached to the end, so that it will either stick in the ground or into a building: 'Throw like a *shuriken*.'

What is a Ninja School?

The Term '*Ryu*' is often used in the modern martial arts world and a host of modern clubs have adopted the suffix of '*Ryu*', or school, to their name. We often hear of a 'ninja school' or *ninja-ryu*. Historically, was there any such thing? *Ryu* or 流 is often translated as 'school', however, it also has connotations of 'line' or 'line of transmission', the stream of information from one generation to another. The term and the concept of 'school' changed over time.

There is not a single 'pure' ninja-school that can be traced to the Sengoku period, as we do not find mention of a *ninja-ryu*. Ninja-schools can be defined in two ways. The first is a military school that teaches the arts of war and includes ninjutsu in its curriculum. So it is not wholly a 'ninja' school, it is a *Gunpo* or military arts school. The second version would be a school that claimed solely to teach ninjutsu as a subject. Remembering that many ninja scrolls are still to be revealed, there is currently only a very select number of references to a 'ninja school' where *only* the arts of ninjutsu are taught. The *Shoninki* states in its opening chapters that other 'experts in robbery' have passed on their thieving skills as '*Ryugi*', or schools of the shinobi arts, but that they are only common thieves. The *Bansenshukai* claims that 48 ninja schools were created between Iga and Koka along with the teaching of the eleven greatest ninja infiltrators. Fujibayashi, Natori and Hattori Hanzo never define their own school as ninja or refer to it in any other way than 'our school' or '*Tou-ryu*'. It appears that most if not all schools focussing primarily on ninjutsu were named after the family that taught them. The official records for the Kishu-

Tokugawa family state the family name '*Natori-ryu*', the *Bansenshukai* states that some of its tools are from other families and names the school using a family name.

Enter *Iga-ryu* and *Koka-ryu*. These names appear to represent ninja schools in the Edo period. However, the ninjutsu writings of Iga and Koka, such as the *Shinobi Hiden* and the *Bansenshukai,* never refer to such a unified school or even the concept of a defined ninja art. Rather than talk of an *Iga-ryu*, Fujibayashi states that he has collected his information from various schools, hence the translation of *Bansenshukai* – 'A Myriad of Rivers Collecting into An Ocean'. So the concept of an Iga or Koka school is most likely a later attempt to utilise the fame of the Iga and Koka warriors. Some of the documents that claim *Iga* and *Koka-Ryu* are not connected to the ninjutsu of Iga or Koka, and some of them do not even deal with ninjutsu as a subject.

Back in the Sengoku period, when clans were vying for power, the concept of '*Ryu*' was more fluid and was connected to the family teaching the arts, with less distinction between the subjects taught. This means that families of Iga and Koka had their own style of ninjutsu, most likely very similar to all the other families, yet with a focus on practical ability and no interest in what is and is not a 'ninja-school'. With the coming of peace, boundaries appear to have been set and the fluid transmissions of practical ninja skills start to find structure and dogma under terms such as *Iga-ryu* and *Koka-ryu*, amongst others.

What Style of Martial Arts Did the Ninja Perform?

With the rise of the ninja boom in the latter part of the twentieth century, the idea arose that there was a specific form of 'ninja hand-to-hand combat', which was taught only to ninja, in secret. This new line of '*ninjutsu*' or '*ninpo taijutsu*'[128] has no backing historically or logically and is considered a modern invention.[129]

The concept of a martial art solely used by the ninja is illogical, as it would need a unified ninja training system and there was none. It would require the ninja to be outside of samurai culture and not subject to their own family arts. Also, it would have to contain elements that are not a part of recognisable 'samurai arts'; but we cannot even define 'samurai arts' in order to differentiate – the reality of martial arts combat in the Sengoku period is not fully understood. Only a handful of schools from the Sengoku period exist and are now very formalised, clearly the product of the accretion of hundreds of years of dogma and lack of application in warfare. Many believe that the traditional martial arts taught in Japan today are the warring arts of the samurai, but this is not true; most traditional martial arts were born in the Edo period and move away from applicable military skills, arts such as Kendo.[130]

Each clan would teach their own warriors their own family traditions, all the arts needed for war, such as horsemanship, tactics, the use of the sword and spear etc, but also, to a select few, the arts of ninjutsu. Ninjutsu is not therefore a distinct martial arts system.

The practice of these 'ninja martial arts' today may very well be highly skilled but it does falsify and distort the history of Japan as year by year, 'high ranking' members of these new schools find their way on to the bookshelves or into documentaries or films, as advisers or hosts. Slowly, this misleads historians, including authors with no agenda. The well known academic Turnbull has been influenced by this misinformation in his popular works, and the contamination is starting to reach further. Dr Waterhouse's article 'Notes on Kuji', which is found in Kornicki and McMullen's book *Religion in Japan* shows such a tendency and was published by Cambridge University Press in 1996. Eventually, the history of the ninja and connected areas of Japanese history may be beyond recall.

This leaves us with the question, what martial arts did the ninja actually use? First, the question is flawed, as it would require that the ninja was a single entity, uniform across Japan, which we know is not true, as whilst ninjutsu does have a recognised curriculum there are multiple variations. Second, the tasks of the ninja do not require him to fight. Ninja manuals often warn ninja *not* to fight. The *Gunpo Jiyoshu* states that a ninja should never enter a fight but should run away; the *Bansenshukai* says if a spear fight is joined, a ninja must get out of the way. A ninja must return with his information undetected – a ninja may kill some of the enemy in a fight, but his information could kill many more.

The *Bansenshukai* does state that as ninja are used as criminal catchers[131] and pursue wanted samurai and targets, they should learn the art of *Kenjutsu* or swordsmanship, or *Iai,* which is the art of quick response (normally with a sword). There is no mention of a secret 'ninja martial art'. A ninja's use of a martial art would depend on his upbringing and social situation. If he was of a samurai house, he would learn the martial arts of that house or that family and from those around him, alongside his ninjutsu. An active shinobi in the Sengoku period was most likely a great fighter and a brave character, as his job would take him to the heart of the enemy.

The Okimori version of the *Shinobi Hiden* has a section inserted after the 1730s, nearly 200 years after the document was first written, and this text appears to be an inserted statement by a ninja. He writes in an extremely 'sloppy' cursive writing and uses the idiom 一騎と一騎, which means 'mounted warrior to mounted warrior', which later came to mean fighting. The text is nearly illegible. However, in the Nagata version, in 1843, over 100 years after this paragraph was inserted, the transcriber has the statement as 'shinobi excel in fighting.'

There are ninja manuals that explain what a shinobi should do in a combat situation. They are specific to circumstances. For example, when chasing down a thief at night, run on his left side and behind the scabbard of his sword, as he has to draw and turn at a difficult angle, or when entering a dark house, go through a door in a certain manner, or have a servant use a torch to illuminate the enemy whilst you use the shadows to fight from. Similar advice appears in samurai literature. These are tricks or ways to gain an advantage, they have no *Kata* specific to the ninja, they do not teach strikes or hits.

In truth, the shinobi were probably ruthless killers and mean fighters, but not with some secret 'ninja martial art'. The modern art with its hand springs and *shuriken* is simply not linked to the ninja, a shinobi would use the martial arts of his family and any war tricks he had picked up as a frontline wartime soldier.[132]

Ninjutsu is dramatic enough without fabrication. These were warriors of a blood-thirsty age, trained to kill with weapons, trained to scout, clutching hand grenades and rockets and setting landmines and traps, writing secret codes and launching fire arrows, climbing rock faces in the dark and walking amongst the enemy in the day. They are the ninja, they are samurai, and their history is remarkable.

A Drop in Status for the Ninja

When trying to understand where the idea of a 'peasant ninja' originates, we have to look at the social changes in Japan. The idea of samurai as a class has been in existence for over 1000 years, yet it was relatively late on that it became a fully separated and unobtainable position. Families were ruled by the warrior elite, as they were in Europe, and the samurai was at the top of that chain; active service alone could create a samurai from a lower class. The term samurai is vague. He could be land owning or in service or retained by a lord for a short period of time, or be a mercenary. The later in Japanese history you go, the more concrete the status of samurai becomes, with a halt to social mobility as the Edo period takes a hold.

In the early Edo period, which is looking back on the Sengoku period, we see the ninja described as retained warriors and as samurai, a status that does continue into the Edo period. However, the defeat of Iga was a massive turning point. Before the defeat of Iga, the warriors of Iga were known as samurai and were hired as such. The heads of the families in Iga were powers unto themselves with no overlord to answer to, their 'kingdoms' uniting at times to fight off invasion. The warriors of Iga were samurai and the famed shinobi who came from there were hired out, retained and employed as samurai. Issues of class start to appear when the families of Iga were displaced from this powerbase in the 1580s. This defeat placed them lower on the social ladder and many of the Iga families lost samurai status. In one generation, we see the highly trained samurai, hired out across Japan, fall in class. The wars end and their skills are no longer at a premium. At the same time there is a halt to any movement between the four major social classes, preventing any promotion to samurai. This means that a 25-year-old Iga warrior of samurai status, trained in ninjutsu in the year 1575, would by the age of 50 be an unwanted but skilled semi-peasant in a time of growing peace.

The governor Todo Takatora who governed Iga after its fall ordered a return of all *Iga no mono* from across Japan and introduced the social status of *Musokunin*, a move designed to pacify the now angry men of Iga. A *Musokunin* was neither peasant nor samurai, he had a foot in each camp. This gave the men of Iga some status back, and raised them above the peasants they once controlled, yet kept them under the new ruling samurai elite.

All the way through the Edo period, we see the use of ninja to perform duties such as capturing criminals and basic policing and spying. They were also given the label *Doushin,* which which meant they were below samurai but above peasants.

So the ninja's skills ar no longer required, their ancestral families are displaced and they are engaged in mundane tasks. Combining these truths with the myth of the Iga peasant families and comic book stories of the ninja versus the 'evil samurai', the idea of the ninja 'underdog' took root and has left us with an incorrect version of their history.

Ninjutsu in the Second World War

Circulating around the ninjutsu community is the idea that ninjutsu was used by the Japanese government in the Second World War and more specifically that it was taught at the Japanese espionage and special agent training facility known as the Nakano School of War. This school taught members in guerrilla warfare and clandestine missions. The late

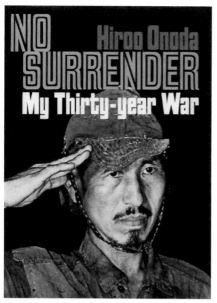

The cover to the English version of Onoda's book.

ninja researcher, Mr Fujita Seiko, is rumoured to have taught the art of ninjutsu at the school.

As would be expected, the Japanese are not fond of revealing their clandestine operations of World War II to the public and most veterans have now passed away. However, one pupil of the school, a highly controversial and popular figure, is the army officer Onoda Hiroo. Mr Onoda is the agent who conducted clandestine warfare in the Philippine Islands for over 30 years, continuing the war and refusing to believe that it had in fact come to an end, choosing instead to believe that this information was propaganda. In 1974, his wartime commanding officer came to order his surrender and return to Japan.

To try to pin down the story of ninjutsu at the Nakano school, I contacted Mr Onoda to ask him directly if ninjutsu was ever taught at the

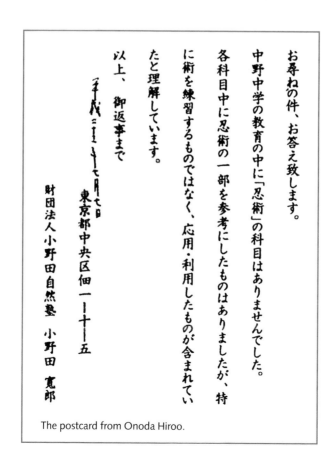

The postcard from Onoda Hiroo.

school. I received a brief reply with an answer that did not in fact confirm or deny the use of ninjutsu:

> Dear Antony Cummins
> I am writing to you to answer your questions. In the curriculum of Nakano school, there was no subject of 'ninjutsu'. Though in some subjects, there were elements which contained [or referenced] parts of ninjutsu, it was not exactly the study of individual skills but simply had the applications [of ninjutsu]. That is my understanding.
>
> Regards
>
> Onoda Nature School Foundation
> Onoda Hiroo

Mr Onoda states that whilst he was there, no direct teachings of ninjutsu were undertaken, yet he implies that sections of what they did learn could in fact be considered to reflect the ninja arts, leaving room for Fujita's claims to refer to the period after Onada's departure from the school and entry into the jungle.

Stephen C. Mercado's well researched book, *The Shadow Warriors Of Nakano* has no mention of either ninjutsu nor Fujita Sekio and in fact mentions the ninja just once in the opening, stating that these figures were the spies of a bygone era. He does not connect them to the Nakano School. The claims of Fujita's connection to the school and the teaching of ninjutsu are dubious. It appears that whilst sections of the curriculum had echoes of ninjutsu, it was not a skill taught to the students there.

The Double Shot Musket and the Attempted Shooting of Oda Nobunaga

As stated earlier, there are some records which specifically mention ninja assassinations; the attempt on the life of warlord Oda Nobunaga was one of them. However, what makes this especially amazing is the fact that the assassination attempt appears to use a secret ninja skill which is found in the *Bansenshukai* manual, the Double Shot Musket.

Sasaki Sakyo-dayu Jotei instructed Sugitani Zenjubou to kill Lord Nobunaga whilst he was travelling near Mount Chigusa. According to the records, the shooter was at a distance of twelve or thirteen Japanese Ken and shot 'two bullets'. The drama was recorded in the document Shincho Koki by an attendant to Nobunaga. The Japanese quote is as follows.

杉谷善住坊と申す者　佐々木左京大夫承禎に憑まれ　千草山中道筋に鉄砲を相構へ　情なく十二三間隔て信長公を差付　二つ玉にて打ち申候
されども天道照覧にて御身に少づゝ打ちかすり　鰐口御入洛遁れ候て　目出度五月廿一日濃州　岐阜御帰陣

The interesting section here is the use of the ideogram 二つ玉 *Futatsudama* or 'double bullet'. This has never been questioned in the Japanese historical community and is simply considered as two shots, most likely from two muskets. The main question here is, did he shoot from two separate guns or from one? To reload a musket would take far too long and Nobunaga would be well protected seconds after the first shot, so the best answer would be that he shot from two loaded weapons. However, the most likely answer is found in ninja documentation. The *Bansenshukai* sheds light on this as a ninja skill, with its instructions on the 'Double Shot Musket':

The Double Shot Musket

Put gunpowder and a bullet as normal into a musket. Next place wet paper [down the barrel] on top of the first bullet and then place a second charge of gunpowder down the barrel. Then, insert a bullet which is slightly smaller [than the first one] and cut a *Hinawa* fuse down to one *Sun* in length, light this fuse and put it down the barrel. When the *Hinawa* ignites the gunpowder, the outer bullet fires and then you may shoot the normal bullet as usual [giving you a second shot].

This method gives you two shots in very quick succession, allowing a single shooter that extra advantage. It is impossible to know if this was the skill used that day but it is without doubt a possibility, as the shooter and the *Bansenshukai* are both from the same area and this is an attributed shinobi skill. Unfortunately (for the shinobi) the shots did not kill Nobunaga and according to the document *Zenjubou*, the shooter was captured at a later date, buried up to his neck in sand and cut with a bamboo saw until he bled to death over time.

18

The Death of the Ninja

his book has attempted to reconstruct the history of the ninja in the Sengoku period from their writings in the Edo period of peace. The life of an Edo period ninja was simply the life of a spy, no different to any other spy in the world. As time passed, the need for highly trained infiltration agents who could climb castle walls and burn castles to the ground had come to an end. Just as the samurai warriors became bureaucrats and public servants, the ninja had changed from elite commandos and spies to half-trained shadows of their forerunners, employed in police and spy networks. Little is known either of Sengoku period training or training in the Edo period, but there a few small glimpses.

The *Okayama-han Hokogaki* is a record of all the retainers for the Okayama domain that served the clan over the last 200 years of the Warring period. It states that during the Sengoku period there were 50 ninja who were hired by the clan and whilst in the last days of the Shogunate, just before the 1868 switch to the Meiji government, the clan had just ten hired shinobi. Associate Professor Isoda comments on this record that it shows the quality of ninja steadily declining. One ninja retired complaining of backache! The record shows that as time progressed, there were fewer accidents, suggesting that training no longer took place.

So what did happen to the ninja at the last? As the story of the above Okayama clan and the tactical failure of conventional samurai strategy in the final days of the Tokugawa government show, shinobi were still hired and retained as ninja until the first days of the Meiji Restoration in the 1860s.

The original Edo castle guards made up of *Iga no mono* under the guidance of the Hattori family faded into obscurity, but were referenced as late as 1727 in the commentary of Ogyu Sorai, in his work *Seidan*. He mentions the Iga servants and criticises their greed, the requirement to compensate them for any favours or services done within the castle. In addition to this, we know that ninja retained in Kawagoe were used to retrieve information on the Hidatakayama peasant's rebellion in 1773 and also the 1779 rebellion of Oshi, showing that the ninja were still in use as government spies towards the end of the eighteenth century.

We have to consider the spies that were brought from the Kishu domain who were used to create the now infamous *Oniwaban,* or secret spy network of the Shogun in the early eighteenth century. They are considered to be shinobi, but without documentary evidence. Logically, the connection between the ninja and the *Oniwaban* is obvious; the *Oniwaban* were made up of spies from the Kishu–Tokugawa clan when that clan took the place of the Shogun in 1716, and at that time, the *Natori-ryu* was the clan's secret war school. Of course, the *Natori-ryu* are famous for the *Shoninki* ninja manual, making the teachings of the *Shoninki* the most likely basis for the *Oniwaban* spy tactics. Or the spies were taken from the *Iga mono* that worked for the same clan.

The true history of the ninja ends after the Meiji restoration; there appear to be no more references to the ninja being retained by any factions, or by the military.

Rise of the Pretenders

Japan has never lost its love of the ninja. Stories of the ninja continue to be told, such as those of the Sanada Ten Braves, ten ninja heroes who had adventures in comic and story books and had fictional ninja schools.

By the mid-twentieth century, some researchers had started mixing their research with claims to actual ninja lineages and a surge of new claimants started to appear. Their claims generally consisted of unsupported lineages that appeared to mimic comic book ninja and the demonstration of acrobatic 'ninja' fighting skills (such as hand springs and flips whilst distributing *shuriken* against the 'evil samurai' figure) and being dressed in black. There were some circus tricks, like walking on glass and nails. These ninja pretenders wrote on the subject of ninjutsu, resulting in the contamination of the historical approach and making the shinobi a taboo subject for Japanese academic research. No claimant has ever been able to supply any form of evidence that proves a lineage before the 1950s, and all of them show vast inaccuracies pertaining to the shinobi arts, making the *Natori-ryu* and the Okayama clan the last records of the use of the ninja to date.

The ninja died out at the end of the Tokugawa period, leaving only a handful of stories and documents in some families and a small amount of information to be passed on in certain sword schools.

19

The Ninja Found

At the start of my attempt to recreate the correct history of the shinobi I had to throw off any preconceptions about what I wanted them to be and to allow myself only to concentrate on what the ninja actually were.

Various problems have arisen during this research. There is the refusal of private collectors to reveal their manuals to the public; understandably they withhold the information owing to the astronomical costs of the manuals themselves, fearful of devaluing their investments. Many private concerns, such as the Iga Ueno museum, guard their treasures fiercely, and even during a high budget documentary I was involved with, they refused to show them to the camera. With ninja treasure hordes such as these, and collectors scouring the market for ninja manuals, a great deal of the information is withheld. Luckily, there are small libraries and collections that allow access to their shinobi works and of course some of the manuals are open for public viewing, especially those which are considered the canon. The manuals actually help authenticate each other and even though the selection is limited, what is available clearly identifies a core curriculum for ninjutsu and establishes the ninja as a very real figure in military history.

It is not only our generation that fictionalised and tried to claim ninja ancestry. The Edo period sees a rise in ninja manuals, but it also heralds an increase in fake documents and stories, which is one possible reason for some collectors or museums to keep their documents under wraps. There are also documents that include fiction yet at the same time hold truths. It is here in this middle ground where the danger for ninjutsu research lies, yet with iron bars and zealous guardians at the gates of ninja research, it will be hard to separate the wheat from the chaff.

Let us reprise what we do know for sure. The *shinobi no mono*, or ninja, was forged in the 'Dark Ages' of Japan and came to us as a whole concept at the end of the fourteenth century, where they appear to have some form of foundation in the 'robber-knights' of the century before. The origin of their skills has a clear connection with the skills of China, making the arts of ninjutsu of Chinese ancestry, yet with an unquantifiable level of identity. Were the skills brought in person by Chinese immigrants, or were they imported by Japanese travellers abroad, or did the arts of the ninja arrive in Japan from the written words found in the Chinese classics? China appears only to be a source of information and not a direct 'teacher'. China itself has the Dog-thief, the Incendiary-thief, the Spy and the clandestine warrior armed with guerrilla warfare, all of which make up the skills of the ninja. But it is only in Japan that we see the forging of all these elements into one person. So it would appear that ninjutsu arrived piecemeal from China, where it was assembled by the Japanese and utilised by people like Yoshitune, Masashige and Shingen. From here it then moved to Iga and Koka, a pit of violence and bloodshed, which carved the glamorous image of the Men of Iga and Koka as experts in the arts of *shonobi no jutsu*, who were hired out across the length and breadth of Japan. They carried their clandestine skills across the armies and developed a loose spy network across Japan. The Sengoku or Warring period utilised these uniquely skilled warriors and had them engage in espionage and clandestine warfare. The romantic image of the ninja is not in itself a lie: the ninja burning castles and climbing to cliff tops, secret flute messages on the wind and hidden messages furled inside arrows; the scout in the grass and the sleeper agent in his shop, poison in a lord's goblet and a sword thrust in the night. Add to this the more horrific images of infanticide, head-hunting, rape, sexual slavery, homosexual paedophilia, murder, theft, drugs and betrayal, and the ninja truly starts to come into focus. A far cry from the black-clad comic character, the shinobi is a spy, thief, warrior, infiltration agent, explosives and fire expert, secret scout and killer. Undercover in enemy territory, he truly deserves the fame which he has acquired. He is one of history's greatest military assets, the *shinobi no mono*, the ninja of Japan.

From left to right: Masako (Natori) Asakawa, Yasuko (Natori) Hine , the author, Yoshio Hine, Mr Asakawa and Juho Yamamoto.

20

Historical Ninja Manuals

Here the Historical Ninjutsu Research Team has translated a selection of short ninja-related documents. This collection will help you understand the political world in which the *shinobi* lived, the tools of the trade, and the feel of the different forms and styles of the documents themselves. The following documents have been translated by Antony Cummins and Yoshie Minami.

The Story of the Sata Brothers

The following story is taken from the seventeenth-century *Intoku Taiheiki*, a war chronicle which revolves around the Mori clan, and was written between 1688 and 1704.

This episode of 'sword-theft' reads just like sword-theft ninja test often portrayed in film. More than one historical record, written by real samurai, actually advises warriors to sleep on strings attached to swords to prevent shinobi from creeping in and stealing weapons. The *Bansenshukai* retells sword-theft tales and other ninja manuals highlight the importance of taking away the enemy's weapons in secret and destroying them. Therefore, before we push episodes like this into the realms of legend, we must remember that the job of the ninja was theft and swords were quite a valuable asset. Therefore, whilst the sword stealing has become a cliché, it is most likely a real description of the arts of the ninja.

Sata Hikojiro, Jingoro and Konezumi or Little Mouse were three brothers who were considered to be excellent ninja (*shinobi no Jozu*) and who were formidable thieves. Because of this, the Ashigaru foot soldiers and others of the Sugihara family all studied the shinobi arts under these Sata brothers.

The Sata brothers could elude people's eyes or fool their minds as well as foxes or raccoons can and some people say they can do it even better.

An example of their skill: several people were sitting around a sunken hearth which had lots of pieces of firewood within it, despite the fact that they all kept an eye on the firewood sticks that were there, the brothers could steal them one by one without anyone noticing it at all. Another example was shown when a man named Irie Daizo challenged the Sata brothers to take his sword that very night, as he knew they were *shinobi no Jozu* or great shinobi. Upon his request, the Sata brothers inquired if they could successfully steal the sword then would he give it to them? He assured them that he would give it to them but he warned if he could hear or notice them at all, then he would prevent them by any means he could.

Thus, Irie returned to his home and secured all the locks on the doors of every corner of the house and remained awake with his eyes open. When the Sata brothers secretly arrived at the home of Irie, they saw all the doors were guarded securely. However it is the first lesson for shinobi to open the doors or break through walls, so there was no difficulty for them to open an entranceway. After infiltrating, they secretly observed the situation and found that Irie was lying there yet he was fully awake. So one of the Sata brothers took paper from the folds of his kimono and soaked it in the water which was kept in a bucket [somewhere in the residence], and dripped drops of water, one by one onto his head. So, Irie thinking it might be a leak in the roof, raised his head up a little, and the Sata brothers took the opportunity and stole his long and short swords secretly from under his pillow and then retreated [back into the night].

Kusunoki Masashige's *Ikkan No Sho*

Kusunoki Masashige was a fourteenth-century warrior. No writings contemporary to his lifetime survive, however, it was common for a system to latch on to a famous name, and it does not make the following seventeenth-century information less valuable. In fact this manual has a foreword which can be dated to the mid-1600s, which is considered old for ninja information. The passages are from different points in the original text.

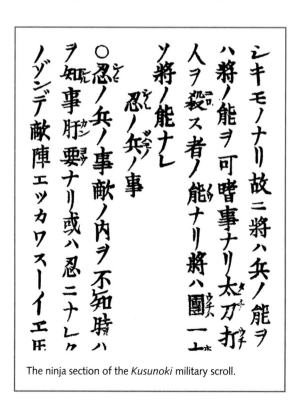

The ninja section of the *Kusunoki* military scroll.

The Art of the *Shinobi Tsuwamono* or shinobi-soldier

You need to obtain inside information on the enemy. However, experienced shinobi may lie to you, and in fact may not have even got close to the enemy and may simply talk about what is most plausible, as they are clever. Because of this, select a talented one from your men and give him enough reward [to satisfy him] and make a prisoner of his wife and children,[133] so that he will not trick you.

Also, you should send around five to seven [shinobi] to go undercover in the enemy territory and do this for either half a year or a full year before [any attack], so that you have inside information. Unless you know the inside of the enemy, your plans will not be achieved and any general should be resourceful about this issue [of using shinobi]. As even in peace times you should send shinobi to various provinces so that they can know a place and be familiar with the people's ways, this is because this information cannot be gained instantly.

The Art of Discovering Shinobi by Speech

In order that Shinobi Tsuwamono, that is shinobi-soldiers, will not become mixed in with your troops in your castle, you should check [those who pass] everyday with passwords. Also, the language and dialects of each province[134] [in Japan] are different from each other and you should be careful of the way people talk.

When a man is leaving a castle, you should check with his master [*Sujin*] who he is and check if people have the daily passwords when they go in or out.

The Way of Castle Guards

In a position where it is hard for the enemy to attack, you should position older soldiers of the age of 40 and beyond as guards. This is done to protect against and to prevent shinobi [infiltration] and night attacks. These guards will not fall asleep and they think of everything and with care. For a place where the enemy are likely to attack from, put younger guards of under 40 years old but mix in a few older soldiers. Also, for every station and posting, you should place someone who can guard against deception 鴈番.

The *Iga-ryu Gunjutsu Youka*

The *Iga Military Schools' Essential Way of Fire* (1728) has been included to display two major points; one, the 'down to earth' and pragmatic style of authentic information in connection with the shinobi; and two, the problematic nature of working with scrolls that have suffered the ravages of time. The importance of fire and explosives to the shinobi must never be underestimated.

The Iga Military Schools' Essential Way of Fire, Volume Jo

[The Table of Contents[135]]
- The Fire Calling Paper [a fire starter]
- An alternative of the above but in board or cylinder form
- Tinder [illegible text] paper
- The Flying Ball of Fire

The author with director John Wate during research for the documentary *Ninja Shadow Warriors*.

- An alternative for the above
- A further alternative for the above
- The Donohi Body Warmer
- Fire from the Inside of Your Kimono
- The Water Winding Light [waterproof or underwater torch]
- The Rainproof Hinawa Fuse
- The Wind Winning Fire [windproof torch]
- The Dry Torch
- The method of Short Burning[136]

[End of the Jo section][137]

- The Grinding Tool
- The Attack Lantern
- The Wheel Candle
- [damaged text] Hook Candle – As this tool is not used for military purposes, I have put it in the Table of Contents but have not recorded the recipe as it was in the original.[138]

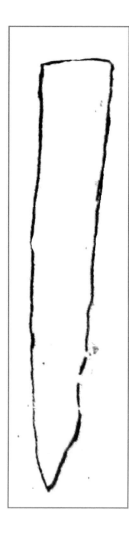

- The Deep Secret of the Short [distance] Fire
- The Cutting Torch

[End of the Table of Contents]

The Fire Calling Paper
- Saltpetre   [?] Momme
- Cinnabar 3 Momme
- Sulphur   8 Momme

Finely powder the above and then thinly apply glue to paper, sprinkling the above powder on to the paper. Next take a second layer of paper with glue and place them together. Then cut out the shape [in the diagram].[139]

An alternative of the above but in board or cylinder form. Make a powder as in the above tool, however, this time apply glue to both sides of the paper and powder it on both sides and add an extra layer of paper on to each side [making three layers].[140]

Tinder [illegible text] Paper
- Mugwart (Artemisia princes) 10 Momme
- [damaged text] crumpled   10 Momme
- Saltpetre   8 Momme

Put this in a pot and cover with water so that it reaches just above the materials and bring to the boil and dry it over the fire and make as you would thick paper.[141]

The Flying Ball of Fire[142]
- Camphor   12 Momme
- Sulphur   9 Bu
- Charred [illegible text] 5 Bu
- Pine Resin   2 Bu

Mix the above with a decoction made from pine wood/bark, which is saturated with pine resin. Then harden the mix and make it into small balls of one centimetre in width.[143] If needed you may also boil sulphur [to make a paste] and apply it to the outside [and let it dry].[144]

An Alternative Recipe for the Above Tool[145]
- Saltpetre   100 Momme
- Camphor   100 Momme
- Sulphur   50 Momme
- Ash   2 Momme

Roast the saltpetre and place 50 Momme of [illegible text]/pine resin [on top of the saltpetre] and when it melts knead in into the rest of the powder above and then harden it into any shape you need, which will be dependent upon the purpose of its usage, but this can be made into a long [throwing fire weapon].

A Further Alternative for the Above Tool
This way is especially secret!

- Camphor   10 Momme
- Sulphur   [?] Momme
- Mouse droppings   three pellets
- Cinnabar   1 Bu

Need the above with 'Juice of Pine'[146] and then wrap with paper. It is good to [damaged text] with this method.[147]

The Donohi Body Warmer
Use white bleached[148] cloth that has been soaked in water for 100 days and then roast it like you would to make tinder. Next wrap it in paper and twist into three strands.[149]

Fire from the Inside of Your Kimono or Pocket Fire
You should carry this tool and the above Donohi body warmer wherever you venture on a shinobi activity.

Use two sections of thin bamboo of one [Shaku][150] long and put the two together side by side [as in the drawing]. On one piece make a [long] vent and put your torch [material] in the second one. For this second cylinder it is best to fill it with the 'Dry Torch' described later on. However, make sure the [rod of 'Dry Torch'] is thin enough to fit in the cylinder.

- The cylinder on the left is the housing for the torch
- The cylinder on the right is the housing for the Donohi body warmer material.
- There is a secret way to put lead in this cylinder[151]
- It is good to use lead [at the top where the two lines point too].

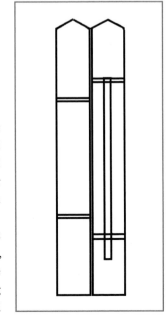

The tool is a combination double-tube which appears to be fully lead lined in one cylinder and only lead lined at one end in the other. One is filled with a hardened mixture which when ignited acts as a torch and the other as a body warmer/ignition tool that can be kept inside a kimono 'when infiltrating an enemy house'.

The text here displays all of the inherent problems when dealing with this type of scroll. First, the context, that is we are not ninja and thus have never used these tools and what may be obvious to a shinobi is lacking in our understanding. Secondly, there is *Kuden* or oral tradition, which tends to be the details that are too hard to explain in the written form but which are desperately needed to make sense of all. Thirdly, illegibility, often the style of writing used is archaic and illegible. Finally, damage, the scroll has been eaten away and bookworm trails criss-cross the texts. This is the charm of working with manuals and adds to the excitement but always with the possibility of disappointment. The scroll is still a fine example of *Iga-ryu*.

The Water Winning Light [waterproof or underwater torch]

Cut bamboo that is two and a half centimetres wide and is eight Sun long and remove the internal joint walls but leave the bottom one in place.

- Camphor   30 Momme
- Pine resin   2 Momme
- Sulphur   1 Momme

Put the above approximate mixture in to the bamboo and ram it down firmly, then wrap the bamboo in paper, there are some oral secrets here. If you wish for the torch to not be extinguished in a windy storm or in water then you should…[152]

The Rainproof Hinawa Fuse

Soak a bamboo fuse in Kanemizu[153] solution until the [bamboo] is fully stained, take it out and dry it in the sun and use it as you wish. No matter how long this fuse is left unused, it will always work.

The Wind Winning Fire [windproof torch]

The first four are of the same amount

- Dry lacquer   middle amount
- Mercury[154]   middle amount
- Sulphur   middle amount
- Saltpetre   a middle amount
- Chinese wax   large amount
- Cinnabar   small amount
- 'White' powdered stone[155]   large amount
- Bitumen   large amount

Melt the bitumen over a fire and melt wax into it and then put in the above mixture and blend well and knead. Soak cloth in water [which has been dried] and is the same as the cloth used for the Donohi but which has not been dry roasted and cut this cloth finely and put this also, into the mixture. Wrap this covered cloth tightly [around the torch] and fasten the edges with hemp thread and apply wax on to it so that it will not go out in strong winds. For daily use, there is an alternative recipe but this one here is for military use.

The Dry Torch

- Lacquer
- Black Soya bean

- Japanese Cypress [sawdust]   [?] Momme
- Saltpetre   2 Momme
- Cedar resin   2 Momme
- Pine resin   [?] Momme
- Sulphur   1 Momme
- Sashime[156]   [?] Momme

Mix oil with lacquer and knead the above mixture and harden it to make a thin and long rod. If you travel one Ri with this torch, the rod will burn down less then one Sun and it will endure both rain and wind.

The Short but Long Burning Tool

- Japanese wax   1 Kin
- Pine resin   2 Kin
- Chinese wax   1 Kin
- Japanese Pagoda Tree
  (Styphnolobium japonicum)   1.5 Kin
- Ukishoseki; this is sparkling white sand
  found in the waters of a mountain rivers,
  it is not stone but extremely fine sand
  and of a certain moisture   40 Momme

Melt the above with fire and wrap in a cloth [making a cylinder] of two centimetres across. Also, pack cotton seed into paper and put into a [holder[157]]. If you use this tool for one day and one night, it will burn down less than one Sun.

The *Sokoku Ikki*

The *Sokoku* is a set of commandments or rules established amongst some of the clans of Iga to help prevent invasion by 'foreign' powers. The document was found amongst others passed down in the Yamanaka family in Koka and was at first thought to have been a commandment of Koka. However, Professor Ishida Yoshihito discussed the possibility that the title '*Sokoku Ikki*' means the self-governing organisation of the Iga district.

The document itself is not signed or dated and appears to be a draft version. Professor Ishida speculates that it was written at some point between 1552 and 1568, for two major reasons. Article 7 of the document prohibits servitude to the Miyoshi clan, however, before 1552 the Miyoshi was only a retainer clan to the more powerful Hosokawa clan and thus would not have been referred to without the name of Hosokawa taking precedence. In 1552 the Miyoshi succeeded in leaving the service of the Hosokawa and took hold of independent power within the Shogunate. Furthermore, the document does not mention or discuss Oda Nobunaga. If it had been written later than 1568, when Rokkaku Jotei, the Shugo governor of Omi province had fled to Koga, then Nobunaga's name and attack would have been known.

If this document is in fact from Iga, of which researchers are almost certain, then it is the only document left concerning the *Iga Sokoku Ikki* as any other documents were destroyed in the *Iga Tensho no Ran* War of 1581. The document was an agreement made between the ten *Bugyo* commanders from Iga to settle conflict amongst the warrior families. Contemporary documents support this and state that twelve representatives were selected to make decisions for the land. Also, it is speculated that there was an equivalent organisation in Koka called *Gun-Chuso,* which is thought to have consisted of many *Domyoso*[158] factions. There are two documents from this union left in the Ohara family (1560 and 1570). According to those documents, within the *Domyoso*, each family had equal rights and decision making was done by discussion and a majority vote. Alongside this some of the *Domyoso* seem to have formed a larger regional group. One of them is the Kashiwagi Three Families; this consisted of the Yamanaka, the Minobe and the Kashiwagi. Two sets of the commandment made among the three families have been left to us (1522 and 1556). The meetings held between Iga and Koka were called '*Noyoriai*', which means 'field meeting'. The ten *Bugyo* from each region met at the border of their lands and discussed issues of interest concerning Iga and Koka.

The title of the document *Iga Sokoku Ikki* reflects the alliance formed among the *Jizamurai* (land-owing samurai of Iga), which is also referred to as the *Sokoku – So* 惣 'self-governing village', *Koku* 国 'country or land', *Ikki* 一 揆, a military unit formed as a means of resisting the increasing powers of regional migrants or Shugo military governors (which was often cemented through oaths). They oversaw matters of a local nature, such as self-defence, irrigation, water control and land management.

The document itself does not concern ninjutsu, however, it is a 'living' testament to the fact that ninja were not set in opposition to the samurai and that the people of Iga and Koka were in fact of samurai status. Also, it is a rare glance into the world of the people of Iga, people who were without doubt the greatest ninja of their time.

I

When any other domain's army is intruding on our province, the collective of the Sokoku should fight to defend against them, with each other as one.

II

Upon the alert sent from a gateway when the enemy are spotted, all the bells in every village should be struck and everyone should take up their position immediately. Everyone should prepare himself with food, weapons and shields and set up an encampment so as not to allow them to enter the gateways of our realm.

III

All people of the ages 17–50 should be stationed for war. If a battle is a prolonged one, and they have to be stationed for a long period, they should rotate via rota. In every village and every area, commanders should be appointed and all the men in the village shall follow the orders of those commanders. As for the temples in the Sokoku, the elders should carry out devotional service for the prosperity of our province, whilst the young should take part in the camp.

IV

All of the Hikan[159] lower people of the Sokoku should write a solemn oath, stating that they will follow their lord whatever the situation of our land.

V

Ashigaru of our land may even capture a castle of another domain. Therefore, those who serve as *Ashigaru* during a siege and go beyond the borders and attack a castle in another land and succeeded in capturing it, they should be rewarded liberally for their loyalty and promoted to samurai status.[160]

VI

Anyone who intentionally lets an army of another domain enter our land, the combined *Sokoku* will subjugate him and his clan and annihilate them without leaving any trace and their land will be put under the use of a temple or shrine. Similarly, anyone who communicates with the enemy secretly and gives them any inside information about our land will be treated just the same as those who let the enemy army within. If someone brings information of anyone's treason in the above manner, he will be highly valued.

VII

Any samurai or *Ashigaru* foot soldiers of our land should not serve the Miyoshi clan.[161]

VIII

If there is someone who does not accept the Yumiya Hanjo Tax,[162] he, his father, sons or brothers will not be eligible for the benefit from the fund for ten years. Neither should they be allowed to take charge of the Yado Okuri Transportation System.[163]

IX

When positioned in a village or camp, all disorderly behaviour or violence should be prohibited within our alliance.

X

As Yamato province has unjustly attacked our province over a prolonged period of time, you should not employ any *Ronin*[164] who once served the generals of the province of Yamato.

XI

As we have controlled our province without any problems, it is of utmost importance for us to obtain cooperation from Koka, Thus, we should have a meeting with Koka at the border between Iga and Koka.

The above commandment will come into effect with the signatures of all who are concerned.

16th day of November

The *Koka Shinobi no Den Miraiki*

The *Koka Shinobi no Den Miraki* (*For the Prosperity and Future of Koka Shinobi*) is one of the most important non-instructional ninja documents in the collection of the Historical Ninjutsu Research Team and highly significant in the world of shinobi research. It was dictated by Kimura Okunosuke Yasutaka to his student Chikamatsu Hikonoshin Shigenori in 1719 (transcribed in 1805). It outlines the Master's fears for the ever-declining *Koka shinobi* and predicts the fall of the ninja with great accuracy. The document is actually one part of a four-part work, which confirmed Chikamatsu as a master shinobi. Chikamatsu on the day of the presentation was given a copy of an unknown ninja manual that contained the school's secrets, the oral traditions which are attached to all ninja schools, a certificate of mastership and Kimura's words, which make up this following document. It was to be passed down the ages to shinobi of the future.

Kimura says that anyone under the age of 70 at the time of writing (born after 1650), has no connection to anyone who was living in the Sengoku period and thus the practical skills have been diluted and are second rate, which ties in with Natori and Fujibayashi and their desire to start recording ninja teachings, the reason for many other manuals that exist. It removes any doubts as to the samurai heritage of the ninja, as Kimura himself states that they are retainers and were relatively well paid and could command their own salary during the warring years, being retained for considerably less in the period after. It also shows that shinobi could command extra money on top of their retainer allowance and could demand a substantial mission fee.

The end signature shows that ninjutsu was practised in military compounds and that within the schools of ninjutsu there were multiple levels of knowledge, which were kept secret from others. The higher levels concentrated on the more esoteric and the 'magical' aspects of ninjutsu, which makes it harder to establish which esoteric practices are real. Kimura's position as a retainer to the Owari-Tokugawa clan and his position as a *Koka no mono* give his words authority. He states that there are magical' or esoteric elements in the higher forms of ninjutsu (elements that the 'new' shinobi were ignoring). Normally the absence of any actual practical skills and simply a collection of magic brings any document into question, but here, a real shinobi is saying that the higher secrets of ninjutsu, beyond breaking and entering and night time raids, contain magical elements, so every scroll needs close scrutiny. The *Shoninki* states there are many 'magical' secrets in ninjutsu but that in this manual the greatest are listed. As we know, the *Bansenshukai* states in the Table of Contents that it contains 'Occult Writing of *Ninjutsu*' but mysteriously, they have been taken out.

Kimura was a man of Koka who was hired by the Owari-Tokugawa clan and is similar to Natori Masatake. Both of them served the Tokugawa family in secret military affairs and in the ways of the shinobi. Kimura himself is listed in the *Bugei Ryuha Daijiten* encyclopaedia as the founder of *Koka-gunnery* and *Koka Takeda Ninpo*. However, there is no supporting evidence presented for this and in all likelihood he simply taught both subjects within his clan. On the other hand, the student and transcriber, Chikamatsu Hikonoshin Shigenori, a personal retainer of Tokugawa Yoshimichi, is a celebrated samurai, who wrote over 100 books on warfare and other subjects and who was renowned for his tactical ability. A master of the martial arts, he founded a school called *Zen-ryu*

全流which he later changed to *Ichizen-ryu,* which suggests that any form of *ninjutsu* within *Ichizen-ryu* school is in all probability, of Koka lineage.

Lastly, Chikamatsu wrote a collection of stories translated into English under the title of *Stories From a Tea Room Window* and whilst not based on ninjutsu, it is interesting to note that a popular Tea Ceremony book is actually the work of a real life Koka-trained shinobi.

On the whole, this document is of vital importance, showing us how ninja were close to their lords, how the ninja fell from power, and how, as Natori says in the *Shoninki*, the ninja of Koka were one band. The manual states that the Battle of Sekigahara had some hidden secrets that were forbidden to be spread, and those secrets were the actions of the ninja.

> **STORIES**
> **FROM A**
> **TEAROOM**
> **WINDOW**
>
> LORE AND LEGENDS OF THE
> JAPANESE TEA CEREMONY
>
> by Shigenori Chikamatsu
> translated by Kozaburo Mori

The following writing is the oral transmission of Sensei Kimura Okunosuke Yasutaka and is given to and written down by his student Chikamatsu Hikonoshin Shigenori.

Stories From a Tea Room Window, the unlikely book written by a real Koka-trained samurai, which is often passed over by the modern ninjutsu community.

Those who are given the traditions of the Koka shinobi arts should all understand the concept of 'Sansei' or the three stages of 'past, present and future', before they enter into study in this school.

1 Past   that which has gone before
2 Present   that which is now
3 Future   that which will come

In ancient times those originally from Koka used to consider themselves as one people and that they were all of the same origin, this was their standpoint for generation after generation and they treated each other like brothers from the same family. This even continued after they became scattered across the provinces and lived in various places, or in far-away territories, even then, they continued to know each other's names, and kept in constan contact. Also, if needs arose they communicated without hiding their intent and displayed everything [about the situation] and arranged to help each other to perfectly to fulfil any shinobi mission at hand, and they did this without fail. They also made it a rule not to pass down any of their traditions to anyone who was not from Koka, which formed the core and guiding principle of their ways [of inheriting their arts]. Even today [in 1719] the above two[165] major principles are still observed and those Daimyo lords who want to hire *shinobi no mono* prefer to hire those of Koka.

It is unlikely that any warrior from Koka cannot find employment and that even if he is retained for only a small fee, he can easily gain service. In fact, there are many people [of Koka] who are given fees even whilst they themselves remain stationed in their homeland. Also, people think that simply being from Koka makes a person an expert in the shinobi ways, and this thought has arisen because Koka is run on the two old traditions [mentioned above and has its foundation in these] strong principles. Until now, this principle [of a strong union] has been fulfilled and those [of Koka] have let each other know who is in which province and also, those who are in important or larger provinces keep in contact more often than others and if an emergency arises, they will resolve any issue very quickly, so the reputation of the shinobi of Koka has been maintained and is renowned; therefore for this reason they are hired by any and all clans.

As I am old, I am now considering the status of those who now do this same task [as I once did] and are spread out across various provinces and thus I am deliberating on the future prospects of our ways. Therefore, I will now make clear the present status and situation in detail, concerning our future[166] and I surmise that these following predictions will turn out to be correct in nine out of ten cases. Also, I hope that my student writes down exactly what I say and shows it to all future students.

[The following points will be the cause of the demise of the arts of Koka]

I

Those people who instantly understand the importance and way of these two ancient principles and our traditions are those who lived within a short period after the turbulent times[167] and they have seen much, which has allowed them to fully understand their family arts 家業 without conscious study. And if you do not follow the way of these ancient traditions, then you cannot fully serve in an emergency and cannot fulfil the requirements of the appointed shinobi tasks of your family.

Those people around the age of 70 think of keeping these traditions alive as an important rule and still write to each other and do not break their promises which were made to their ancestors, sparing no effort in preparation, so that in an emergency situation and if needs arise they can be immediately be ready the next day and therefore, those around 70 years of age will serve the clan 家 well. Those who are younger than 70 years cannot serve [their clans] very well and this should be a point for future discussion. The reason for their uselessness is that it is a time of peace in this land and there have been no crises in which those people from Koka can achieve greatness and show the arts of their family. Thus, because of this they have no opportunities and receive no rewards or recognition.

II

As there are no emergencies then there is no chance for our men to get close to their own lords and receive his orders directly or even converse with him. In olden days there was the saying 'from the mouth to the ear' and *Koka no mono* used to talk to their lords directly and receive his orders and they built a good relationship, however, as this is not the case now, we have become lower in position and are of the level of *Geshoku*.

III

Because of this lack of emergencies, *Koka no mono* cannot achieve greatness nor accomplish feats, and there will be scarcely any lords who will want to use Koka people or appreciate them in the future and they will have no chance to prove their worth.

IV

As there is no demand to serve a lord or conduct official business, [new shinobi] will not maximise their own creativity.

V

As I mentioned previously, it is now a time of peace and so [the *Koka no mono*] will become accustomed to an easier life and will become negligent and have zero inspiration or will to push their arts.

VI

[*Koka no mono*] are spread across all provinces but are now generations apart. In older days they used to be fathers and sons or even brothers who were spread about the land, but now they are almost unconnected by blood and are strangers to each other, like those other people around them, and because of this they seldom write or communicate with each other.

VII

In times of peace, people do not remember times of war and what it is like and become comfortable, so they feel that there is no need for the shinobi and they no longer carry detailed information about each province nor do they give gifts to each other. On top of this, they do not know who is in which area or who good people are.

VIII

Today, in every clan [shinobi] are not needed so they are left stagnant and 'left to hang'[168] and many are given small fees and at a relatively low level [to how it used to be]. Therefore, they are occupied with feeding their wives and children and can simply not afford to hone their family arts, which makes them underachievers within their own profession.

IX

Generally speaking, in days gone by, when we used to receive orders direct from our lords, [the men of Koka] were given large amounts of money in payment for their missions, as much as they required and even if they spent hundreds of Ryo gold coins and if they [the ninja] are asked 'on what was the money spent' they did not need to divulge the answer. This was the normal way for *shinobi no mono* both in Japan and China and they did not have to balance any accounts. Thus the better *shinobi no mono* were for missions as spies, then the more money they were supplied. This made everyone do their best to perform great shinobi arts but in modern days, there is simply no demand and they have no opportunity to earn extra money outside of their regular allowances. Therefore, both skilled and lesser skilled [shinobi], are financially poor, thus there are no *shinobi no mono* that now make constant efforts to become great.

X

As [the arts of the ninja] are a matter of extreme secrets, then even when teaching those people who are in the same school, the traditions [of the school] are taught so discreetly that they are found in a setting of three or even five stages or levels. In principle, at the first or second stage, you should teach unimportant or useless things until you determine whether the person is trustworthy or not or what abilities he has; if you find him to be serious and resourceful, then you may give him all the traditions. Such a person is only 1 in 1000 people and the other 999 are just taught the first to second stage, which are made to look important and which makes them think they have learned all the traditions of shinobi. However, because of this, the school is now managed by those who know only the first or second stages of the arts, yet think they have the complete skills, which hinders the progress of our arts; therefore you must understand that this system is now pointless.

XI

As most students in a school are only at the level as described above, they tend to think that *shinobi no jutsu* is almost the same as skills of illusion, but there is only one in a multitude who can master the arts to such a deep level that they truly understand that the teachings of the Gokan[169] five types of spy are of the utmost importance and of vital use. All this happens because the teacher does not teach the traditions openly and the students only have limited capabilities.

Though such techniques as hiding yourselves, disguise, crossing over a pond or marsh, crossing a river, climbing a wall or infiltrating a gate are included in the skills of shinobi, they are only trivial and rarely of service to you, making it hard to achieve a great accomplishment with these skills alone. Though the Gokan five types of spy comprise all that is essential, no one teaches it in detail [any more] and as a result even ambitious people in the school think that such minor skills [as mentioned above] are all secret skills and ways that are important for a shinobi. Because of this, eventually, the skills of shinobi will be become lesser and find limits, this is a certainty.

XII

The difference today is that people are culturally enlightened and tend to learn academically and be more reasonable. Many people do not use or learn hidden secret skills which have been passed down from ancient times, for example: *Mitsume* and *Kikitsume* 見詰聞詰 'listening and hearing with intensity', *Yojigakure* 楊枝カクレ 'Toothpick Hiding' and *Karametsume* 搦ミツメ 'Catching[170] Fingernail' are regarded as unreasonable and magical and even heretical skills and people often follow up by quoting the following saying: 'There should be nothing mystical about any righteous path.' This retort of theirs is truly an example of the saying, 'Shallow cleverness prevents you from travelling on the righteous path.' In those secret ways or skills invented by ancient people there are a numerous things that look unreasonable or unrighteous to the eyes of modern people but in fact have actual benefits and miraculously do work. These miraculous skills seem unreasonable, but this is because others do not reach down deep inside of the way of these things, but you must note, there is reason found within these ancient ways [if you understand the truth of them]. Not having realised such deep reasoning, a lot of people do not believe and abandon those skills thinking they are evil and magical.

XIII

As these traditions are kept so secret, it is often the case that they are discontinued or passed down in a very wrong way because of their very secrecy.

Considering the above thirteen reasons, it can be safely said that there is a huge difference in skill levels found within those who call themselves *Koka Shinobi no mono* and the main differences can be seen between those who are above 50 years old and under 50 years old, but this has always been the case.[171] Eventually, in the future it will turn out that only one of every 10,000 people can serve well when any emergency arises. Those Daimyo who keep *shinobi no mono* will only retain them for the name of Koka and for them simply being from Koka. Those who are employed only for that reason are doing nothing more than selling the name of Koka and when an emergency arises, they will not be able to serve in any way. And, if at such a critical point they cannot perform, it will result in not only his ruin but it could also lead to serious danger for that province. Alongside this, such an event would be a great dishonour for the traditions of Koka and cause the decline of the line itself.

Therefore, those who receive my teachings should be aware of the above reasons before anything and keep training without deviating from the ways or principles of the ancient traditions of this school and should achieve great feats.

Therefore, I here leave these articles recorded to give a warning to those in our school and for the consideration of the future prospects [of Koka ninja].

This document was written on the fifteenth day of the first lunar month in the period of Kyoho 4 (1719). Also, all the important points from Hara Yuken Yoshifusa's [ninja] scroll and the associated oral traditions have been passed on and have all been given, together with a certificate of qualification [to me, Chikamatsu the transcriber of these words].

On this very day mentioned above, my Master dictated this Future Account and I wrote down every word he said, word for word with due respect. On the sixteenth day of the month, I visited my Master to thank him for this and he again told me to record his words which are about a further two matters and are placed here in the following text. This also I wrote down word for word without any difference. These are all essential points of the school and should not be neglected in any way.

Employing or being employed

Those who employ [shinobi] are tacticians or lords whilst those who are employed are *shinobi no mono* and even today there are only 10 out of 100 who can truly serve [as ninja]. Alongside this, there might be only one good tactician or lord out of a multitude who is able to utilise his agents very well and this is because good tacticians or lords need to be well versed in military skills and have a grasp of the subtle essence required in employing spies, and should also have a good knowledge of the specific skills of the shinobi. If this is not the case, they cannot judge exactly if a certain action is feasible or not when using shinobi, because of this factor, just under five out of out of ten [missions] will fail to be successful. [Usually] those [people] who are capable and can determine if a plan is reliable or not do not hold the authority to actually utilise such skills. Thus it can be said that there are only one in a multitude of lords or tacticians who have the understanding needed in this area. Also, if they use [*shinobi no mono*] in a wrong way, it could threaten the survival of a country or cause the destruction of an entire army. But all that the *shinobi no mono* can do when used in any way is to perform the best they can to fulfil the orders given to them by their superior.

Being a shinobi appears to be difficult but it is in fact not as difficult as it seems, for if his life is endangered, nothing other than his life will be lost. All throughout the history of Japan and China, the lords who used [shinobi] very well were Jinbei, Masamoto, and later on, the late Lord Tokugawa Ieyasu (Toshogu). These are the only three [good lords] throughout Japan and China who actually used [ninja] well but there are a countless number of lords who were defeated and killed as they could not use their agents properly. At the Battle of Sekigahara, from the beginning and right through to the end, the spies who served Toshogu did very well and fulfilled their aims each and every time, so that many of their secret ways or skills have been passed down in our traditions, whilst the shinobi who served Lord Ishida Mitsunari [Tokugawa's opponent] used the arts wrongly and could not succeed at every point so they were defeated and ruined. This art [of using shinobi] seems to have been the only point that mattered and was integral to Mitsunari's outcome and was the deciding factor as to whether he should win or lose the Battle of Sekigahara.

[As you can see from the above] if the person who uses [shinobi] are not proficient then it is useless and is exactly as the saying, 'A horse who could run 1000 Ri cannot be found without a man who can recognise talent (Hakuraku).' This is exactly the case with a good shinobi, if there is nobody who can use him very well.

Be sure to remember this saying, 'Hawks and musha-warriors will perform dependent upon the person who uses them.'

[Postscript by Chikamatsu]
For your information, during the Battle of Sekigahara, there were secret episodes which utilised the traditions of Koka and it was prohibited for anyone to write these episodes down, so as to not give them away them to others, including the written records about the battle which were spread throughout the country afterwards. Fortunately, my Master has been given the tradition and sometimes he taught these exploits by mouth and from time to time in a series of lectures which ran for three years.

[Returning to Master Kimura's words]
The incomparable and indispensable essence found within military ways
In military tactics the shinobi arts are incomparable and indispensable to its essence. It might sound as if I am promoting my own interests and should be reproached for self admiration; however, this is simply not the case and neither is it simply my personal opinion. For proof that these arts are the deepest secrets, you should investigate the thirteenth chapter of *The Art of War* by Sun Tzu. After describing all kinds of military techniques, he discusses the matter of using spies and ends his writing, saying:

'It is the enlightened ruler and the capable general who are able to use the most intelligent ones from within their ranks to be deployed as spies and secret agents so as to achieve the greatest and complete victories in war. Secret operations and espionage activities form an integral part of any military campaign as the planning of strategies and the movement of troops depend heavily upon them.'

Sun Tzu emphasises his point by saying 'heavily' or 'complete' as it is of great importance.

As is mentioned in the traditions of 'Niso Daigo' 二相大悟, everything originates from ears and eyes and this is exactly what shinobi do as they travel thousands of Ri across mountains and rivers, serving as ears and eyes and report all they see and hear [to the lord]. Whoever the great generals of all ages were, how could they have gained this intelligence without sending out shinobi? Shinobi are the ears and eyes of the entire army and so 'the movement of troops depends heavily upon them.' Therefore, it can be said this is the deepest essence of warfare, more important than any other arts.

People from most military schools in Japan are barely literate and can not read *The Art of War* in very fine detail, therefore, they are not aware of what it means and do not think that using spies is essential or important, they even think it is no better then shinobi-stealing[172] 竊盗, which is actually in complete contradiction to what Sun Tzu teaches in his work, and for this reason you should try to understand fully the subtle meaning of what Sun Tzu's work means and build the basis for the success of your entire army from that chapter. Those who do not understand the true and deepest of secrets of military warfare should know that they can all be found in Sun Tzu's *The Art of War* and those who do not know this are not worth conversing on the topic of warfare with.

[Postscript by Chikamatsu]
I write here for your information, that the lectures on the chapter of using spies in the Art of War has been complied into a series of ten lectures and were recorded with commentary.

This future account and the above two important matters were both dictated and checked by my Master, and copied on the third day of second lunar month and in the year of the Kinoto-Boar in Bishu (Owari province) and transcribed by me Nogen (Chikamatsu) of the Renpeido soldier training complex.

Further transcribed in the year of Kinoto-Ox in the eighth month of 1805 in Osaka by Suzuki Sadayoshi, a warrior of Bishu and given to Mizu no Gentadamichi.

Extracts from the *Gunjutsu Kikigaki*

The following are small extracts from the military manual *Things Heard About Military Ways*, written in the fourth daimyo of the province of Tosa (1641–1700) concerning the arts of war in Japan. The author, Yamauchi Toyomasa, makes an interesting point about the use of *Suppa* and *shinobi*. *Suppa* is often considered to be an alternative word for ninja. It is difficult here to ascertain if the author is using them together to demonstrate that they are in fact identical in skill or if he is using them in such a manner because they have differing roles.

Question:
When you build a battle camp, it is an established formula to have a twelve Ken distance between the outer bamboo fences and the barracks; however, this can be reduced to a distance of between five and seven Ken according to the situation. On what grounds is this done?

Answer:

If a night attack comes, the enemy will have shinobi hide beside the fence, and they will light a signal fire, light torches, make war cries for their allies etc., all with the intention to cause confusion among the camp. If your men see a signal fire sent out, all in the camp will think that they are about to fall victim to a night attack and will fall into confusion. The enemy will take advantage of this confusion. However, if there is enough space between the fence and the camp quarters, you will be able to assemble a formation inside the camp or you will not have too much confusion if you get out of the barracks and into such a space immediately. If there is not enough space between the quarters and the fence, and if you are under a night attack, it will make the confusion even worse, therefore, the distance should be twelve Ken. Generally it is desirable to have enough vacant space within a camp.

Question:

Is there any difference between performing a night raid upon a castle from one made against a battle camp? Also are there any cases where a night raid ended up in failure? If so, what are the details?

Answer:

There have been so many cases where night raids ended up in failure, for example, the case of Umijiri castle, [where the Murakami clan were raiding and the Takeda clan defended, 1540] or the case of Miterao of Joshu [where the army of Koshu made night raids but failed and ended up withdrawing in 1548]. Also, there was the case of Kushunoki Masashige when he raided Heguri castle.

Taking the above in to consideration, there are also other cases of night attacks on castles, such as when Suyama and Komiyama night attacked the palace of Kasagi, when Iwakikumaru night attacked Yoshino castle [where Prince Morinaga of the southern court defended], or the case of Yoshitsune attacking Ichinodani, where he attacked from the direction the enemy least expected.

As mentioned in the volume of *Gunpo*, you should send *Suppa* to an area where you require a thorough investigation and do this in advance to help you decide. After this, you should have shinobi infiltrate and set fires whilst you take advantage of the confusion which is caused because of them and attack from outside. Even if the castle is not very large, you will not be able to obtain fruitful results unless you send in shinobi after investigating what the land is like thoroughly. This should be done almost in the same manner as when deciding where your *Suppa* should be positioned. You will never be able to attack a castle successfully without having shinobi infiltrate and set fires. When Mitsuuji attacked Umijiri castle, they could not succeed in setting fires by sending shinobi and were trying to take any advantage of a gap found within the castle.

The essential principle when night attacking a castle is have *Suppa* sneak in and set fires first, then attack from outside taking advantage of the confusion. Without causing any confusion among the enemy, it is hard for you to attack them successfully. For castles that are well defended and where it is hard for shinobi to infiltrate, you will not be able to attack successfully without adopting correct tactics.

The *Rodanshu* Scroll

The *Rodanshu* translates roughly as 'A Collection of Ancient Military Wisdom'.[173] Within the circle of ninjutsu researchers, the *Rodanshu* scroll needs little or no introduction; however, it is not a 'stand alone' ninja manuscript but rather a collection of military skills which, at certain points, reflects ninja information. Dated to 1846, it claims to be a transmission of skills used by Yamamoto Kansuke and is thought to outline his secret military equipment and strategies. Yamamoto Kansuke was a Sengoku period retainer to the famously successful warlord Takeda Shingen, who was later renowned for using the shinobi and their arts. It appears that the *Rodanshu* is a later and heavily reduced transcription of information that came from a scroll of a similar name orginally transcribed in 1668, and later transcribed by the *Daimyo Toki Masakata* (Sengoku Masakata) in 1865, giving it further credibilty. However, even with this early transcription date it is impossible to know if it was ever connected to the famous Yamamoto himself or if it is even based on the warfare of Shingen at all.

How has this scroll come to be known as a 'ninja' scroll? Within the manuscript you can find a small selection of 'classic ninja tools and skills' that were recorded in other manuals such as the *Bansenshukai* and which clearly display a certain amount of shinobi information. It is the inclusion of diet pills, collapsible war-boats, the infamous 'water-shoes',[174] grapples, and water crossing floats that place this scroll within the realms of ninja technology; however, it only uses the word shinobi once. Strangely, it is the limited use of the word shinobi that gives this manual its authority. This is because if the manual was simply an invention of the nineteenth century (and not a continuation of ancient knowledge), then it would have 'played up' its ninja connection. Also, the ninja-like apparatus is mixed in with other 'samurai' tools, which to some could be considered mundane, lists of samurai horse-gear and the like make up a large section of the work. Therefore, we can rest assured that this is a genuine article and an accurate transmission of older military skills. Further reasoning for this is that the skills contained within match those of older manuals and are not 'exciting'; in some cases, they are actually quite drab,[175] which from a historical angle, makes the scroll more credible.

This scroll includes sections dedicated to mounted scouting, or *Monomi*, discussed earlier in this book. The information is a mix of mounted battle and scouting skills which concentrate on equestrian elements but which also include collapsible boats, explosives and fire equipment. This manual is a collection of information for mounted scouts, who at times would have to dismount and possibly split up, allowing a few members to go deeper into enemy territory whilst others stayed with the horses. It describes a mixture of *Monomi* scouting skills and shinobi tools to be used by the same person but at different times, depending on if their task was long range scouting or a deep penetration of enemy lines. There are general battle skills for mounted samurai combat and horsemanship, which can be seen in the contents of the text at the end, such as the two standards or banners and the 'battle-camp collapsible water bucket', items found in 'conventional' samurai life.

The *Rodanshu* is primarily a 'picture scroll' with text information at the end, here the illustrations have been placed in the order they were found and the descriptive text orginally next to the tools has been numbered with explanatory notes in square brackets that I have added. Throughout the scroll, the term '*Kuden*' is used, which as described before is the concept of passing on information by word of mouth alone and has been translated as 'secret' or 'oral tradition', however, it must be remembered that *Kuden* in itself does not imply secrecy but means that more information is required.

The *Rodanshu* is one of the classic scrolls referenced by collectors and is a positive step in understanding both mounted scouting and the skills of shinobi.

Japanese Measurements

Shaku	30cm
Sun	3cm
Bu	3mm
Ryo	15g
Momme	3.75g
Kin	600g
Sho	1.8 litres
Go	180ml

The Tengu Chain Reins

1   The circumference should be 9 *Bu*
2   The ring should measure 9 *Sun* 8 *Bu* in outer diameter
3   This measurement is over 1 *Sun* in diameter

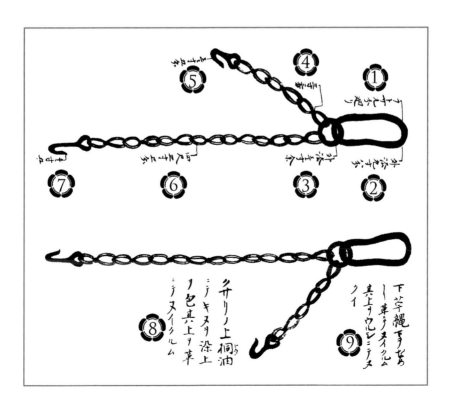

4   3 *Sun* 3 *Bu*

5   1 *Sun* 5 *Bu*

6   4 *Shaku* 5 *Sun* 5 *Bu*

7   1 *Sun* 5 *Bu*

8   Cover the chain with cloth soaked in Tung oil and bind and sew over it all in leather.

9   Use a rope made from the *Ramie*[176] plant as the core of this ring and bind it all in leather and lacquer it.

'The Reins of a Rock Pulling Against a Stone'

1   Make this rope of the *Ramie* plant and cover with leather

2   Tie the *Ramie* rope with firm knots, like this.

[The use of this item is unknown, however it appears to be alongside a pair of horse reins and itself is titled as a form of rein. Therefore, on the small amount of evidence available it is possible that this is a form of martingale, a section of tack that connects the horse's head to a strap along its chest, preventing the horse from raising its head up too far.]

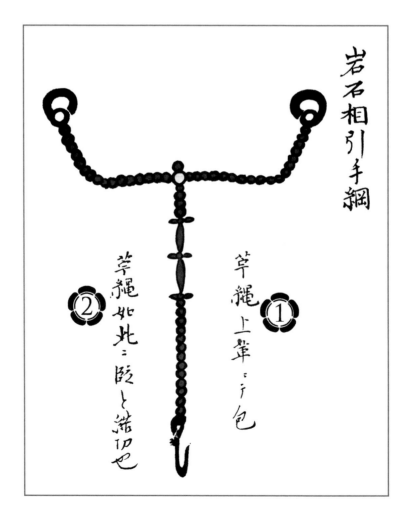

'Short Rods [For Prompting a Horse]'

A one *Sun*[177] rod or whip

The same as the last tool.

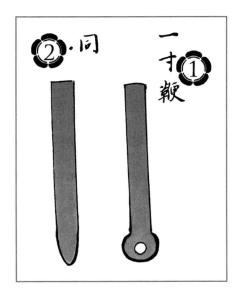

'Lacquered Waist Attachment for a Sword Scabbard'

1   Attaching hook

3   Tanned leather with lacquer

4   Tie *Ramie* rope with a line of firm knots, like this [the ball configuration]

[This is an attachment from the waist to the scabbard of your sword. What is unknown is if this was the construction used in day-to day-life or if this was for equestrian purposes only.]

'Standard Iron'[178]

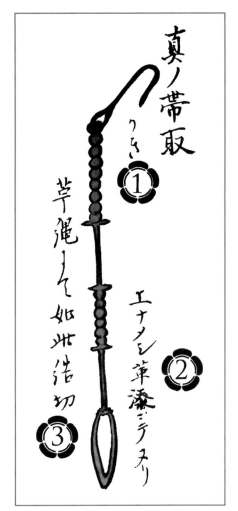

'Dream-like Iron'

[The military war manual found at the end of the *Bansenshukai* ninja scroll talks of 'hinges' used to hold spears, and comparing these with the 'Spear Rest' which appears a little further down the scroll, then it would seem that these are also those 'Spear Rests', most likely a platform for a lance-type weapon. The translation of 'real and dream-like iron' is a literal translation and is based purely upon the meaning of the ideograms, if the word is based in a phonetic understanding – which it originally may have been – then its meaning has been lost.

'A four *Sun* Horse-bit'

1   Also known as a *Mukotsume*

'Reins That Pull Together and Fill the Mouth'

1   Ring
2   2 *Sun* 1 *Bu*
3   This is a three foot cloth
4   Use Cloth
5   Make with cloth and double up
6   The same as the other ring

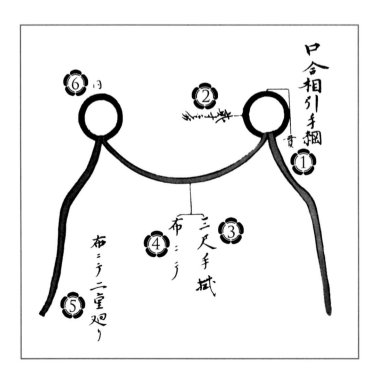

'Spear Rest'

[As described above, this is most likely the 'Spear Rest' discussed in the *Bansenshukai,* however the full meaning is unknown.]

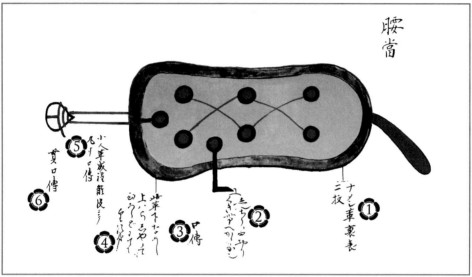

'Sword Belt'

1   Two sided with tanned leather on the back and the front

2   Brass hook to be attached to the sash

3   Oral tradition

4   This leather is tanned on the back and the front[179] and is lined with woollen cloth or white [illegible text].

5   The leather can be made of good quality skin and should be 9 *Sun* long, this is an oral tradition

6   The clasp[180] is an oral tradition

'Water Flask'

1   The length should be one *Shaku* and the top should be made according to [illegible text].

3   Attach it to your belt and cover[181] with copper. Details on its construction are an oral tradition.

'Horse Girth Band'

1   Tighten [with the two strings at the ring]. This is 'Fast Riding Saddle' and also a double Horse Girth.

2   Ring: oral tradition

[Accompanying text]

There are various types of horse girth bands, such as the *Kanto-haraobi*, the *Kurishime-haraobi*, the *Neji-haraobi*, and the *Hayagura niju-haraobi*. Further information is an oral tradition.

[When a scout or mounted warrior pushed his horse to a fast pace, this tool was used to help strap him down in the saddle.]

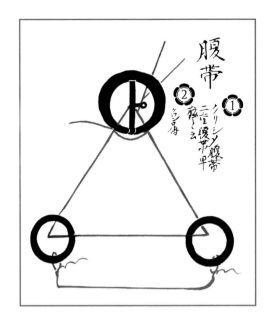

'The Horseback Lantern'

1   Oral tradition

[This is probably a torch that attaches to the rider behind the saddle and illuminates the area around him. It would render the rider visible, therefore it was probably used for riding at night and in a group.]

'The Battle-Camp Water Flask'

1   Oral tradition

[What may appear to be a basic item to modern readers would have been an essential tool in Asian summer heat and a standard requirement for any scout who was out for days on end. There is no explanation for the black nodule on the right hand edge.]

'The Battle-Camp Water Bucket'

1   Supporting shaft
2   The bottom of this bucket is made of wood.
3   The sides of this bucket are made of cloth.

[This is a common medieval water bucket and is constructed of material and is collapsible, it is possible that this was taken with a rider to hold water for a horse or to take water to a makeshift camp when the mounted warriors were on the move.]

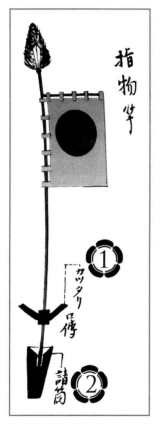

'The Standard or Banner'

1   This is a *Gattari* fitting [to attach the standard to your back] This '*Gattari*' attachment is an oral tradition.
2   This is the bottom cylinder housing for the banner.

1   This tool is the same as the one above
2   This grip[182] here has oral traditions.

[These standards or banners would most likely be used in actual combat, as keeping a low profile in mounted scouting may not have been a high priority and generally, banners and standards are used so that commanders can identify sections of their troops in combat.]

'The Floating Bridge'

This tool is made from a spear.

1   There is a ring near the top of the spear shaft.
2   These two red circles are 'floating shoes' and are
     secret.
3   There is a rope to hold on to.[183]
4   This is the butt of the spear.
5   Here you will find the 'pointing eye'.[184]

[Floating bridges are without doubt connected to ninja
and are mentioned in many manuals. However, this
version appears to be a variation, as other floating bridges
are normally anchored on the banks of a river. This device
is a flotation aid for one man and could have been used
either to cross over a river or to travel down river through
into enemy territory. The construction of the two floats is
unknown, however it is most likely lacquered and sealed
leather or animal skin with a 'stopper' cap for filling with
air.]

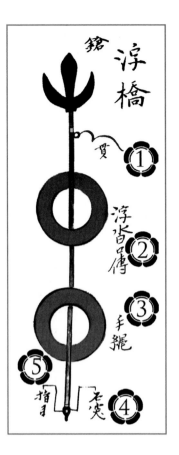

'The Life Jacket'

1   Oral tradition

['Life jacket' is the closest translation,
however its literal translation would be
'Floating Shoe'. It is mistakenly believed
that the 'Water-Spider' ninja tool is a set
of floating shoes, an idea spread by the
late ninjutsu researcher, Fujita Seiko, as
discussed earlier. It is here where Mr
Seiko may have derived his ideas, as this
is a similar tool. Both this tool and the
latter are forms of inflatable flotation
buoys that tie around the waist. The
Bansenshukai manual states that these
tools sometimes have 'screw caps' to
aid inflation, which could be one of
the secrets which are referenced in the
manual as an oral tradition.]

'The Rapid Boat'

[There are no notes for this tool, not even a *Kuden* oral tradition mark. It is simply titled 'Fast Ship' or 'Rapid Boat'. The *Bansenshukai* has a full description of one of these vessels. The *Bansenshukai* version of this craft is a selection of plates (not unlike the ones presented here) that fold away and can be used to construct the basic framework of a boat, which is then covered in a treated leather skin to form a waterproof hull. This version clearly has sections missing and no instructions on its construction. The hooks and metal brackets in the image appear to not match the plates next to each other. It is unknown if this is a 'V' shaped hull or a square-bottomed boat and if the thinner sections are bottom boards or not. The bow and stern construction is unknown and not illustrated and nor is the skin of the hull. Its use is understood but its construction is an oral tradition that has yet to be fathomed.]

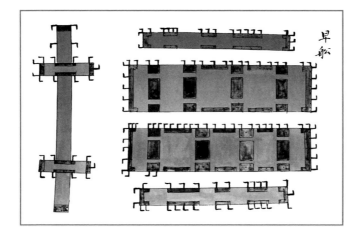

'The Horseback Shield'

1   The length is two *Shaku* and eight *Sun*.
2   This window is a Monomi or scouting window.
3   The red arches here are wooden arm grips.
4   The cross here is made of rope.
5   The width of this shield is one *Shaku* and five *Sun*.
6   There are more secrets here.
7   The two red strings at the bottom are hemp rope.

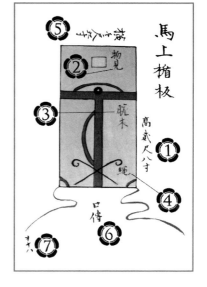

[The Horseback Shield appears to be a variation of the shield found in the *Gunpo Jiyoshu* manual, both have viewing ports. However, the difference here is that this version appears to be used by *Monomi* horseback scouts and is most likely use to ward off arrows when openly spying on the enemy, or when retreating after infiltrating the enemy territory.]

'The Fire Boat'

1   This red line is the 'Sending Fire'.[185]

2   This is a rudder.

3   The large yellow section is the main hull.

4   This is also a rudder.

5   This section of the red line is also a 'Sending Fire'.[186]

[Fire craft have been used in the East right back to ancient China. This version has a few details that are unknown. Firstly, the size of the overall craft is not commented on. This could be a series of small boats or larger 'ships'. This fuse or 'sending fire' appears to be lit on one side, so could be an explosive directional propellent. The craft appears to work on a twin-rudder system, however, it is not mentioned if these rudders are manned, that is if the ship is big enough, and if the said pilot abandons the ship at the last moment, or if these rudders are controlled by long ropes as the craft makes its way downstream and towards the target, or if they are fixed rudders used to help keep a straight course. The fire in the centre is made of 'tied grass' and in all probability is straw saturated with flammable oil. This may also be terminology for a hardened substance, which in fact contains no grass at all.

All in all, this is a very interesting device and fits well within the ninja ethos of the guerrilla tactician and explosives expert as well as with samurai naval warfare.]

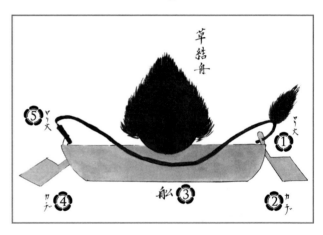

'The Broad Breath-Hiding Cloth'

1   Oral tradition

[This is a cover that hides the trace of warm breath hitting cool air and thus helps to hide a scout. The name itself literally translates as 'Breath Meeting Thirty Centimetre Cloth (*Tenugui*). This was most likely used on a horse, as its construction appears to be designed as a muzzle. It appears that the 30cm cloth is rolled up lengthways with a knot placed in one end and in one corner of the cloth, as can be seen by the red nodule

in the upper left corner of the image. The end of the cloth tapers off and is entwined with a black string that appears to secure to the 'tied knot' then the apparatus goes around the horse's mouth and nose and is pulled tight, clamping the horse's mouth closed. The four strings probably secure the cover to the horse's bridle. A similar system is used by the *Otsubo hon* school and was mentioned earlier.

'The Overhang Climbing Bridge'

1 This is a sickle and there are secrets here.
2 Jute rope
3 There are more oral traditions.
4 This is a sickle and there are secrets here.
5 The grapple is made of iron and has oral traditions attached to it.

Of all the tools within this scroll, this is possibly the most difficult to interpret. When literally translated the tool becomes 'The Reverse Wall Climbing Bridge',[187] which leaves a selection of various functions. The tool itself is a grappling iron that allows a rope to pass through in two directions, a rope which has sickles attached to both ends. The *Shoninki* ninja manual talks about using a grappling iron and spikes to help ascend walls, which could mean that this tool is use in this way. The Japanese connotations in the title give the feel of a 'rising curve', going back over itself, therefore the primary meaning is something to with an 'overhang' when climbing outer castle walls, as the walls in question, within the title, are outer defensive walls and not those that support buildings. It is possible that a shinobi would grapple up on to the top of the wall and insert the sickles into the masonry below –under an overhang – which would give him a double rope 'bridge' to shimmy up. This would explain the reason

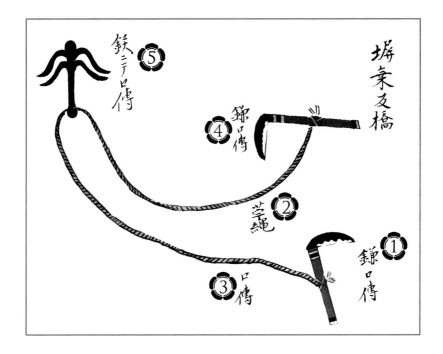

for the tying of the rope to the hafts at the half way mark, as when used on an overhang any pressure on the haft from the rope at this angle would cause the sickle to jam against the roof of any crevice. To imagine this tool in use, you have to see an agent climbing face upwards towards an overhanging turret wall with his back resting on the two ropes below him or scuttling along face down.

An alternative usage would be to use the grapple in a standard way but with the addition of the infiltrating agent standing on the sickles, which have been inserted into holes in the stonework, using them to create a series of foot holds. He then uses the rope to pull on and free each sickle, shaking the lower sickle free to pull it up after him, ready to find a suitable hole for his next step, and so on to the top. This is a second possible reason as to why the ropes are tied in the middle of the sickle haft, helping the ninja rattle them free.

A third alternative would be that a shinobi could tie a loop in each rope, a short distance below both sickles. This way he could hold a sickle in each hand and hook them into a suitable hole and place his feet in the rope loops, transferring all his weight onto the two sickle points. He could then transfer all of his weight on to one side and move one sickle up as high as possible and then step up. In this example, the ninja would allow the grapple to hang below him and carry his equipment as he ascends, which could account for the 'reverse' element in the title. Lastly, it could be a version of the shinobi tool called the 'Kuribashigo' which is a grapple with two ropes. A shinobi would tie rungs onto the rope and climb up section by section.

'The Night Attack Torch'

1   Oral tradition
2   This is made of 'tied grass'.[188]

Youichi Taimatu means 'night attack torch', and is a close cousin of the *Torinoko*, a form of hand-held torch used for work at night. These balls are made of tied grasses with flammable insides, such as ears of straw our pounded wood. The tool can be held in the hand or thrown into an area to give light so that you can see, or to set fires. The first image here is of interest as the black 'pips' are most likely to be iron spikes. This tool is straw on a metal frame, used to throw and stick into buildings to cause them to ignite.

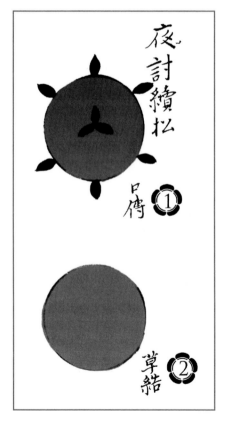

'The Donohi Live Embers Case'

1 It can be made of Iron or Copper – according to the metal's hardness

2 This is called a 'Tanpo'.

A Donohi is a material treated to burn slowly and to retain embers for a prolonged period so that you can warm your body and hands and also so you can start fires or commit arson. The version in the *Shoninki* comes with a copper cylinder to hold the materials; the *Bansenshukai* has some versions that need wrapping to carry. The box is a container to keep these materials in and in fact matches perfectly with a description given in the *Shinobi Hiden* manual.

Hyorogan 兵粮丸 - **A Soldiers' Campaign Rations**
Energy Food Pills

Hakurogan[189]

Glutinous rice	5 *Go*
Rice	5 *Go*
Lotus pips [seeds without their husk]	1 *Ryo*
Japanese yam	1 *Ryo*
Cinnamon	1 *Ryo*
Coix seed	1 *Ryo*
Asiatic ginseng	5 *Bu*[190]
Crystallized sugar	1.5 *Kin*

Mix the above with water, knead very well and steam in a basket steamer. Make small balls and consume five to seven of these a day. It is also beneficial to give them to horses too. Crush it with your teeth and put it into the mouth of a horse, along with water.

The Red [Hunger] Pills of Lord Imagawa

Asiantic ginseng	3 *Momme*
Licolis	2 *Bu*
Cinnabar	4 *Momme*
Musk	2 *Shu*[191]
Chinese bellflower	2 *Momme*
Bukury (Fu Ling) *Poria sclerotium*	2 *Momme*
Kudzu root	1 *Bu*
Cyperus rhizome	3 *Momme*

Mix the above with honey and knead well.

An alternative for horses only:

Decoct the roots of the *Ibara* red thorny plant and feed the decoction to the horse.

For *Tsumeuma,* which is 'breaking in' or exercising horses you should give the above decoction to them with vinegar mixed with stream water or *Funori* 'glue' made from seaweed.

For *Baritsume,* which is hard 'breaking in' or exercising, you should give the above decoction with vinegar or a further decoction of the shrub, *Akebia quinata.* To calm its breathing, remember give it to the horse with water.

The Torch called *Ariake*

Saltpetre	50 *Momme*
Elm tree	26 *Momme*
Camphor	32 *Momme*
Powdered moxa	3 *Momme* 5 *Bu*
Pine tree saw dust	5 *Momme*
Pine resin	3 *Momme* 5 *Bu*
Ash	2 *Momme* 3 *Bu*
Mouse droppings	1 *Momme* 8 *Bu*
Powdered *Azuki* bean	1 *Momme*

Put the above mixture into a bamboo cylinder and firmly ram it down, then shave the surface of the bamboo until it is as thin as paper. Mix alum with glue and apply it on the surface of the cylinder. The mixture should include alum, *Nomono*[192] and glue with a ratio of 3:2:1.

The Waterproof Torch

Elm tree [sawdust?]	38 *Momme*
Sulphur	30 *Momme*
Pine tree saw dust	30 *Momme*
Perilla oil [*Perilla Frutescens*]	5 *Go*

Put the above into a bamboo cylinder and compress it firmly. Shave the surface of the bamboo and apply a mixture of a little borneol and glue. Alternatively you may apply a coat of wax.

The Tied Grass Fire[193]

Sulphur	100 *Me*
Cinnabar	10 *Momme*
Shu vermillion [Mercury Sulphide]	5 *Momme*

Compress the above firmly into a bamboo tube and shave the outer skin of the bamboo cylinder. Bore a hole in to the bamboo and tie it onto a ship with wire.

To store this before use, put it into a bamboo cylinder and insert powdered *Azuki* beans into the cylinder. However, if it is exposed to the air, then the fire will not last long. There is an oral tradition for this.

An Alternative Recipe for the Above

However, this one is ignited directly instead of using *Tsukegi* lighting taper

Camphor	45 *Me*
Elm wood [sawdust?]	25 *Momme*
Saltpetre	3 *Momme*
Ash	3 *Momme*

Construct this as described in the previous tool, however, this version should be ignited directly [instead of with a taper]. Also, it is less waterproof than the previous one; however, it can be used around water [but with care].

Sending Fire

Saltpetre	15 *Momme*
Elm wood [sawdust?]	1 *Momme* 5 *Bu*
Ash	5 *Bu*
Pig Iron (broken in to the size of poppy seeds should be fine)	1 *Momme*

Put the above into a cylinder and ignite it. It is advisable to wrap paper around this with moxa and with a small amount of saltpetre mixed in.

The Greater Torch, which is a torch to be used during a night battle

Chop *Konara* oak wood into two, soak it in water for fourteen or fifteen days and then dry it in the sun. Decoct an amount of saltpetre in water at length and apply the decoction to the wood. After applying all of the decoction onto the wood, you should then dry it in the shade. When it is completely dried, cut it into pieces of the length of one *Shaku* two *Sun*, or one *Shaku* eight *Sun* or even as long as three *Shaku*. Put the pieces together and construct a tool with a circumference of about one *Shaku* two *Sun* and secure it with wire, then wrap it in paper and apply resin. Then use *Yoho* elm wood on the end [as a handle].

The *Donohi*[194] Body Warmer
Charred Fruit of the Chinaberry
Charred stems of *Polygonum longisetum*
Ground tea

Grind the above in powder and knead it with unrefined sake until it solidifies. Ram it firmly into a bamboo cylinder so that it forms a bar of charcoal and so that you can cut it in to sections ready for use. Bury this in the ash [beneath] a hearth for three days without igniting the tool [but allowing it to dry roast]. To carry the *Donohi*, you should char the leaves of Japanese cedar and make an ash of them, and put the *Donohi* solid bar in to this ash of cedar, and then put all the contents inside a bamboo cylinder. The cylinder should be made like a hand basket [i.e., with a handle] and should be attached to your waist.

Shields

Fix the leather of a buffalo onto a board with lacquer and smooth the leather with a hot iron. The board should have a double layer of smoothed leather fixed onto the shield with glue. When fitting the leather to the shield, grind the ash and powder[195] of a blacksmith's bellows into fine powder and mix it with lacquer and apply it to the shield 100 times. The shield should be six or seven *Bu* thick and capable of defending against muskets.

How to decoct *Nibear mitsukurii* 'fish skin'[196] for the above purpose

Use the skin of the face and head of a boar with all of the hair removed, then add *Kadsu* roots and knead it whilst warming in a vessel in hot water. A thin piece of deer skin can also be used.

How to Seal and Oil the Surface Skin of a Life Jacket

Decoct *Perilla* oil for up to three or four days, to test if it is ready put pieces of straw in the oil and see if they become crooked like *Suegi*. Then scoop up one *Sho* of the oil and mix well with six *Momme* of lacquer and apply the mixture [to the life jacket]. After that, apply normal and undiluted lacquer.

How to Apply Oil to Ships[197]

Mercury chloride	3 *Ryo*
Pine resin	3 *Ryo*
Aizu wax	2 *Ryo*
Perilla oil	1 *Sho*
Lime	5 Ryo

Grind the above into powder, decoct to the measurement of seven *Go* and then apply it to the ship.

Night Attack Torch or Area Illuminating Fire

Camphor	100 *Momme*
Saltpetre	10 *Momme*
Elm wood [sawdust?]	60 *Momme*
Ash	6 *Momme*
The sawdust of Pine wood	10 *Momme*
Pine resin	5 *Momme*

Grind the above into powder and ram it into a large bamboo cylinder, compress it firmly, [when set][198] this will make a bar so you can cut into pieces for use. In case of heavy rain and wind, it is preferable to use the way of the Grass Tied Fire, which uses a three parts mixture of Camphor, Cinnabar and Vermilion. Also, it is ideal if you can use this recipe even in normal times. The diameter of the throwing ball[199] of this tool should be about three *Sun*. This is to be thrown into the enemy and one piece can light up a ten *Ken* square area.

Concerns About Horse Gear[200]

A saddle with gold and silver edges is not recommended and soaked cow's leather moulded into shape and lacquered should be used instead.

You should have three layers of spreads under your saddle. The *Umahada* – which is the spread to be put directly on the horseback – should be made of cattail, so that it will not irritate and make raw the horse's back.

The *Nogutsu* straps which attach to the skirts of the horse's saddle should be straight and not hooked, as hooked ones often get caught.

Shiode saddle rings [used to attach things to] should be made in the style of *Mekurinuki*,[201] and also they should desirably be attached with rings made of leather. Normal *Shiode* rings cannot be easily reattached once they have broken off. Also, looped versions of this are not good because they will strech the horse's crupper.

Metal stirrups should be used.

Fur saddle flaps should be used as they are beneficial in cold weather.

The hems and fringes of saddles should be made of linen with a chain sewn inside of them.

The leather cords used for stirrups sometimes break. Therefore it is preferable to double them up with a rope of linen and put them through the hole for the stirrup cords which is on the saddle uprights [which support a rider in the saddle].

Reins should be made of fabric weaved with thick yarn. *O-no-tazuna* reins which are made of cord are not good as they are too thin in your hands, especially they are of no use in the rain. Nowadays many people use purple dyed versions but in the days of old it was hard to use such reins without permission from the lord. If you have a particular liking for *O-n-tauna* reins, you should use silk-crepe instead.

The *Umazura* horse mask has disadvantages, whilst having not so many advantages and horses can have trouble breathing when using it. However, it is useful when your colleague's horse becomes angered, thus you should use it if needs arise.[202]

The horse bit should be cross shaped. Decorative ones such as ones with carved crests are not good.

Horse shoes should not be made of the 'false nettle' plant.[203] This is a secret.[204]

The *Hana-neji* 'nose twisting stick[205] should be equipped with a sickle. How to make this is an oral tradion.

There is oral tradition for the Horse Ladle.

The 'Travel Nose Leather' should be connected with *Karamushi* false nettle rope.

Horse feed bags for bran should be sewn with the stiches on the inside of the bag and should be attached on the both sides of the back of the saddle. Those colours which stand out are not good.

For a temporary saddle stand whilst travelling, use the [horse] shoe basket, make sure it has a hinged lid.

The above [horse] shoe basket should be woven in the '*Ajiro*' style of weaving and also you should apply lacquer to the basket so it can be strong enough to be used as the horse washing tub, however there are oral traditions on how to make this.

The Art of Horses

Larger horses are better for crossing rivers, whilst smaller horses are good for ascending and descending. Horses with short body-trunks are good for fields and mountains, whilst those with long trunks and a high head are good when in deep rice paddies, ponds and marshes. *Same*-horses which are cremello and perlino horses do not stand out in the morning sunlight. Horses of 'dual-colour' should be avoided on the battlefield. 'Dual-colour here means *Buchi,* that is those horses with big white dapples, *Ashige,* dappled grey and *Yukifumi,* those who 'step in snow' that is have white sections at the lower part of the leg. Remember, you should consider what kind of horses will suit your purpose.

On a battlefield young horses are not recommended and should not be ridden. A horse around eight years old is good and should be used.

'Difficult' horses or those who are fearful should not be used, those horses which are too hard to control are simply not good. Before a battle, if a horse is agitated and 'chomping at the bit' and you have to restrain it, then this is not proper at all. Also, if you are taken by such a horse and killed in vain, then this is truly regretful. Remember that you must be able to freely control a horse with the reins in one hand.

Oroshi-horses, which are Russian horses will not stay or go to the gallop unless the rider lifts his rear off the saddle. However, armoured warriors [*Musha*] are heavy therefore you cannot ride [risen off the saddle] as can be done at normal times. Therefore, it is desirable to use horses from Hitachi. Alongside this, it is also said that *Oroshi*-horses are not recommended when you have to cross over difficult terrain, rocky areas and down rocky trails and pathways. Remember you should ask people who know of these things.

A horse should not have a long mane because it will tangle with the gear or even the reins.

The Art of Horse Riding

When mounting and dismounting from a horse and in armour, there is an oral tradition which involves the stirrup. Also, there is something to be passed down by mouth about the saddle-girth.

There is a secret way to carry reins and hunger pills when on horseback, this is called the 'Seven *Sun*' [way].

How to tighten the saddle is an oral tradition.

Remember the art of tethering a horse to grass.

If a horse suddenly becomes nervous or loses control, then you should wash its mouth out with water and rest it before riding on.

Push your right stirrup forward and pull your left stirrup back and ride like this, with your feet not straight [and opposite each other]. This is done to maximise your grip around the horse and to keep the horse calm.

How to ride horses that have one-sided mouth[206] or are untamed should be orally transmitted.

[To re-train] those horses who lie down near a river or who lie down when they see water, you should put a tooth pick or a firm twisted paper string, deep in to their ear, this method is also good for horses that anger quickly.

After riding a horse fast for five or six *Cho* in distance you will find that the horse gets out of breath. Therefore, you should ride it in a circle two or three times or even in a zigzag manner. You should ask experienced riders about other ways.

If you want to pull ahead of other horses, you should ride a fast-footed horse or fine horse.

There are secret ways to cross a horse over water.

When you ride to a river bank, take care and consider the horse. Wash its mouth and then ride into the river with the reins loose; also, the 'front' of the horse should be unrestricted. There are vast amounts of things to be orally transmitted for these ways.

When you ride into a river, go in facing downstream. It is desirable that the horse is familiar with water so you should train it at normal times.

After a hard ride, if you plunge straight in to water then the horse may die. Therefore, wash its mouth and cool down its head before a river crossing.

When crossing a river untie the forward cords of the skirt that goes underneath the saddle and tie them back on themselves [which will pull the skirt backwards and help the crossing].

[When crossing a river] lift up the stirrups and cross them over the top of a saddle.

When in water, if someone comes to hold the tail of your horse, fend them off with the butt of your spear.

If in a big river, you should still ride your horse until you get to the deeper sections, there is an oral tradition for this.

To cross over a moat, dry or water filled, show the horse the moat by riding up and down the moat, so he can see it, then retreat and then go at them at speed, talking to your mount and giving him the whipping rod [so that he crosses].

When you ride in a deep paddy field you should raise the head of the horse and gently pull backwards and raise your bottom off the saddle. The 'reins of rock pulling against stone' [illustrated at the start of this manual] are good for this, but there are more secrets.

When you ride upon a road at night you should follow a pale horse, a dapple grey horse or any animal that is distinct. There are many things you should be aware of and it is like a cart following another cart, for if the forward cart is overturned, then the cart at the rear will learn by the mistake of the cart at the front.

When on the march, going out on a shinobi mission[207] or if you are on a mountain or even in a steep and rocky area, then you should use an unsaddled horse.

If a horse is out of breath and you have no water, then use your own urine to wash its mouth.

Apply salt to the tongue of a horse every morning and wash and apply 'medicine' to calm its breathing.

Wrap the above 'medicine' in a cloth and attach it to the bar of the horse's bit [so it dissolves in its mouth].

The above volume is what Babamino no Kami Yamamoto Kansuke, who was a retainer of the Takeda clan of Koyo studied at all times and should be kept secret. However [the receiver of this scroll] was very eager to obtain it, therefore, I will pass this on, but be sure not to reveal this information to anyone.

[The giver]

Mabuchi Ruiemon

Transcribed on the 27th day of the second lunar month in the year of 'Koka[208] Two' [1846] which is considered as the year of Kinoto-snake.[209]

[The receiver]
Iikura Ken'nosuke

The Sixteen Tools of the Sawamura Family of Iga

This is a list of sixteen tools that are considered to be shinobi tools passed down in the Sawamura family of Iga. Their content – including the 'shinobi-lantern' – secures these items well within the realm of the ninja and can be found in multiple manuals. The original writing is in *Sosho* or 'Grass-style' and is some of the most difficult we have come across yet. Therefore, for the benefit of those familiar with Japanese, the original text has been transcribed here into Kaisho or Block-style by Mieko Koizumi (pictured on page 213). The order is English, then the original Japanese and lastly the simplified Japanese below that. Note that the numbers do not appear in the original text.

覚

Memorandum

1

Hikibashi 'the retractable bridge' – a tool needed when you are crossing over a moat

引橋 － 堀越申時入申候道具

引橋 － 堀越し申す時いり申し候道具

2

Uke 'life Jacket' – a tool needed for swimming

うけ－ 水于をよぐ時入申候道具

うけ－ 水をおよぐ時いり申し候道具

3

Kunai 'digging tool' – a tool needed to climb up a stone wall or used when digging away at a clay wall

く奈い － 石垣于の本' 里又ハ塀爾あ奈を阿計申時入申候道具

くない － 石垣をのぼり又は塀にあなをあけ申す時いり申し候道具

4

Hikinawa 'pulling rope' – a tool needed to cross over a place you are unfamiliar with

引縄 － 不知所候之行渡リ仕時入申候道具

引縄 － 知らぬ所候これ行き渡りし時入り申し候道具

5

Uchikagi 'grappling hook' – a tool needed when you cross over a fence or wall

打可ぎ－ 塀于越之申時入申候道具

打かぎ－ 塀を越し申す時いり申し候道具

6

Makuribashi 'rolled ladder' – a tool needed when you cross over a fence or wall

まく里橋 － 同断

まくり橋－ 同断

7

Nokogiri 'saws' – a tool needed when cutting through a fence or wall – it has an edge on both sides.

のこぎ里 － 塀于き里申時入申候但両刃ニ而御座候

のこぎり － 塀をきり申す時いり申し候但両刃にて座候

8

Kamanata 'the sickle hatchet' – a tool needed to cut something, it is the same as the normal version

かま奈多－ 何事毛き里申時入申候道具徒年のごとく申耳候

かまなた－ 何事もきり申す時いり申し候道具つねのごとく申すに候

9

Hakagi 'winged key' – a tool needed to probe for Kuroro door-latches
者かぎ - くろろたづ年申時入申候道具
はかぎ - くろろたづね申す時いり申し候道具

10

Do[nohi] 'fire carrying tool' – a tool needed to carry fire
とう - 火を持申時入申候道具
どう - 火を持ち申す時いり申し候道具

11

Torinoko 'fire egg' – a tool needed to make fire
と里のこ - 火をた天申時入申候道具
とりのこ- 火をたて申す時いり申し候道具

12

Taimatsu 'torches' – a tool needed at the time of Youchi night attacks
たいまつ - 夜うちの時入申候道具
たいまつ - 夜うちの時いり申し候道具

13

Shinobi Chouchin 'shinobi lantern' – a tool needed to observe a guardhouse or any other such place
忍ちやうちん- 番所与ろ川見申時入申候道具
忍ちょうちん- 番所よろづ見申す時いり申し候道具

14

Nobusuma 'field blanket' – when you lay ambush in a field, have your men 'wear' this
[野]ふすま-人数を[野]にふせ申時きせ申候道具
[野]ふすま-人数を[野]にふせ申す時きせ申し候道具

15

Nagabukuro 'the long bag' – a tool needed when you are cutting through a wall
長袋- かべき里申時入申候道具
長袋- かべきり申す時いり申し候道具

16

Hiya 'fire arrows' – a tool needed when you burn down military quarters
火矢 -小屋をやき申時入申候道具
火矢 -小屋をやき申す時いり申し候道具

End of the 16 tools
以上拾六具

The author with Meiko Koizumi and Mr Yoshida, an expert on scrolls and manuals.

夜討之書 *Youchi no Sho*, The Night Attack Scroll

Transcribed in 1689, presumably by Ito Jin-emon Yukiuji, it is believed that Koike Jin-no-jo Sadanari wrote this scroll earlier and it is considered to be a part of *Ogasawara-ryu*. Primarily this is a night attack scroll and the skills listed are for conventional samurai to use. However it is a great look into how commanders used shinobi during night raids. Some additional text has been inserted in brackets to aid understanding.

- If the enemy have travelled over a steppe or difficult area or have traversed a long distance you should obtain information on their situation and status in secret and commence a night attack.

- After a full day's battle or after you have been defeated you should gather the remnants of your men and conduct a night attack.

[This is a regular theme in military manuals and plays on the enemy's neglect after they feel they have secured a victory; therefore other military manuals caution that after a victory should come prudence and attention to defence.]

- You should attack an enemy position when they have been encamped for a prolonged portion of time and have thus become neglectful. To know the situation of their camp you should send shinobi.

- On the night when the enemy arrives to construct battle camps you should commit surprise attacks.

- On a night of heavy wind and/or rain make sneak attacks 窺ヒ討.

- When the enemy are retreating over a long distance you should attack and take advantage of the gap they create during the move.

- A night attack troop should be fifty in number and you should assign *Kashira*-captains for every unit of ten men and all the people on the night raid should be dressed in black.

- On a night raid you should bind the tongues of the horses and wrap cloth around the metal sections of the bits that jangle.

- On night attacks you should not take long weapons with you, however that being said, long swords 長刀 are acceptable. Also, bows should be the primary weapon in the first attack.[210]

- Passwords should be arranged before you set off on a night raid.

- Identifying signals 相形 should be arranged before you set off on a night raid.

- When making your way to the enemy position, it is often the case that your troops may lose their way. Place one unit in the middle of the route behind the troops so that they can make sure of the direction they are going by calling to each other.

- *Shinobi no mono* should be sent to observe the internal set-up of the enemy forces or position.

- In the case where you attack an enemy camp by surrounding it, prepare torches for use.
- War cries should be made from a direction that the enemy do not expect you to be – this is a stratagem.

- Instruments should be used to send signals.

- Ambush troops 伏兵 should be used.

- Send *shinobi no mono* to ignite fires in the enemy camp.

- Perform hit and run actions, whether or not to make further repeat attacks depends on the extent of the enemy's negligence.

- Before you infiltrate the enemy camp, do not light any torches – then upon the order of a *Kashira*-captain, throwing torches should be utilised in unison.

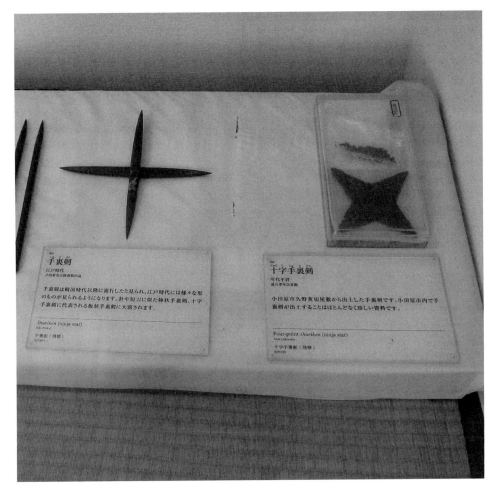

To date, no references have been found to *Shuriken* throwing stars in any of the known ninja manuals, but this may change.

- Torches should not be carried by combatants.

- Night attacks should be done in the Hours of the Boar or the Rat [between ten and two o'clock] or also when horizontal clouds appear above the mountains [at dawn] – however, you should not always stick to these ways, especially if the enemy are negligent at night.

- When you return from a night raid, identifying signals [as described above] should be used to identify your men before you let them enter the compound.

- When troops are returning from a victorious night raid, a reserve troop should be stationed [around your camp] as the enemy may try to follow the returning men – have this reserve troop deal with the enemy and let those who have returned enter the camp [and rest].

- Construct watch fires on both sides of a castle gate and question everyone before they enter.

- When your troops return from a night attack and go through the gate, send out *monomi* scouts and investigate before they enter the gate. When the enemy soldiers persistently follow your troops back and try to infiltrate your castle you should secure the castle gate and have ambush troops placed there to kill them.

- In the case where the enemy is far away and you have to travel over a long distance to commit the night attack and it is not easy for you to reach them quickly, in this case you should send *monomi* scouts and/or shinobi in the daytime to observe them closely. Next divide your entire attack number in to groups and then following signals from these aforementioned scouts, send these groups one at a time.

- When attacking on mountains or slopes or in valleys, it is difficult to attack at once with a massive army. Therefore, up to day six, seven, or even day eight of the new lunar month your forces should commence night attacks and they should do this around the time of moon-set. During the day before these attacks have your troops wait in appropriate places and in position and then at moon-set, descend on and defeat the enemy. It is essential to consider if the distance is far or not and when the attack is [to be initiated]. You should not light torches.

[It should be noted here that this differs from the previous instruction to attack in the hours of the Boar and the Rat, however, this situation is different, being a specific attack on an incline. The first few days of a new moon are the darkest and by day six and up to day eight of the moon's cycle it will be hitting the half full stage of its orbit and after this the increasing moonlight will help give away any movement by one's forces, therefore it is best to stop after this day.]

- On a pitch dark night and when you have to advance through mountains, valleys, fields and streams you should assign guides to take point and place them in front and rear. If you are afraid that you have lost your way, you should halt your troops and confirm your direction. Also you should have some men go between the front and the rear.

- In a situation where you think that some troops may lose their way, then you should attach paper to a tree or to bamboo, this will act as a signal for the forces behind you. This [technique of marking] is called *Go*.

- When there are bushes on either side of the path and you are suspicious about that area, considering it a good point of ambush, you should shoot arrows into the bushes at random – then take one unit of the troop and have them line up [on either side of the path] in defence and have the rest of the troop move through the area. Also, if *Fushikamari* ambush troops are there, your horses will sense their presence – more to be passed on in oral tradition.

- When on a night attack your forces need to know the direction of their base camp for a safe return. Observe the heavens [to get your bearings]. Also, concerning the land, you should remember: the flow of the water, the shapes of mountains, the sounds of the river and the direction of the wind.

- Send shinobi close to the enemy camp and have them set fire to the enemy camp huts in the direction you are going to attack. At the same time as the flames reach upwards into view, your attack group should give war cries and you should observe the situation inside the camp. If they are confused and surprised, move through their camp, just like a howling wind. It is not good procedure to perform this raid in a sluggish manner. If the enemy try to follow you out after you have raided, have ambush troops set up to attack them from the flank.

- If you have set flames in their camp, if you have given the war cries yet their defence is quiet and reserved, then in this situation, you should retreat. If you are not aware of this point and try to attack them without such considerations, then it will be harmful to your forces.[211]

- Divide your attack force into between five and seven groups and distribute among them ten good men who are trained in the way of the shinobi 忍. These shinobi should wear the clothes of a labourer. When the groups attack and move through the enemy camp, the shinobi from each group should remain behind in the confusion and pretend to be labourers who belong there – to make this work have them shout and react as they should during the attack, shouting out warnings to others that there is a night attack, then they should steal weapons and horses. Afterwards, at dawn, a new set of attack teams should get close to the enemy camp and when they attack from the front, the shinobi on the inside will attack the rear of the defenders. Also, the shinobi-captain should signal his shinobi-group 惣ノ忍 by means of instruments and they should go around the camp fighting. Also they should set fire to the enemy's huts, this is done to disturb their movement and at which point the shinobi should also release the horses and let them stampede away from the camp. Sometimes they let the troops placed outside in ambush come in.

- Send troops close to the enemy battle camp and have them hide on either side of the enemy position. Next, shoot fire arrows at the enemy vanguard, at this signal [other] troops should descend and make a raid on the enemy and this is also the time for the use of muskets. If the enemy retaliate and fight back, you should cope with it and then retreat after a whilst. This is the point when you initiate your hidden troops to attack them from the sides. Meanwhile, if you can, find a gap and push forward into the buildings and fight your way forward, trying to find the enemy *Hatamoto* command group. Take note, according to the situation, you should withdraw as quickly as possible. You should cause consternation in the enemy headquarters by shouting around that (insert name) is our ally or that we have killed the enemy general. Then according to the movements of the enemy, make a full force attack and defeat them.

Do not take any heads at this point and attack using shields, if you do not have shields use bundles of bamboo.

- Concerning successive attacks – you should attack or close in on an enemy camp for two or three successive nights in a row. You should make war cries to draw the enemy out, when they come out you should retreat at speed, this is done to exhaust them. To make sure you do not exhaust your own men, you should send alternating troops on these fake raids. If you do this repeatedly you will bring them to neglectfulness after a couple of days and when they let their guard down, remember to take advantage of this and attack them at these points. In addition to this you should conspire so that enemy shinobi listen to the sounds of your army in preparation for a night attack. This is done so that any enemy shinobi [near your camp] will report back and this will make the enemy prepare for this fake attack every night and they will tire in the end. This is a virtuous tactic, as it uses the enemy shinobi to weaken their own army without ussing up your allies' strength.

This scroll is a secret writing passed down in our school for generations. Be careful in passing this information on from person to person and do not show it to anyone outside of our school.

[Names written afterward in what appears to be a different hand and in an extremely cursive and unintelligible style]

Koike Jinnojo Sadanari
Uehara Hachizaemon Sadampbi
Mizushima Bokuya Motonari
Ito Jin-emon Yukiuji – [transcribed in the] twelfth month of the year 1689
Ito [unintelligible text]
Ito [unintelligible text]
Ito [unintelligible text]
[Unintelligible text]
Sakata [unintelligible text]

Bibliography

Primary Sources

Bansenshukai 萬川集海 (1676)

Choken Jutsu Hiden 町見術秘伝 (1846)

Dakko Shinobi No Maki Ryakuchu 奪口忍之巻略註 (Edo period)

Fukashima Ryu Mitsunin no Chu Sho 福島流蜜忍之註書 (1774)

Heiho Nukigaki Hippu No Sho Gunshi No Maki 兵法抜書匹夫抄 (1689)

Iga-ryu Koka Ryu Shinobi Hiden 伊賀流甲賀流竊奸秘伝 (Edo period)

Iga-ryu Kanpo Mizukagami No Maki 伊賀流間法水鏡之巻 (unknown date)

Iga-ryu Ninpo Gokuhi No Maki 伊賀流忍法極秘之巻 (1716)

Igazuke Sashidashi Chu 伊賀付差出帳 (1636)

Inko-Ryu Ninpo Chusho Tsuketari Chokaden 引光流忍法註書附長家伝 (1774)

Izu-ryu Kohi no Furoku 伊賀流炬火之付録 (unknown date)

Gokuhi Gunpo Hidensho 極秘軍法秘伝書 (*c.*1570–1650)

Gunpo Jiyoshu 軍法侍用集 (*c.*1612)

Koka Ryu Bujutsu 甲賀流武術 (Edo period)

Koka Ryu Densho 甲賀流伝書 (Edo period)

Kusunoki Ryu Ninpo Dakko Shinobi No Maki Chu 楠流忍法奪口忍之巻註 (Edo period)

Kusunoki Masashige Ikkan no sho 楠正成一巻書 (*c.*seventeenth century)

Kaisei Mikawagofudoki 改正三河後風土記 (1610–1837)

Murasami Diahi No Maki 村雨大秘之巻 (1715)

Shinobi Hiden 忍秘伝 (1560)

Ninpo Mizu Kagami 忍法水鏡 (1798)

Ninpo Sho Ka-zamurai Techo 忍法書　賀士手牒 (1720)

Oieryu Shinobi Hiden 御家流竊盗秘伝 (unknown date)

Omiyochishiryaku 近江與地志略 (1734)

Onmitsuhiji Shinobi-dai 隠密秘事忍大意 (1724)

Otsubo Hon Ryu 大坪本流 (unknown date)

Shinobi No Maki Te Kagami 忍之巻手鏡 (Edo period)

BIBLIOGRAPHY

Shoninki 正忍記 (1681)
Toryu Dakko Shinobi No Maki 当流奪口忍之巻 (Edo period)

Secondary Sources

Block, R.A., Arnott, D.P., Quigley, B. and Lynch, W.C. 'Unilateral Nostril Breathing Influences Lateralized Cognitive Performance' *Brain and Cognition* (1989)

Cummins, A. and Minami, Y., *True Path of the Ninja: The Definitive Translation of the Shoninki* (Tuttle Press, 2011)

Cummins, A. and Minami, Y., *True Ninja Traditions: The Shinobi Hiden and the Unknown Ninja Scroll* (Wordclay Press, 2010)

Mafee, M.F., Valvassori, G.E. and Becker, M., *Imaging of the Head and Neck* (Thieme, 2005)

Needham, J., *Science and Civilization in China: Volume 5* (Caves Books Ltd, 1986)

Sansom G., *A History of Japan: 1334–1615* (Stanford University Press 1961)

Sawyer, R.D., *Fire and Water: The Art of Incendiary and Aquatic Warfare in China* (Westview Press, 2004)

Sawyer, R.D., *The Severn Military Classics of Ancient China* (Westview Press, 1993)

Sawyer, R.D., *The Toa of Spy-craft* (Westview Press, 1998)

Sung Y., *Chinese Technology in the Seventeenth Century: T'ien-kung K'ai-wu* (Dover Publications, 1997)

玉林晴朗. 傳記聚芳. 日本青年教育会出版部 (Tokyo, 1942)

Various Authors, *Iga Koka Shinobi no nazo* (Shinjinbutsu Orish, 2005)

Notes

1   The *Gunpo Jiyoshu* and the *Shinobi Hiden* have been translated into English under the name *The Secret Traditions of the Shinobi;* the *Shoninki* manual has been published in *True Path of the Ninja*.

2   The word 'killer' is used here to avoid the connotations of 'assassin'. A shinobi was not a trained assassin, his role was information gatherer in the main and if opportunity presented itself or it was required, they were used as assassins. However, the evidence often points to the destruction of whole families and their homes as opposed to single targets. On the rare occasion, direct assassination does appear in historical documentation, such as the *Bansenshukai*.

3   It is important to note here that the term *shinobi* 忍 as a military function has been recorded since the fourteenth century, whilst the word *shinobi no mono* or ninja 忍者 is first found here in this document, making the first recorded use (to date) 1656. However, the term *shinobi no mono* with the radical 'no' does appear as early as 1639. There is no difference between the jobs or connotations between shinobi 忍 and *shinobi no mono* 忍者. Also, it must be understood that more and more documentation is being found and examined and only time will tell if this remains the earliest record.

4   A symbol broken into two sections so that when they meet they match and identification is confirmed.

5   The original text is ambiguous, however by cross referencing this point the translation given appears to be the best option.

6   The word '*shinobi*' is used twice here, once to mean 'stealthy' and second to mean 'ninja' as a person.

7   The text is ambiguous.

8   A Chinese military scholar who is thought to have arrived in Japan.

9   This is the recording of an oral tradition which is over 1000 years old and cannot be considered historically correct without validation.

10 Whilst the term 'China' is used throughout the book, it must be remembered that influences on Japan came from much of mainland Asia.

11 The Historical Ninjutsu Research Team believes that volume one of the *Shinobi Hiden* postdates the other volumes and was written 20 years before the *Bansenshukai*.

12   It is interesting to note that this implies they were samurai. This contradicts the information given in *The Ninja – Ancient Shadow Warriors of Japan*, where it is stated that ninja do not commit suicide, which as can be seen is incorrect.

13   Translation by the late H.C McCullough, Tuttle Press.

14   At this point, the men of Iga, who are later famed for their ninja skills, are unaware of the stealthy tactics, showing that the origin of the ninja may not lie in Iga as commonly held.

15   The reading of '*shinobi*' is confirmed in the *Gunpo Jiyoshu* manual c.1612.

16   This aspect of criminal or military use is discussed in depth later on.

17   It must be noted that this is an Edo period document.

18   Written before 1612, this is technically an Edo period manual, however its early date and the history of the author suggests Sengoku period information. It was probably written within the first few years of peace.

19   The transcription of the *Taiheiki* war chronicle discussed previously is from the mid-sixteenth century and places the shinobi at the height of the Sengoku period.

20   The text can not be accurately dated, it was published in the mid 1600s; however, the author is a Sengoku period warrior. The current theory is that it was either written in his lifetime or that his family wrote it from his notes at the turn of the 1600s and it was published in block print later on.

21   Presumably, the shinobi takes the alcohol with him or pays for it, being liberal with his coin.

22   Translated into English in the author's work *The Secret Traditions of the Shinobi*.

23   Masashige had two sons who took control. The first son Masatsura soon dies, when it was transferred to his brother Masanori.

24   There is no evidence to show if any of these lines came directly from the Kusunoki family or if they are simply using the name to promote the reputation of the school in question.

25   Translated by Sawyer as 'Roving Officers'.

26   Remembering that no contemporary records exist, this information comes from later sources.

27   His death is not fully understood, reports of old wounds or snipers abound.

28   The original text actually says 'within', which is geographically incorrect. His meaning here is that both shinobi of Iga *and* Koka are considered premier.

29   Iga is hiring its own men, as before the invasion of Oda Nobunaga, Iga was independent. However, this campaign is in 1615, when Iga was annexed and under the rule of the Tokugawa regime and thus obliged to supply troops for the first time in its history to meet the army requirements of an 'overlord'.

30   Evidence for this is provided in a later chapter.

31   This is based on the payment level of Hattori Hanzo's father, Natori Masatake and the following grandmasters of the *Natori-ryu* and the work of Associate Professor Isoda. It may change with subsequent findings.

32 A unit of pay based on a rice exchange economy. Twenty-five Koku is considered pay for a low level samurai, but above an *Ashigaru* foot soldier. A samurai of 10,000 Koku was a warlord.

33 Both of which are translated in full later.

34 The list represents those words which are considered to either be shinobi or close to the meaning.

35 C.585–473BC, a state during the Spring and Autumn period in China.

36 A treatise on military strategy in ancient China, believed to have been written by Jian Taigong, military adviser to King Wen and King Wu, which helped them to establish the Zhou Dynasty. Considered to be one of the Seven Military Classics.

37 'Our school'.

38 In this manual the pronunciation '*Suhha*' is used.

39 There is more confusion as there are even more ways of pronunciation.

40 The scroll often shows the '*nin*' ideogram next to the character for heart, pointing to a 'determined will'.

41 Literally, 'lower officials'.

42 Literally, 'spare' but the latter part of the quote establishes that you need it to change your guise into a different social class.

43 You should not travel in luxury but place yourself in lower quarters and mix with dubious people to display that you are not a member of the government, helping to strengthen your cover as a lowly traveller.

44 This is made up of two classic ninja elements, '*togiki*' meaning listening scout and '*nawa*' or rope. To 'carry a *togiki*' would make no sense, therefore it appears to be a tool as yet unknown, some kind of a rope that is either used for listening by scouts, or to detect listening scouts.

45 Often misnamed *Kishu-ryu*.

46 This mention of *Doushin* comes from the 1844 listing, however, the men of Iga probably were *Doushin*, just below samurai level, a status they assume after the loss of their territory in Iga.

47 There is a complex argument about the use of *Kamari* and *Kusa*. *Kusa* (grass) is considered an alternative to ninja, however, Fujibayashi in the *Bansenshukai* uses both *Kamari* and *shinobi* in different ways. The '100 ninja poems' used the term *Kamari* alongside *shinobi*. It appears that the two jobs overlapped but were not identical.

48 Both are made up of two ideograms and both include the ideogram 盗 – steal.

49 Often read as *Yutei*, but which is phonetically spelled out as *shinobi* here, however, it appears that the author simply copied a Chinese encyclopaedia and substituted the word *shinobi no mono* to suit a Japanese audience. This means that the two may not be directly linked and that the author was explaining what this Chinese word would be translated to in Japanese, or alternatively, it could be that *shinobi no mono* is the correct reading for this ideogram in Japanese.

50 One possible reading.

51 The term *Gotonpo* has become a popular word in the modern ninjutsu community, however, it has not been found in any historical ninja manual to date and was introduced to the Japanese popular culture via this encyclopaedia. It is evident from this document that these are not practical ways of hiding as they are based on magic and are Chinese folklore. Also, it must be understood that the author had no actual training in or knowledge of ninjutsu, he simply translates a Chinese document and overlays the Japanese word *Shinobi no mono* and attributes these magical skills to the Japanese ninja. This makes this skill of *Gotonpo* dubious as, at present, it has no direct reference to an actual ninja manual and unless an example can be found, it must be concluded that this skill set was inserted into ninja history without documentation.

52 At this point the quote from the Chinese manual ends and the Japanese commentator continues.

53 It is worth noting here that some Japanese researchers attempt to show a wholly Japanese origin to the ninja and that China played no part in their development. These researchers tend to come from the post-Chinese invasion and World War II generation and naturally are prejudiced against any form of Chinese connection. On the whole, the evidence points to a mainland origin of the skills of the ninja.

54 The original radical was moon.

55 In the *Bansenshukai* one anecdote was a story of vengeance whilst the other shows the primary aim was the death of the lord.

56 A form of segregation in a battlefield camp.

57 An alternative version of this appears in the *Gunpo Jiyoshu*.

58 The context shows that this is a human and not an animal.

59 This section is possibly one of the closest Chinese examples of a ninja–like figure.

60 The example given is that of a sparrow.

61 According to Needham.

62 This is due to bird flight being a tell–tale sign of an active *shinobi* within the area. If the birds are being scared by the gunfire it will be difficult to locate the ninja.

63 Literally, 'physical training' however, it means 'actual' training in this context.

64 Most likely, herbs and treatments.

65 This simply states '*Sake*-farming' and could mean the production of *Sake* or possibly selling *Sake* and farming as individual tasks. It seems more reasonable that this means production.

66 These almost replicate the above five items, however this is by design, the first five are elements to be learnt whilst these seven are the actual methods of infiltration. The titles are expanded on here as the original document simply has an ideogram that would be understood within the context by a Japanese speaker.

67 With the exception of a shinobi connected to an army; as the army is on the march he has no need of disguise.

68 Whilst the form of horseshoe is not described in the manual, Japanese horse shoes where not constructed of metal but were a form of straw sandal. The instruction not to use them is presumably due to the need to change them often.

69 This is a reference to the Taoist belief in the red phoenix defending the south; the text suggests that using the blood of sparrows will help you gain energy from this defending phoenix.

70 Possibly a line of *Natori-ryu*.

71 The ideogram can be used as both, making it hard to determine which was in the mind of the author.

72 To date, no practical controlled tests have been performed.

73 Some manuals talk of insects and worms, more so than mammal blood.

74 This formula is based on blood and water having a similar density.

75 Nutritional data supplied by Alex Allera of the Chemistry Department of Turin University.

76 This ingredient has been noted for its medicinal benefits.

77 '0' here means negligible in amount and 'Nil' means not found.

78 Also an ingredient with medical qualities.

79 A kilocalorie is equal to what we commonly refer to as a 'calorie' with an average of 2000 needed by a male per day, according to most sources.

80 That is to maintain his weight, to simply survive it would require less.

81 Depending on the amount of hours a person sleeps, an individual can go through, up to five Sleep Cycles a night. One cycle can measure from 90 to 120 minutes.

82 The black-clad guise of the ninja is most probably an Edo period phenomenon and masked intruders were probably thieves who wished to hide their identity. As discussed previously, some shinobi may have also been involved in theft.

83 In the image, the writing to the right states 'This is *shinobi no jutsu*'. This is interesting for two reasons. Firstly, it shows the author felt he had to explain that ninjutsu also included mathematics. Secondly, to date it is the only record which shows how to pronounce the word as *shinobi no jutsu*. The name for the arts of the ninja is *ninjutsu*, however with the addition of the partial 'no' this makes the term *shinobi no jutsu*, adding to the building evidence for the preferred use of the term *shinobi* over *ninja*.

84 An unknown skill.

85 In this case the original has not been seen and I am working from secondary sources.

86 In the past this has been mistranslated and many modern images show the sword on the last or outer six centimetres of the blade, which makes a long probing arm supported by a string. However, the original text states that the blade itself should only come out of the scabbard by six centimetres.

87 The earliest reference found to date of the mix up of the 'Rabbit Step' as a form of walking on the hands and its attachment to the *Bansenshukai* version

can be found in the works of Yumio Nawa, published in 1972. He adds further confusion by stating that the 'Rabbit Step' appears in the *Shinobi Hiden* manual – it does not.

88   Often translated as *Toho* but which can be read as *Uho*.

89   One variation has cloth wrapped around the hands and a sliding of the foot-hand combination little by little.

90   This magical step is combined with a form of *Kuji* magic to protect from demons etc. The etymology of the name of this step '*Uho*' shows that it used to be employed to describe a crippled walking gait in ancient China, after a Chinese Emperor who worked so hard for his people he became crippled.

91   It is possible that Nawa had access to a manual that describes the 'Rabbit Step' as the same walk found in the *Shinobi Hiden*, however he himself did not declare this.

92   One ideogram is illegible in the text and reads '*Ka[?]nawa no koto*' which leads the Team to conclude the missing ideogram is '*gi*' making this '*Kaginawa*' or grapple and rope.

93   Being copied does not make the manual or its information less real, and it too has its place in history, yet this needs to be before 1868 to be a form of reliable information.

94   Natori Masatake was without doubt a samurai under the rule of the Kishu-Tokugawa and Fujibayashi was most likely a *Koshi*, a form of displaced samurai, following the invasion of Iga under Oda Nobunaga.

95   Presumably this has a handle on the inside and is light weight and painted black. It would probably work extremely well.

96   Cylindrical bamboo.

97   This literally says block-wood and it is unclear if this is a tool the shinobi uses or the bar used on the door.

98   A person who is part of a group who are relatively higher ranking samurai and who are attached to divisions, literally 'supporting groups'.

99   The same term for the same tool is used in the *Shinobi Hiden*.

100   This is most likely a reference to the blade having different size teeth on each side, according to the *Bansenshukai* one side should be a general cutter whilst the other is for bamboo.

101   Most probably a hole made by a drill.

102   The scroll in this image is not the manual quoted in the text and is in fact a different manual with this same skill, further confirming its usage across ninjutsu. As described in the other scroll, the plate under the sound amplifier can be seen. Interestingly, this scroll is signed by two ninja, Kido Hachiroemon of *Iga Otoaa* and Azumatarozaemon of *Koshu Tsuchiyama Koka*.

103   A helpful guideline for ninjutsu manuals is the idea that a manual should be practical and have some form of psychological magic to aid the ninja; if a manual is purely magical with next to no ninjutsu, then it is more than likely a later

fiction. However, some manuals fall into a middle category and each manual must always be tested independently.

104   Next to no ninjutsu is actually recorded within this manual.

105   The original states to 'chant in the mouth' meaning in silence, or in your head.

106   At present this *mudra* is unknown, but the best theory to date is the *mudra* of Zen. The *Kuji* for 'Zen' is connected to both the word *Ongyo* and the goddess *Marishiten,* which would make it the best option for this skill.

107   This is a literal translation and is probably an idiom used for an unknown skill.

108   Literally '*Juji* pushback'.

109   The original word in the text can be used as the name of a temple or for beggars. By its context there, it appears to mean 'ways'.

110   The *Tenshin Katori Shinto Ryu* still holds an oral tradition of ninjutsu, which is not considered a school of ninjutsu, simply a collection of knowledge to help defend against shinobi attacks.

111   A form of defensive cape to protect against arrows.

112   In the Sengoku period the vanguard was a prestigious place and where battle hardened troops would form, as is so often the case in warfare. As the Edo period continued, the reputation of these detachments changed and in the early 1700s records start to mention their 'uselessness'. The connotation here is that this Natori was a military man on the front lines of Sengoku period battles making him a fighting samurai.

113   Most likely at 250 Koku or more.

114   There is confusion as to whether Masazumi or Masatake is correct, as both are used historically.

115   Sometimes listed as *Fujinoissuishi* Masatake.

116   Whilst the suffix '*no kami*' is less important in the Edo period, its appearance still makes this man a samurai, adding to the growing list of samurai-shinobi evidence.

117   This list takes precedence over the now incorrect list published in the *Bugei Daijiten Ryuha* listings.

118   Myself included.

119   This quote is paraphrased from Ikeda's article, where he directly quotes the document.

120   Hanzo I is the Sengoku period *Iga no mono* who moved to work with the Mikawa clan, soon to produce the Tokugawa regime. This Hanzo was the father of the famous Devil-Hanzo, who here is Hanzo II, in turn the father of the troublesome Hanzo III.

121   This warrior was later sentenced to commit ritual suicide due to his involvement with a rebellion against his Lord Hanzo, which was motivated by the class difference.

122   This is his reference to the ideogram for female.

123   This text was purposely blocked out and is considered to be a comment so strong it was removed by a later transcriber.

124 This text is ambiguous because of the deleted parts.

125 *The Gateless Gate* is available in multiple editions and translations.

126 It is beneficial to separate the document, which shows you the way to get through the gate, and the idea of enlightenment itself, both of which are the Gateless Gate.

127 The earliest surviving copy is a transcription from 1733.

128 A purely modern combination of words, which never appear in Japanese history.

129 The *Iga Ueno* ninja museum research section states ninjutsu is not a martial art, as does the Momochi Koka Ninja House/Museum and other ninja researchers such as Nakashima, Seiko, Kawakami and Otake. They consider this new line of 'ninja arts' as 'entertainment' and in no way a real line or a replication of historical ninjutsu.

130 Kendo teaches the student to hit armoured areas, not ideal in real warfare.

131 Fujibayashi here is determined to state that this 'criminal catching' is *not* ninjutsu and is not the role of the ninja and then complains that the shinobi are having to perform this duty more and more; a reflection of the fact that the status of the ninja was in decline at this point.

132 Research has shown that Sengoku period combat was harsh, brutal and unromantic, glorious deeds are stripped away with headhunting and murder taking their place.

133 The *Bansenshukai* advises that a fake wife and child should be used and you should feed them false information, which sounds plausible. Unbeknownst to the author of this manual, the shinobi they dealt with were probably enemy shinobi. We do not know if the women and children die.

134 It is not often that defence against shinobi discusses the art of dialects, which is always present in actual shinobi manuals.

135 It appears that this was a two-part book, the second scroll is missing.

136 Literally three centimetres, however it is a colloquialism for 'short'.

137 The author comes to the end of the tools in the first book and then lists the tools that appear in the second and missing volume, these tools are not featured in the scroll.

138 This is the original author's note in the text; he appears to reference an 'original' manual of unknown title.

139 Presumably a ninja would place this paper in the embers he is carrying to catch fire.

140 Presumably you roll this into a cylinder.

141 The text is highly ambiguous here and appears to mean using the pulp to form a paper, which can be used as tinder. There is a reference to a 'bitter taste' but it has been taken out here for clarity.

142 These are small flammable balls which were most likely used in night raids by throwing them, possibly in high numbers, into straw or thatch.

143 The text says 'this size' and draws a circle, the circle measures one centimetre.

144　There is an illegible section of the text and all that can be made out is 'mouth – ball'.

145　This is a much larger tool that the one above.

146　Most likely a decoction of pine wood and resin, however, he uses both terms earlier on.

147　This is a thrown fire weapon, so the missing text will reflect that point.

148　This word is damaged in the text, however, often bleached cloth is used for this tool.

149　This twisting is supposition, the text is beyond legibility, however, often they twist them together to prolong burning.

150　Most likely length.

151　Probably so that it does not burn as it is inside the ninja's kimono.

152　The text has one more illegible sentence here which discusses 'rubbing', 'sand' and 'stone'.

153　A liquid used for blackening the teeth.

154　Literally 'water metal'.

155　*Pagodite* or chalk?

156　Unknown component.

157　The text is not clear on the addition of the cotton seed.

158　Families of the same name.

159　*Hikan* are lower level people who serve the elite.

160　This statement is exceptionally important for the history of Iga. Some academics believe that the people of Iga did not hold samurai status before their defeat; however, the people of Iga most definitely considered themselves as samurai.

161　The Miyoshi were in league with the enemies of Koka and Iga.

162　Literally *Yumiya* means 'bow and arrow' and *Hanjo* translates as 'signed document'. There is another word in use at that time which was *Yasen*, 'Money for Arrows', which translates as 'war tax'. By analogy, the *Yumiya Hanjo* is a request to pay a share of the war funds for the province.

163　*Yado Okuri* (or *Mukae*) or 'transportation system'. It was often conducted by local leaders who could provide a number of men in that area and probably yielded some profit for them.

164　Mercenary samurai.

165　Throughout the entire text, Kimura insists on the two principles of constant communication and keeping the shinobi teachings only with those from Koka.

166　The author constantly switched between the present and past tense.

167　Senguku period.

168　There is an ambiguous idiom here, however by context it means unused.

169　The author is saying that many people get caught up in the 'shallow ends' of deception and states the truth shall be found in the way of the five spies, a concept of Sun Tzu's.

170 Here the 'catching' has a connotation of a winding motion, possibly the 'Spider Hand' of *Fukushima-ryu?*

171 Here he does not seem to be referring to the end of the Sengoku period generation but the difference in understanding between the old and young. Fujibayashi also states that older shinobi are better than younger ones.

172 This sentence should not be missed by any student of ninjutsu. Kimura is implying that those who perform this form of shinobi are merely thieves. The difference is in the use of the ideogram, the one here is found in various writings and sometimes together with the classical ideogram for shinobi.

173 *Rodanshu* literally translates as 'A Collection of Ancient People's Talk'. As it is a military manual the distinction needs to be added.

174 Not to be confused with 'Water-Spiders'.

175 The *Rodanshu* scroll starts a little 'dry' but ends up as a very exciting read towards the end.

176 *Boehmeria nivea.*

177 The measurement here is not meant to be accurate, it is an idiom for 'short'.

178 This ideogram normally means gold, however in this context it means iron.

179 This could be translated as top and bottom but the translators feel back and front fit more with the description.

180 This ideogram is used earlier in the text to mean ring.

181 It is unknown if this is inside or on the outside, however the grammatical connotations slightly favour the outside.

182 Literally, 'side hand'.

183 The rope does not appear near this ideogram, however it is most likely the rope attached to the ring at point two.

184 This could either be a reference to the direction the tool goes when crossing or travelling down a river, meaning that the spear butt would face downstream, or it could be a reference to an unknown use of the hole in the butt of the spear that appears in the diagram.

185 Literally, 'Sending fire'. It could be that this is a bamboo tube filled with propellant that forces the craft in one direction when lit, however, the image lends itself more to ignition fuse.

186 The same ideogram as above.

187 This ideogram is often used in ninja manuals as 'ladder' and is interchangeable with 'bridge' and ninja manuals often switch between the two.

188 This may be the 'Tied Grass' recipe found later in the book and may not actually be made of grass.

189 Unknown, presumably some kind of pill or tablet. *Haku* means 'white', *ro* is the plant *Pennisetum alopeculoides*, and *gan* means pills.

190 The text says *To*, however the *Bansenshukai* says *Bu*.

191 Unit of weight, one *shu* is 1/24 of a *Ryo*.

192 An unknown element.

193 Literally 'Grass Tied Fire' however, as discussed earlier, this term 'Grass' can mean 'temporary'. This tool is possibly connected to the fire ship.

194 For a full description of the *Donohi* body warmer see Cummins and Minami, *True Path of the* Ninja.

195 Either the leather of the bellows or ash scrapings.

196 No actual fish is used.

197 This implies that the ship in the image section has a skin of leather. An alternative version of this skin is given on the 'ninja-boat' in the *Bansenshukai* manual.

198 In all probability, the bamboo chamber is removed.

199 This could be a short cylinder shape.

200 A small selection of points have been removed from this section due to their mundane nature.

201 Unknown style.

202 A rider will sometimes hold the nostrils of a horse to calm it down.

203 Animal shoes used to be made of straw and plant material in Japan.

204 This is probably a reference to the fur style ones used by the *Otsubo* school.

205 A stick with a circle of rope at the end, to be placed over the horse's nose and twisted, to control the animal. A form of twitch.

206 A horse who leads with one side that cocks its head.

207 Shinobi horsemen are samurai who act as ninja and who quiet the horse by restricting its mouth and dampening its footsteps for stealthy missions.

208 Not the 'ninja' province of Koka.

209 The Chinese astrological label given to that year.

210 The text here is ambiguous, it could either mean bows are the primary weapon throughout or they are the first weapon used as the distance closes.

211 Most military manuals, both Japanese and Chinese, caution that a quiet enemy is a disciplined force and perhaps prepared for such an attack.

Index